THE PROOF OF GOD'S AMAZING LOVE

Catherine Martin

The Proof of God's Amazing Love

Quiet Time
MINISTRIES

PALM DESERT, CALIFORNIA

Cover by Quiet Time Ministries.
Cover photo by Catherine Martin—myPhotoWalk.com

Interior photos by Catherine Martin available at MYPHOTOWALK.COM—CATHERINEMARTIN.SMUGMUG.COM

The Proof Of God's Amazing Love—Embrace The Power Of The Gospel Of Christ
Copyright © 2024 by Catherine Martin
Published by Quiet Time Ministries
Palm Desert, California 92255
www.quiettime.org

ISBN-13: 978-1-7375747-8-1

Printed in the United States of America
24 25 26 27 28 29 30 31 32/ LSI 2024 / 10 9 8 7 6 5 4 3 2 1

Dedicated to …
the Lamb of God,
Who takes away the sins of the world,
Who is my Redeemer, Reconciler, Savior, Justifier,
Sanctifier, and my Righteousness,
the Lord Jesus Christ.

Dedicated to my husband
David G. Martin, M.D.
who has been my beloved companion
on this journey of faith.

Dedicated to
all those hearts who follow Jesus
and are His ambassadors sharing the gospel
throughout the world, and to those who are my co-laborers
in sharing and teaching the gospel of Jesus Christ
who partner with me in Quiet Time Ministries

May we embrace the power of the gospel of Christ,
be established in our faith, so the world may know
the proof of God's amazing love,
that it was while we were sinners
that Christ died for us.

The proof of God's amazing love is this:
that it was while we were sinners
that Christ died for us.

For I am not ashamed of the gospel,
for it is the power of God for salvation
to everyone who believes,
to the Jew first and also to the Greek.
For in it the righteousness of God is revealed
from faith to faith; as it is written,
But the righteous man shall live by faith.

For God so loved the world, that He gave His only begotten Son
that whoever believes in Him shall not perish, but have eternal life.
For God did not send the Son into the world to judge the world,
but that the world might be saved through Him.

Contents

And can it be that I should gain an int'rest in the Savior's blood?
Died He for me, who caused His pain? For me, who Him to death pursued?
Amazing love! How can it be that Thou, my God, should die for me?
Refrain: Amazing love! How can it be that Thou, my God, should die for me!

Tis mystery all! The Immortal dies! Who can explore His strange design
In vain the firstborn seraph tries to sound the depths of love divine!
Tis mercy all! let earth adore, let angel minds inquire no more.
Refrain: Amazing love! How can it be that Thou, my God, should die for me!

He left His Father's throne above, so free, so infinite His grace;
Emptied Himself of all but love, and bled for Adam's helpless race;
Tis mercy all, immense and free; For, O my God, it found out me.
Refrain: Amazing love! How can it be that Thou, my God, should die for me!

Long my imprisoned spirit lay fast bound in sin and nature's night;
Thine eye diffused a quick'ning ray, I woke, the dungeon flamed with light;
My chains fell off, my heart was free; I rose, went forth and followed Thee.
Refrain: Amazing love! How can it be that Thou, my God, should die for me!

No condemnation now I dread; Jesus, and all in Him is mine!
Alive in Him, my living Head, and clothed in righteousness divine,
Bold I approach the eternal throne, and claim the crown, through Christ my own.
Refrain: Amazing love! How can it be that Thou, my God, should die for me!

CHARLES WESLEY, 1738

astor and theologian, R.C. Sproul begins his speaking message series on the Apostle Paul's Epistle to the Romans with whimsical caution, "Fools rush in where angels fear to tread." The sheer scope "fiercely intimidated" him. I so relate to these words. However, at this stage of my life, with Romans, I feel something different – a sense of awe and wonder. It's all about the majesty of God and His incomprehensible ways and works. And the Lord has taught me that the best thing I can ever say when He calls me to write a new book, especially a quiet time experience, is, "I can't, but He can," and then I trust Him to show me the way. I am counting on the great promise in 1 Thessalonians 5:24 – "Faithful is He who calls you, and He will also bring it to pass."

I have been living in the book of Romans for years, really, ever since I became a Christian. A teenager, I met weekly with a mature Christian woman, Thea, who taught me from Romans and Matthew Henry's Commentary. I used to drive home after our times together filled with amazing truths that just boggled my mind. That was my introduction to the wonderful world of theological truths. I truly love theology and thinking deeply about all that God says in His Word. I love taking difficult ideas and themes, then sharing them with others in a way they may be better understood and applied. I guess it's the teacher in me, and I learned it first from my mother, a teacher, who was my greatest mentor in life.

In Romans, there is deep thinking and a wide landscape of biblical truth. Truly in a lifetime one could never traverse its vast treasure. And yet, we are going to travel on the journey of Romans together. And quite honestly, I'm excited. I can't wait.

The Lord has encouraged me with the words of John 14:26 and I have held to His promise throughout the writing of this *A Quiet Time Experience* – "But the Helper, the Holy Spirit, whom the Father will send in My name, He will teach you all things, and bring to your remembrance all that I said to you." I offer you these same words as you embark on *The Proof Of God's Amazing Love*, realizing that the Lord is going to teach you all things through the Holy Spirit whom the Father has given you as your Helper to bring His words to your life.

Frederic Louis Godet, a Swiss Protestant theologian of the nineteenth century, in his *Commentary on St. Paul's Epistle to the Romans*, makes a profound statement, worthy of thought as we begin studying Romans together. He writes, "The probability is that every great spiritual revival in the church will be connected as effect and cause with a deeper understanding of this book." I agree! The truths contained in Romans are so powerful that when they penetrate the mind and heart, they will, as Godet intimated, spark revival. My prayer as you study Paul's letter to the Roman church, is that your heart will be revived as never before, that you will be set on fire with a great love for Jesus Christ, and that you will deeply experience the power of the gospel of Christ for salvation, sanctification, spiritual growth, and service in His name. And ultimately, the gospel brings the realization of the hope of its promise – eternal life with Jesus Christ (Romans 6:23).

I remember, early on in my own faith journey with Christ, reading the words of Romans 5:8 in J.B. Phillips' *New Testament In Modern English*, and finding my heart warmed with the love of Christ: "Yet the proof of God's amazing love is this: that it was while we were sinners that Christ died for us." Indeed Paul elaborates in Romans 5:11, that "we may hold our heads high in the light of God's love because of the reconciliation which Christ has made." A number of years ago, from those inspiring words of Romans 5:8, I wrote an *A Heart on Fire* (Quiet Times for the Heart) companion speaking message entitled, "The Proof Of God's Amazing Love," surveying the wondrous cross of Christ. That was a big step for me in my journey through the book of Romans, and this concept is at the heart of my motivation for writing this quiet time experience.

Another aspect of my education in Romans came when I sat under the teaching of my New Testament professor at Bethel Theological Seminary, and one of the translators of the *New International Version* of the Bible, Dr. Walter Wessel. I have pages and pages of notes from that incredible class. I think what impressed me more than anything else was the heart of Paul, the

Pharisee, responding to the lightning strike call of Jesus to preach the gospel of Jesus Christ as an Apostle.

What does the Lord intend for us to learn as we travel chapter by chapter through Romans? We are going to linger long in the infinite beauties of the gospel of Jesus Christ as laid out and explicitly expressed in Romans. As we live in these truths, we are going to experience the real power of the gospel, not only to save, but also to sanctify, grow us spiritually through the work of the Holy Spirit, and set us on the journey of serving our Lord as we live out our days on earth. We will look specifically at important words that the Lord gives us like faith, gospel, righteousness, love, grace, and hope. As a result, His message for you is going to come alive through the power of the Holy Spirit, as He teaches you in His Word.

You will discover that the gospel is undeniably "good news;" it is good news that you and I cannot live without. It is the best news you will ever know, and by the time we are finished with our journey, you will realize how safe and secure you are in Christ, and that your fantastic adventure in trusting Him has only just begun. We will find ourselves face to face with the Triune God—Father, Son, and Holy Spirit. You are going to grow spiritually in your intimate relationship with God as never before experienced. This book of quiet times is not meant to be a doctrinal or theological treatise, nor is it intended to be an explanatory or interpretive commentary. This study is intended to be a devotional quiet time experience for you with your Lord and Savior Jesus Christ. Our focus is precisely on the main themes of the gospel with a view to experiencing the gospel's power in our very lives.

There is so much spiritual food in Romans that we could live there for a lifetime. God leads us in His Word as we spend quiet time with Him, and we will tarry long with Him as He leads us to live awhile with Him in Romans. Keep in mind that the great D. Martyn Lloyd-Jones, a Welsh Congregationalist minister and medical doctor of the 20th century, wrote more than 350 sermons on Romans filling 14 spectacular commentary volumes. So, the fact that we are going to delve into this great and deep and wide ocean of God's Word called Romans in only eight weeks makes it clear that we will merely scratch the surface. And yet your heart will be so filled to the core with the glory and greatness of your God that His love will shake your heart and revive and renew your spirit. The truths of Romans are transformative, and so it is, when you plumb the depths, you will be transformed by the power of the Holy Spirit. You will be so changed that you will "grow in the grace and knowledge of the Lord Jesus Christ" (2 Peter 3:18), and you will serve Him well bringing great glory and honor to Him.

W.H. Griffith Thomas, an Anglican cleric and theologian ordained in 1885, and one of the original founders of Dallas Theological Seminary, writes in his devotional commentary on Romans, "It is the heart that must penetrate most deeply into the secrets of this doctrinal, theological, and yet always personal Epistle. The Apostle's own spiritual experience is the main key to his meaning, and those who enter into similar experiences of the profound truths here recorded will possess the best clue to the interpretation."[2]

Romans is considered by many biblical scholars to be the magnum opus of Paul of Tarsus, who was entrusted to lay out the words, inspired (God-breathed) by the Lord through the Holy Spirit. We will become intimately acquainted with the heart of Paul, and as for me personally, I cannot wait to meet this extraordinary personage in heaven. Romans contains many of the secrets as to why Paul had such a powerful ministry and why he was able to run his passionate and stormy race with endurance. We will see how the great doctrinal truths from God lead to a great lion of faith and a heart set on fire to serve the Lord. In Romans, Paul will take you to a new and glorious place in your relationship with Christ.

Paul's detailed and intimate letter is written to "the beloved of God in Rome, called as saints" (Romans 1:7). The book of Romans is after all a message for the church then and now, rather than an expansive text to all the people of ancient Rome or everyone on earth right now. And yet, an unbeliever can read Romans and be saved by grace through faith. But you, the believer, are getting the inside scoop, the up close and personal God-breathed insights of a Pharisee who met the Lord Jesus Christ on the road to Damascus. And so, as we begin this excellent adventure, we need to ask, "What does the Lord want me to know now that I have become a Christian?" You will certainly find the answer to that question as you read and study Paul's letter to the church in Rome.

Permeating the entire book of Romans is the grandeur and glory of God's love for you. His love is at the heart of the gospel. We see God's heart in the words of Jesus in John 3:16-17: "For God so loved the world, that He gave His only begotten Son, that whoever believes in Him shall not perish, but have eternal life. For God did not send the Son into the world to judge the world, but that the world might be saved through Him." Dear friend, when you experience the love of God firsthand in coming face to face with the Lord Jesus Christ, your life will never be the same. And that is exactly what is going to happen when you study in awe and wonder the book of Romans.

I will never forget the day when my beloved husband asked me to marry him. He lovingly presented a small bouquet of three roses to me representing all that he is—body, soul, spirit. He handed them to me, placing them in my trembling hands and then he asked me to be his wife. Roses have often been a symbol of affection and a way to say, "I love you." The red rose on the cover of this book was captured by me at the Principe Corsini Villa Le Corti, Val Di Pesa, Florence, Tuscany, Italy. This "God's Smile" image has long been one of my favorites in my SmugMug myPhotoWalk portfolio, and so I chose it for the cover of this study to help us remember the love of God contained in the gospel of Christ. God loves you, dear friend. And we have only begun to glimpse the depth of His love for us. No matter how much we know, there is always more to know and understand. So, brace yourself for a new and deeper experience of God's love in Jesus Christ. It will happen.

Something God has used over the years to help me know and love Him more is myPhotowalk Devotional Photography. As I have walked out in His magnificent creation with my Nikon, Fuji, and Sony cameras and His Word, looking through the lens has slowed me down to see His intricate design. I have watched Him paint beauty and color into the landscape at sunrise and sunset, and I have realized how He can paint that same kind of beauty and color into the landscape of my life. Nothing is impossible with God. Each day of your quiet time experience in Romans, *The Proof of God's Amazing Love*, will contain a fine art black and white image from my portfolios of flowers, gardens, and landscapes. This will help us remember the power of the gospel not only to save us but to sanctify us as we grow spiritually, and then carry us into His plan and purpose as we surrender to Him and serve Him using our gifts given by the Spirit. All images are processed with Nik Silver Efex Pro and Adobe Photoshop for you to use as meditation and study to see the great power of the Master Designer who created the universe. myPhotoWalk and Quiet Time Ministries proudly offer custom color prints of our devotional photography exclusively through SmugMug at catherinemartin.smugmug.com.

Together we will embark on this journey through Scripture in the form of quiet times alone with the Lord. Each quiet time is organized according to the PRAYER™ Quiet Time Plan™:

Prepare Your Heart

Read and Study God's Word

Adore God in Prayer

Yield Yourself to God

Enjoy His Presence

Rest in His Love

Each week consists of five days of quiet times, photo selections from my devotional photography, and then a devotional reading on Days 6-7. Each quiet time includes devotional reading, devotional Bible study, journaling, prayer, worship, hymns, and application of God's Word. Journal Pages and Prayer Pages (adapted from *The Quiet Time Notebook*) to record your thoughts and prayers are in the Appendix of this book. With *The Proof of God's Amazing Love* and your Bible you have everything you need for rich quiet times with the Lord. Because schedules vary, you can be flexible and you may choose to take more than one day for each quiet time. You may complete each quiet time at your own pace, taking as little or as much time as you can give to spend alone with the Lord.

I want to encourage you to use a Bible in this study with large enough print that you can easily read each passage of Scripture. Your Bible should be easy to leaf through going from passage to passage as you study. Larger Bibles are sometimes difficult to manage. You may have a large study Bible for reference, but your regular Bible should be more manageable. Also, choose a translation that is easy to read like the New American Standard Bible, the New International Version, the New Living Translation, the New King James Version, or the English Standard Version. I love *The New Inductive Study Bible (NASB)*. Feel free to consult different translations as you study. I encourage you to underline and mark up your Bible and your quiet times in this book as you study. As you meditate in God's Word, savoring each passage of Scripture, you are going to find many cherished verses in this quiet time experience. My favorite marking tools are a Papermate Sharpwriter #2 pencil, Micron colored fineliner pens, and the Pentel 8-color automated pencil.

As you study God's Word in Romans, you may wish to consult a commentary for more study—I recommend a one-volume commentary like *The Bible Knowledge Commentary* or *The New Bible Commentary*. I also encourage you to use the study notes in a good study Bible like *The NIV Study Bible* or *The Life Application Study Bible*. Five good commentaries on the book of Romans are *Romans: A Shorter Commentary* by C.E.B. Cranfield, *St. Paul's Epistle to the Romans: A Devotional Commentary* by W.H. Griffith Thomas, *The Epistle to the Romans* by Leon Morris, *Be Right* by Warren Wiersbe, and *The Expositor's Commentary Romans - Galatians, Volume 10*. More recommended commentaries are included in the Appendix. A study tool that is absolutely invaluable and one I use all the time is Logos Bible Study Software (www.logos.com). Then, if you desire to learn more about how to have a quiet time, I encourage you to get my book *Six Secrets to a Powerful Quiet Time*. To learn more about different kinds of devotional Bible studies for your quiet time, I encourage you to read my book *Knowing and Loving the Bible*. I also encourage you to have a good hymnal for your quiet times with the Lord. My favorite hymnal is *Hymns for the Family of God*. I have included many hymns in this study and they will whet your appetite for the wonderful theology of great hymnwriters like Fanny Crosby, Charles Wesley, and Isaac Watts.

VIEWER GUIDES

At the end of each week you will find your Viewer Guide to take notes from the video message. In each message, Catherine teaches from God's Word, and challenges you to draw near to the Lord. These inspirational and instructional messages are especially designed to accompany your studies each week. These messages are available on the companion *The Proof of God's Amazing Love* DVDs, Digital M4V Video, Digital MP3 Audio, as well as HD 1080p Digital M4V of the HD Leader's Kits for a professional large group experience. Search the Quiet Time Ministries Online Store at www.quiettime.org or call Quiet Time Ministries at 1-800-925-6458.

For Leaders

The Proof of God's Amazing Love is a powerful resource for group study including a complete Leader's Guide with Discussion Questions in the Appendix. *The Proof of God's Amazing Love* DVD Leader's Kits or *The Proof of God's Amazing Love* HD 1080p Digital Leader's Kits are available at the Quiet Time Ministries Online Store at www.quiettime.org. You may also call Quiet Time Ministries at 1-800-925-6458. The kit includes the *The Proof of God's Amazing Love* book, *The Proof of God's Amazing Love* video messages, and *The Quiet Time Journal*. Each *The Proof of God's Amazing Love* book is organized into 8 weeks with 5 days of quiet time per week and Days 6-7 for review and meditation. The book also includes 9 Viewer Guides for the group video sessions, Leader's Guide and Discussion Questions, and Journal and Prayer Pages.

Quiet Time Ministries Online

Quiet Time Ministries Online at www.quiettime.org is a place where you can deepen your devotion to God and His Word. Cath's Feature Articles Blog is where Catherine shares about life, about the Lord, and just about everything else. A Walk In Grace™ is Catherine's devotional photojournal, highlighting her own myPhotoWalk photography, where you can grow deep in the garden of His grace. myQuietTime is an exclusive HD 1080p video presented on YouTube at The Quiet Time Live Channel. myPhotoWalk.com is Catherine's devotional photography website where you can view her nature and landscape photography and order custom prints at CatherineMartin.SmugMug.com.

My Letter To The Lord

As you begin quiet time adventure in Romans, I'd like to ask, where are you? What has been happening in your life over the last year or so? What has been your life experience? What are you facing and what has God been teaching you? It is no accident that you are in this book of quiet times, *The Proof of God's Amazing Love*. God has something He wants you to know, something that will change the whole landscape of your experience with Him. Watch for it, listen for it, and when you learn it, write it down and never let it go. Will you write a prayer as a letter to the Lord in the space provided on the next page expressing all that is on your heart and ask Him to speak to you in these quiet times? And then, beloved, I encourage you to grab your Bible, *The Proof of God's Amazing Love*, and get ready for the adventure of your life! I can't wait to study God's Word together with you.

My Letter To The Lord

⚛ INTRODUCTION WEEK ⚛

Every Life Tells A Story

Welcome to *The Proof of God's Amazing Love - Embrace the Power of the Gospel of Christ*. In this study in God's Word, you are going to discover why the gospel is the best news, all that Christ has done for you, God's amazing love for you, Christ and essentials of the Christian life, and the excitement of your adventure with Christ that lasts forever. These Viewer Guides are designed to give you a place to write notes from my *The Proof of God's Amazing Love* messages available on DVDs, Digital M4V Video, and Digital MP3 Audio for your computer or mobile device. In our time together today, we are going to look at 2 Corinthians 2:14-3:3, stories of people whose lives have been changed by Romans, and then important truths about your life story.

"Clearly, you are a letter from Christ showing the result of our ministry among you. This letter is written not with pen and ink, but with the Spirit of the living God. It is carved not on tablets of stone, but on human hearts" (2 Corinthians 3:3 NLT).

Some important truths about your life story

1. Your story is ____.

2. Your story is _______________________________, and grows to the degree you grow in your knowledge of the Lord.

3. Your story _______________________________ of God everywhere. 2 Corinthians 2:14

4. Your story reaches ____around you.

5. Your story is written first by the Spirit of God on the tablet of your _______________.

How our stories are different
1. Each story is unique in details because we are unique.
2. Each story is lifechanging in different ways.

3. Each story speaks in unique ways through your words, attitudes and actions according to the way the Lord chooses to use you during your brief stay on earth.

4. Each story is influential in the unique ways it touches lives and creates a ripple effect.

How our stories are the same

1. We are all created by God. Psalm 139:13-16

2. We are all created for God. Isaiah 43:1-7, Ephesians 2:10

3. We all have in us a longing for God. Ecclesiastes 3:11

4. We all have an awareness of sin. Romans 3:23

5. God reaches out to each of us and invites us into a relationship with Him. Revelation 3:20

6. When we come to the Lord, He dramatically changes us. Romans 8:29

7. God brings people into our lives to lead us and help us grow. Hebrews 13:7

8. We will develop an insatiable appetite for the Word of God. Jeremiah 15:16, Hebrews 4:12

9. Part of our story will include a deep love for Jesus Christ. Philippians 1:21

10. God gifts us and empowers us through the power of the Holy Spirit. Galatians 5:22-25

11. Our stories include a call to ministry to serve the Lord. Colossians 3:24

12. God will ask us to do impossible things where we may feel overwhelmed. Philippians 4:13

13. We all walk a road of suffering. John 16:33

14. God weaves together all the events of our life for good. Romans 8:28

15. All of us have hope in our stories including the hope of heaven. Romans 15:13

What will help you in the development and power of your story?

1. Make ___________________God a priority in your life and in your study of Romans.

2. Pay ______________________________________to God's story in your life.

3. ____ your story.

4. ____ your story.

Video messages are available on DVDs or as Digital M4V Video. Audio messages are available as Digital MP3 Audio. Visit the Quiet Time Ministries Online Store at www.quiettime.org.

FOR SUCH A TIME AS THIS

Romans 1:1-17

This letter is truly the most important piece in the New Testament. It is purest Gospel. It is well worth a Christian's while not only to memorize it word for word but also to occupy himself with it daily, as though it were the daily bread of the soul. It is impossible to read or to meditate on this letter too much or too well. The more one deals with it, the more precious it becomes and the better it tastes.

Martin Luther

THE NEED OF THE HOUR

For this is how God loved the world; He gave His one and only Son, so that everyone who believes in Him will not perish but have eternal life. God sent His Son into the world not to judge the world, but to save the world through Him..

John 3:16-17 NLT

PREPARE YOUR HEART

n the evening of May 24, 1738 a young 34-year old man went unwillingly to a religious meeting on Aldersgate Street in London. John Wesley had spent thirteen years frustrated at his attempts to have a pure heart before God. Finally, he realized what he needed and desired more than anything was an assurance of salvation. His brother Charles had been struggling with the same need. And just three days earlier Charles had come to understand that salvation was by grace through faith in Christ. At that time, he wrote in his journal that the Spirit of God "chased away the darkness of my unbelief." Soon after Charles Wesley's conversion experience, he wrote two hymns, "And Can It Be That I Should Gain" and "Where Shall My Wondering Soul Begin."

So now, three days later, John Wesley was sitting at the meeting on Aldersgate Street listening to someone read Martin Luther's "Preface to the Epistle of Romans." He writes of what happened next: "About a quarter before nine, while he was describing the change which God works in the heart through faith in Christ, I felt my heart strangely warmed. I felt I did trust in Christ, Christ alone for salvation, and an assurance was given me that he had taken away my sins, even mine, and saved me from the law of sin and death." Excitedly, he shared his newfound faith with the group. And later that evening, he visited his brother Charles and shared the wonderful words, "I believe."

Dr. Roger J. Green, Professor of Biblical and Theological Studies, makes this observation of the experiences of Charles and John Wesley: "Until their conversions the Wesleys had what John described as 'a fair summer religion.' They were both ordained. They both preached, taught, wrote, composed hymns, and even gave themselves to missionary work—all to no avail. They had not Christ, or rather, Christ did not have them. They lived by good works, but not by faith."[1]

Is it possible to be religious but never experience a relationship with Christ? The answer is yes. It was happening in Rome when the letter to the Romans was written and it is happening even in the world today. Are people throughout the world putting their faith in many useless things, investing in futile and temporal pursuits, and even giving themselves to blatant immorality while missing what life is all about? Yes. Again, it was clearly occurring in Rome and we see it today in the world where we live. Is it possible to have put one's faith in Christ but never have experienced assurance of salvation? Oh yes, because doubts, fears, and insecurities plagued blessed believers in Rome, and the same thing is happening even today. The greatest need of the hour in every generation is salvation by grace through faith in Christ. And once one puts their faith in Christ, they need to know just how secure they are in their newfound faith. Believers then as now need to be established and grow in their faith in Christ (Romans 1:11).

One of the greatest and best known set of verses is John 3:16-17. "For this is how God loved the world: He gave His one and only Son, so that everyone who believes in Him will not perish but have eternal life. God sent His Son into the world not to judge the world, but to save the world through Him." These words were spoken by Jesus Himself, the one and only Son. They are the best description of the gospel by Jesus Himself while He walked on earth. And now, in *The Proof of God's Amazing Love*, you are embarking on the journey into the best and most complete words about the gospel of Christ that you will read in the Bible—the book of Romans written by Paul the Apostle. Of course, the gospel is seen from Genesis to Revelation. But Romans is the most well laid out explanation of the gospel and everything you need to know to be saved, forgiven of your sins, and inherit eternal life. No wonder the 19th century theologian, Godet, called Romans "the cathedral of the Christian faith." In Romans, you will learn all about salvation and the benefits of your salvation that last forever and ever. You will learn how to live during your stay on earth until you step into heaven, face to face with your Lord. The best news of all is the assurance of salvation that is yours because of the finished work of Jesus Christ. You are going to know beyond the shadow of a doubt, perhaps more than you may have ever realized, that you are eternally secure in Christ. Knowing all this confirms God loves you. And His love is amazing.

And so, dear friend, on this first day of quiet time with your Lord, begin by meditating on the words of Charles Wesley, "And Can It Be That I Should Gain" on page 10 found at the beginning of this study. Then, write a simple prayer, asking the Lord to prepare your heart for this journey.

READ AND STUDY GOD'S WORD

1. It is always exciting to begin a journey in God's Word that you know is going to be an adventure with rich reward. This is especially true in the study of Romans. C.E.B. Cranfield writes in the introduction of his commentary on Romans: "The outstanding importance of the Epistle to the Romans in the history of the Church is well known. Again and again it has played a decisive part in the renewal of Christian faith and life. We shall be wise to approach it with eager expectancy."[2]

Whenever you study an epistle in the New Testament, it is most important to understand who the author and recipients are, the occasion of the letter, when it was written, and the overall theme of the letter. This information is found at the beginning and ending of Romans.

Read Romans 1:1-17 and Romans 15:23-24, 30-32 and write out what you learn about the following:

Who is the author of Romans? (Romans 1:1)

Who are the recipients of Romans? (Romans 1:6-8)

What is the occasion and purpose of the letter? (Romans 1:9-15, 15:23-24, 30-32)

What is the theme of Romans? (Romans 1:16-17)

2. In Romans 1:1-17, we discover that Paul the apostle is the author of this letter to the Romans. The recipients are Christians who live in Rome, the center of the Roman Empire. Rome was a religious city that worshipped many gods including the emperor. Christians met in house churches

with more Gentile than Jewish believers at the time of the writing of Romans. Paul wanted these believers to understand the gospel and to explain it to them himself. He also wanted to prepare the way prior to visiting them firsthand on his way to Spain (Romans 15:23-33). He clearly wanted to strengthen and establish them in their faith in Christ. In Romans, Paul is going to talk about Christ and the essentials of the Christian life that flow from the gospel of Christ. And, as you will see in future chapters in Romans, he wanted to explain the relationship between Jews and Gentiles in God's plan of redemption. This is hinted at especially in Romans 1:16. We also discover at the end of Romans 15 that Paul asks the church to pray for him as he takes a contribution to Jerusalem prior to visiting them in Rome. Paul is writing from Corinth in early spring A.D. 57. What we see in this first chapter is that the overall theme is the gospel and the revelation of God's righteousness and salvation to those who believe. The Greek word for "gospel" is *euaggelion* and means good news. The good news is the revelation of God's righteousness and the power of God for salvation to all who believe, the Jew and also the Greek. And oh, how we need salvation—the Greek word is *soteria* and means safety, deliverance, and preservation from danger or destruction.

Read Romans 1:1-4, 16-17 again and write out everything you learn about the gospel.

3. We are going to learn so much about the gospel in this study. It is mentioned throughout many of the epistles in the New Testament. Read the following verses, circle the word "gospel" in each verse, and underline your favorite words and phrases about the gospel.

Now I make known to you, brethren, the gospel which I preached to you, which also you received, in which also you stand…I delivered to you as of first importance what I also received, that Christ died for our sins according to the Scriptures, and that He was buried, and that He was raised on the third day according to the Scriptures, and that He appeared to Cephas, then to the twelve. After that He appeared to more than five hundred brethren at one time, most of whom remain until now, but some have fallen asleep; then He appeared to James, then to all the apostles; and last of all, as to one untimely born, He appeared to me also. 1 Corinthians 15:1, 3-8

In Him, you also, after listening to the message of truth, the gospel of your salvation—having also believed, you were sealed in Him with the Holy Spirit of promise. Ephesians 1:13

…because of the hope laid up for you in heaven, of which you previously heard in the word of truth, the gospel which has come to you, just as in all the world also it is constantly bearing fruit and increasing, even as it has been doing in you also since the day you heard of it and understood the grace of God in truth. Colossians 1:5-6

4. Do you notice the phrases, "message of truth" and "word of truth?" The gospel is true and is the truth. The word for truth is *aletheia* and means "objective reality." God determines what is true. Truth is discovered by you, not determined by you. You discover truth in God's Word. Jesus, who is the truth (John 14:6), prayed to the Father: "Your Word is truth" (John 17:17). This is important to think about this as we learn about the truth of the gospel. Many in the current culture do not believe in absolute truth and do not know the truth. In our study of the gospel of Jesus Christ, we need to understand that it is truth. Because it is true, it is authoritative for our lives, and possesses the right to command our beliefs and actions. The truth of God's Word is both authoritative and also relevant for your life. Paul encourages us to "Be diligent to present yourself approved to God as a workman who does not need to be ashamed, accurately handling the word of truth" (2 Timothy 2:15). As you think about the truth of God's Word and the gospel of Jesus Christ, how does this motivate you to study God's Word and especially to study Romans?

5. Why do you think the gospel is good news, especially good news for you? Write your thoughts in the space provided.

ADORE GOD IN PRAYER

Jesus said in John 3:16-17, "For this is how God loved the world: He gave His one and only Son, so that everyone who believes in Him will not perish but have eternal life. God sent His Son into the world not to judge the world, but to save the world through Him." We are beginning to see that the gospel is the good news of Jesus Christ and because of all He has done (and we will see this in the weeks to come), you can be saved, forgiven of your sins, and inherit eternal life. Pray the following prayer as a response to the good news of the gospel of Jesus Christ.

> Heavenly Father, I pray that Jesus Christ may become dearer to me. May I love him as a personal friend and hide myself in the hourly awareness of his presence. May I have no taste or desire for things which he would disapprove. Let his love constrain me not to live for myself, but for him.

F.B. MEYER IN DAILY PRAYERS

YIELD YOURSELF TO GOD

> It [Romans] should be studied with earnest prayer and personal trust. Intellectual attention alone is insufficient. The Epistle should be regarded as a personal letter to ourselves. Its deepest secrets will only be revealed to the heart that is willing to submit to its teaching and translate it into action.[3]

W.H. GRIFFITH THOMAS IN ROMANS: A DEVOTIONAL COMMENTARY I-V

> In studying the Epistle to the Romans we feel ourselves at every word face to face with the unfathomable…The Epistle to the Romans is the cathedral of the Christian faith.[4]

FREDERIC LOUIS GODET IN COMMENTARY ON ST. PAUL'S EPISTLE TO THE ROMANS

And the theme Paul lets us know at once, is the gospel of God…Let me put it like this: the good news he [Paul] has got to give them is, that God Himself has introduced the way of saving men through Jesus Christ. "I am not ashamed of the gospel of Christ," he says, "for it is the power of God unto salvation, to every one that believeth…" God is doing something. He is doing it in Christ. And he goes on to tell us in the 17th verse that what God is doing in Christ is that He is giving to man Christ's righteousness. So that what we have now is salvation as a gift from God, who gives us freely the righteousness of Christ, and not salvation as the result of any man's effort. That is what he is talking about; he is thrilled by it…it is altogether new, says Paul. It is good news. It is new news. Henceforth we are not going to think of righteousness in terms of what a man does, but of a righteousness which God gives — a righteousness that comes from God in Jesus Christ through faith. And it is for everybody, Jew and Gentile: not only Jew, but Greek also. And he keeps on playing on that great theme.[5]

D. MARTYN LLOYD-JONES IN ROMANS, EXPOSITION OF CHAPTER 1, THE GOSPEL OF GOD

ENJOY HIS PRESENCE

As you have begun your journey in Romans, what is the most significant truth you learned today? Close by writing a prayer to the Lord expressing all that is on your heart. Thank Him for all He is teaching you for such a time as this.

REST IN HIS LOVE

"He called you to salvation when we told you the Good News; now you can share in the glory of our Lord Jesus Christ" (2 Thessalonians 2:14 NLT).

Abundant Life

I came that they may have life, and have it abundantly. John 10:10
Newport Beach, California, USA
Fujifilm X-T2, ISO 400, f6.4, 1/420sec, Adobe Photoshop, Nik Silver Efex Pro
myPhotoWalk.com—catherinemartin.smugmug.com

THE MAN FOR THE HOUR

*But I do not consider my life of any account as dear to myself, so that
I may finish my course and the ministry which I received from the
Lord Jesus, to testify solemnly of the gospel of the grace of God.*

ACTS 20:24

PREPARE YOUR HEART

ho would the Lord choose from among all the people on earth in the first century to preach the gospel of salvation by grace through faith to both Jews and Gentiles (also known as the circumcised and the uncircumcised in Galatians 2:7)? It would take someone special and the Lord chose Paul to be the one to teach that the gospel is for everyone who believes, "to the Jew first and also to the Greek" (Romans 1:16). Paul considered this a ministry entrusted to him by the Lord Jesus, and so it was.

What makes the Lord's choice of Paul especially profound is the fact that Paul was the least likely candidate. He hated Christians, persecuted them, and worked overtime to have them arrested. He believed Christ to be the enemy. Paul had a stellar pedigree from the world's standpoint. He describes himself as one who was "circumcised the eighth day, of the nation of Israel, of the tribe of Benjamin, a Hebrew of Hebrews, as to the Law, a Pharisee, as to zeal, a persecutor of the church; as to the righteousness which is in the Law, found blameless" (Philippians 3:5-6). He revealed in a defense before the Jews in Acts 22:3 that he was a Jew, "born in Tarsus of Cilicia, but brought up in this city [Jerusalem], educated under Gamaliel (teacher of the Law, Acts 5:34), strictly according to the law of our fathers, being zealous for God just as you all are today. I persecuted this Way to the death, binding and putting both men and women into prisons" (Acts 22:3-4).

Can you imagine the supposed impossibility that someone like Paul would be entrusted with the gospel of Jesus Christ communicating the righteousness of God and a salvation by faith apart from the Law? Well, get ready for the ways of Jesus Christ, who does "immeasurably more than all we can ask or imagine" (Ephesians 3:20). As you begin your quiet time today, ask the Lord to stir your heart and speak to you from His Word. Write a simple one sentence prayer in the space provided.

READ AND STUDY GOD'S WORD

1. The first verse in the letter to the Romans reveals the author as "Paul, a bond-servant of Christ Jesus, called as an apostle, set apart for the gospel of God" (Romans 1:1). Who is Paul? We are first introduced to him as Saul (his Jewish name) at the stoning of Stephen in Acts 7:58. "When they had driven him [Stephen] out of the city, they began stoning him; and the witnesses laid aside their robes at the feet of a young man named Saul." In Acts 8:1 we learn that "Saul was in hearty agreement with putting him to death. And on that day, a great persecution began against the church in Jerusalem." Oh Saul, little do you know what is about to happen! Read Acts 9:1-19 and describe in a few sentences this dramatic and life-changing event.

2. How did meeting Jesus impact Saul? Read Acts 9:19-22 and write out your most significant thoughts about Saul, also known as Paul (his Greco-Roman name, Acts 13:9).

3. Read the following verses and write out your insights related to Paul, his relationship with Christ, and the ministry Jesus entrusted to him.

Philippians 1:21

Philippians 3:8

2 Timothy 1:8-12

Optional: Galatians 1:15-17, Galatians 2:19-21, 2 Corinthians 11:23

4. There is a word that Paul uses more than once in describing the ministry the Lord has given him. It is the word translated "entrust" (see Galatians 2:7, 1 Thessalonians 2:4, 1 Timothy 1:11) and means to have something committed to one's trust or charge. Christ Himself gave Paul the task to proclaim and preach the gospel. Paul considered himself a "bond-servant of Christ Jesus" and refers to Jesus as "Jesus Christ our Lord" more than once. That word, "Lord" is *kurios* and means Lord, master, and owner. Paul took his Lord's assignment seriously and was faithful to all that was entrusted to him. We see his faithfulness in his singleminded focus to the stewardship entrusted to hm. He said, "I do all things for the sake of the gospel" (1 Corinthians 9:23). And we can be so glad he was faithful in all the Lord assigned to him in ministry, for we have the fruit of his faithfulness in so much of the New Testament, especially the letter to the Romans, written after he had served the Lord many years in ministry. Thus, in Romans, we are given a view of the gospel after preaching and teaching it for a long length of time. Read Acts 20:24, Paul's words later in life, and underline your favorite words and phrases.

> But I do not consider my life of any account as dear to myself, so that I may finish my course and the ministry which I received from the Lord Jesus, to testify solemnly of the gospel of the grace of God (Acts 20:24).

5. Think about how Jesus Christ changed Paul. How committed to Christ was Paul? How is Paul an example for you today? What is the most important lesson you learn from him that helps you in your own relationship with Christ? Do you realize that Jesus Christ is your Lord? How does Paul encourage you to be faithful in all your Lord has entrusted to you? Write your thoughts in the space provided.

ADORE GOD IN PRAYER

Pray the following prayer by Peter Marshall entitled "The Grateful Heart": "Lord, I pause to look back on the long way Thou hast brought me, on the long days in which I have been served, not according to my deserts but according to my desires and Thy loving mercies. Let me meditate upon the dark nights through which I have come, the sinister things from which I have been delivered—and have a grateful heart. Let me meditate upon my sins forgiven, for my shame unpublished—and have a grateful heart. I thank Thee, O Lord, that, in Thy mercy, so many things I feared never came to pass. Fill my heart with thankful praise. Help me to repay in service to others the debt of Thy unmerited benefits and mercies. May the memories of sorrows that disciplined my spirit keep me humble and make me grateful that my God is no celestial Santa Claus but a divine Saviour. In His name I offer this sacrifice of praise. Amen."[6]

YIELD YOURSELF TO GOD

For half a century and more I have been a student and teacher of ancient literature, and to no other writer of antiquity have I devoted so much time and attention as to Paul. Nor can I think of any other writer, ancient or modern, whose study is so richly rewarding as his. This is due to several aspects of his many-faceted character: the attractive warmth of his personality, his intellectual stature, the exhilarating release effected by his gospel of redeeming grace, the dynamism with which he propagated that gospel throughout the world, devoting himself single mindedly to fulfilling the commission entrusted to him on the Damascus road ("this one thing I do") and labouring more abundantly than all his fellow-apostles — "yet not I, but the grace of God which was with me."[7]

F.F. BRUCE IN PAUL: APOSTLE OF THE HEART SET FREE

As he [Paul] kept Christ's deposit, so Christ had kept his. And as he gave in the account of his stewardship, who can doubt that the Lord greeted him with, "Well done, good and faithful servant, enter thou into the joy of thy Lord." What a festal welcome he must have received from thousands whom he had helped turn from darkness to light, from the power of Satan to God, and who were now to become his crown of rejoicing in the presence of the Lord… How largely his letters bulk in the makeup of the New Testament. They make a fourth part of the whole. And their importance must be measured not by length but by weight. Consider the precious treasures you are handling…The epistles marvelously reflect his personality. It has been said of one of the great painters that he was accustomed to mix his colors with blood drawn from a secret wound; and of Paul it may be said that he dipped his pen in the blood of his heart. It is not too much to say that, humanly speaking, the gospel of Christ would never have taken such fast hold on the strong, practical, vigorous nations of the West, had it not been for these epistles…"Ah," it has been eloquently said, "what does the world owe to this apostle; what has it owed him; what will it owe: of pious pastors, zealous missionaries, eminent Christians, useful books, benevolent endowments, examples of faith, charity, purity, holiness? The whole human race will confess that there is no one to whom it proclaims with so much harmony, gratitude, and love, as the name of the apostle Paul."[8]

F.B. MEYER IN GREAT MEN OF THE BIBLE, VOLUME II

ENJOY HIS PRESENCE

As you ponder all you have learned about Paul today, why do you think he was the perfect choice to preach the gospel, and write about the gospel in his letters in the New Testament, especially in the letter to the Romans? How impressed were you with how the Lord met Paul and changed his life? According to author and New Testament Greek professor Merrill C. Tenney, Paul "was committed to one position when he left Jerusalem; according to the effect of his whole life he was irrevocably convinced of the supremacy of Christ when he reappeared in Jerusalem preaching the faith which he once destroyed."[9] That is how life-changing his newfound relationship with Christ was.

Talk with the Lord about all you have learned from Paul and why you are looking forward to studying the letter to the Romans. The Lord wants to meet with you also, and knowing Him more intimately will change your life. Write a prayer to the Lord expressing all that is on your heart.

REST IN HIS LOVE

"For to me, to live is Christ, and to die is gain" (Philippians 1:21).

LOOKING UP TO GOD

I lift my eyes to You, O God, enthroned in heaven. Psalm 123:1 NLT
Newport Beach, California, USA
Fujifilm X-T2, ISO 100, f11, 1/100sec, Adobe Photoshop, Nik Silver Efex Pro
MYPHOTOWALK.COM—CATHERINEMARTIN.SMUGMUG.COM

THE PEOPLE OF THE HOUR

*You also are the called of Jesus Christ; to all who are
beloved of God in Rome, called as saints."*

ROMANS 1:6-7

PREPARE YOUR HEART

hen you write a letter or an email, you always write with the recipient in mind, whether a friend, family member, acquaintance, or a stranger. When Paul wrote the letter to the Romans, he had an immediate audience in mind—the people of the church in Rome, both Jews and Gentiles. The population of Christians in Rome was predominantly Gentile, but there were also Jewish Christians as is seen in Romans 4:1, and chapters 9-11. So when we read and study the letter to the Romans, we must always remember the words are written to believers in Christ. And knowing Paul's immediate audience is essential to understanding all we read and study in Romans.

Paul most likely had another audience in mind as well. He clearly knew the ripple effect of the written word of God and discipleship of men and women. He wrote to his disciple Timothy, "The things which you have heard from me in the presence of many witnesses, entrust these to faithful men, who will be able to teach others also" (2 Timothy 2:2). You were also on his mind as he wrote Romans, knowing that his words would be passed on to believers in future generations. Those words we read in Day 1 by W.H. Griffith Thomas are especially important to think about today: "The Epistle should be regarded as a personal letter to ourselves. Its deepest secrets will only be revealed to the heart that is willing to submit to its teaching and translate it into action."[10]

Always remember when you study God's Word, that "All Scripture is inspired by God and is useful to teach us what is true and to make us realize what is wrong in our lives. It corrects us when we are wrong and teaches us to do what is right. God uses it to prepare and equip his people to do every good work" (2 Timothy 3:16-17 NLT). The Bible has been called God's love letter to us. It is God's Word, dear friend. What this means for you is that God intends for you to take what He says personally, as though it is written just for you. This also means that as you read and study Romans, remember that God has something to say to you. When you read and study Romans, get personal and ask, "Lord what do You have to say to me?"

Paul wrote some important words to the church at Colossae telling them how to handle

Scripture. He wrote, "Let the word of Christ richly dwell within you, with all wisdom teaching and admonishing one another with psalms and hymns and spiritual songs, singing with thankfulness in your hearts to God" (Colossians 3:16). May the words of Romans make their way so deeply into your heart that they burst forth in psalms and hymns and spiritual songs to your Lord. Jeremiah regarded the word of God as a rich meal when he wrote, "Your words were found and I ate them, and Your words became for me a joy and the delight of my heart; for I have been called by Your name, O LORD God of hosts" (Jeremiah 15:16). May Romans be like the delicacy of a wonderful meal that is deeply satisfying to your heart. Think about the words Jesus said about His Word—"Anyone who listens to my teaching and follows it is wise, like a person who builds a house on solid rock. Though the rain comes in torrents and the floodwaters rise and the winds beat against that house, it won't collapse because it is built on bedrock" (Matthew 7:24-25 NLT). The truths in Romans will establish you on solid ground so that no matter what you face today or tomorrow, you stand strong in Christ. Finally, you have a personal teacher with you at all times, the Lord Jesus through the Holy Spirit. Jesus said, "But the Helper, the Holy Spirit, whom the Father will send in My name, He will teach you all things, and bring to your remembrance all that I said to you" (John 14:26). May you learn much from your indwelling teacher, the Holy Spirit.

As you begin your quiet time, ask the Lord to speak to your heart today.

READ AND STUDY GOD'S WORD

1. Paul describes his audience in the first chapter of Romans. Read Romans 1:6-7 and write out his description of the recipients of his letter.

2. In Romans 1:8 Paul thanks God for the Christians in Rome because their faith is being proclaimed throughout the whole world. Then in Romans 1:11-12 Paul shares that he wants to see those Christians in Rome established and encouraged. Isn't it interesting how he describes those in Rome? There are three phrases that he uses: "called of Jesus Christ," "beloved of God," and "called as saints." Read the following verses and underline favorite truths about these three phrases. And remember, if you know Christ, these are things that are true about you! Be sure to

think about these truths personally in your own life. For example, "I am called of Jesus Christ and I belong to Him, I am beloved by the Lord, God has chosen me from the beginning for salvation…"

Called of Jesus Christ—Called means you belong to Jesus Christ

But we should always give thanks to God for you, brethren beloved by the Lord, because God has chosen you from the beginning for salvation through sanctification by the Spirit and faith in the truth. It was for this He called you through our gospel, that you may gain the glory of our Lord Jesus Christ. 2 Thessalonians 2:13-14

Who has saved us and called us with a holy calling, not according to our works, but according to His own purpose and grace which was granted us in Christ Jesus from all eternity, but now has been revealed by the appearing of our Savior Christ Jesus, who abolished death and brought life and immortality to light through the gospel. 2 Timothy 1:9-10

Beloved of God—Beloved means you are God's loved one

For I am convinced that neither death, nor life, nor angels, nor principalities, nor things present, nor things to come, nor powers, nor height, nor depth, nor any other created thing, will be able to separate us from the love of God, which is in Christ Jesus our Lord. Romans 8:38-39

So, as those who have been chosen of God, holy and beloved, put on a heart of compassion, kindness, humility, gentleness and patience. Colossians 3:12

Knowing, brethren beloved by God, His choice of you. 1 Thessalonians 1:4

Called as saints—Saint means you are holy and set apart for God

And they will call them, "The holy people, The redeemed of the LORD"; And you will be called, "Sought out, a city not forsaken." Isaiah 62:12

To the church of God which is at Corinth, to those who have been sanctified in Christ Jesus, saints by calling, with all who in every place call on the name of our Lord Jesus Christ, their Lord and ours. 1 Corinthians 1:2

You are a chosen people. You are royal priests, a holy nation, God's very own possession. As a result, you can show others the goodness of God, for he called you out of the darkness into his wonderful light. "Once you had no identity as a people; now you are God's people. Once you received no mercy; now you have received God's mercy." 1 Peter 2:9-10 NLT

3. What is the most significant truth you have learned and how does it encourage you today?

ADORE GOD IN PRAYER

Take some time now to talk with the Lord about all you learned from Him. Talk with Him about what it means that you belong to Him, you are loved by Him, and that He has made you holy and set apart for Him. Then, talk with Him about all that is weighing on your heart today. Lay out each burden in your life, and ask Him to carry them according to His words in 1 Peter 5:7. "Give all your worries and cares to God, for He cares about you." Thank Him for the opportunity and privilege to study Romans and talk with Him about all that He will be teaching you as you study His Word.

YIELD YOURSELF TO GOD

What an inspiration to realize that they were the objects of God's love because they belonged to Jesus Christ. God delights to call us His beloved ones, and as we contemplate this love which finds and takes us just as we are and loves us with an everlasting love, we should rest and rejoice in His love and take it home to our own souls, for comfort, encouragement, and peace.[11]

W.H. GRIFFITH THOMAS IN ROMANS: A DEVOTIONAL COMMENTARY I-V

ENJOY HIS PRESENCE

Do you realize that God loves you and has a plan for your life? We can't leave today's study without asking if indeed you have entered into a love relationship with Him by asking Jesus into your life? Jesus said, "Behold, I stand at the door and knock; if anyone hears My voice and opens the door, I will come in to him and will dine with him, and he with me" (Revelation 3:20). We see in John 1:12 that "as many as received Him, to them He gave the right to become children of God, even to those who believe in His name." You can receive Jesus right now by praying a simple prayer something like this, *Lord Jesus, I need You. Thank You for dying on the cross for me. I ask You now to come into my life, forgive my sins, and make me the person You want me to be. In Jesus' name, Amen.* Oh how He loves you dear friend. His love is the love that reached out to Paul on the Damascus road, the love that held him strong even when his circumstances were seemingly impossible as he preached the gospel, and it is the love that will never let you go. Soon you will see in an even deeper way all that is contained in the gospel. And behind it all is the great love of God for you; "For God so loved the world, that He gave His only begotten Son, that whoever believes in Him shall not perish, but have eternal life" (John 3:16). Will you close your time today by writing a prayer and telling the Lord how much His love means to you?

REST IN HIS LOVE

"For I am convinced that neither death, nor life, nor angels, nor principalities, nor things present, nor things to come, nor powers, nor height, nor depth, nor any other created things, will be able to separate us from the love of God, which is in Christ Jesus our Lord" (Romans 8:38-39).

Trust In The Lord

Trust in the Lord with all your heart. Proverbs 3:5
Rancho Mirage, California, USA
Nikon D7000, ISO 100, f5.6, 1/200sec, Adobe Photoshop, Nik Silver Efex Pro
myPhotoWalk.com—catherinemartin.smugmug.com

WHAT IS ON THE HEART OF GOD

*For I am not ashamed of the gospel, for it is the power of God for salvation
to everyone who believes, to the Jew first and also to the Greek.*

ROMANS 1:16

PREPARE YOUR HEART

hat is on the heart of God? That question is answered so well in the letter to the Romans.
Paul says in Romans 1:16 "I am not ashamed of the gospel, for it is the power of God for salvation to everyone who believes, to the Jew first and also to the Greek." What we see here is that God wants those He has created to be saved. Behind it all is His unfathomable and everlasting love for you. What is on His heart? It could be summed up in one word—you.

Even if you didn't believe in God, just for the sake of argument, let's suppose that there is a God who is Creator. This God is a God of justice and righteousness and love. And just suppose that He created human beings for a purpose—He wants a love relationship with them forever. And suppose in the beginning that this love relationship existed and was idyllic. The fellowship and the exchange of love between God and His creation was perfect.

Within that idyllic existence boundaries existed, set up by God Himself, to allow for this love relationship to flourish. The boundaries were basic: God's creation was not to exist independently of Him, but was to be dependent upon Him as the source of everything.

And then one day, God's human beings crossed those boundaries. They decided on their own, with the help of one who was bent on destroying their relationship with God, to make a choice that was independent and directly against what God had commanded. Once they crossed that boundary, sin entered the world. When sin entered the world, the love relationship with God was affected: their sin separated them from a holy God and they could no longer enjoy this intimate fellowship with Him for which they were designed. This sin created a great uncrossable chasm between man and God and affected all of mankind. The Bible tells us in Romans 3:23 that "all have sinned and fall short of the glory of God" and in Romans 6:23 we see that "the penalty of sin is death." Those who were loved by God were in a hopeless, helpless, depraved state whereby they could not be in a love relationship with God because of His own demands of justice and righteousness and because of their sin and its penalty. Thus God could not bestow His blessings

43

on them and they could not experience His love. Romans 5:6 says that "we were powerless to help ourselves." It is as though all of mankind was and is on death row, "having no hope and without God in the world" (Ephesians 2:12).

We see here what might be thought of as the divine dilemma because of God's justice, holiness, and righteousness. And yet, God loves us with an everlasting love and desires a love relationship with us. Therein is the dilemma. Because of His own demands of justice and righteousness, those God loved could not experience a love relationship with Him because of their sin. Here we also see the human dilemma in that we are created to know and love God, but the depravity of man where all have sinned and fall short of the glory of God prevents a love relationship with God. There is an uncrossable chasm between holy God and sinful man.

And now, you will see the act of divine love. He is just and He is also the justifier (Romans 3:25). Because of God's own love for us, He did something Himself, something only He could do, to bridge the uncrossable chasm of sin and death. Romans 5:8 says it all in just one sentence. "Yet the proof of God's amazing love is this: that it was while we were sinners that Christ died for us." F.F. Bruce explains: "What men can scarcely do for the good, God has done abundantly for the vile and the despicable." Here we see the nature of our God's divine love. It is love for the undeserving. It is a love that takes action on the behalf of the undeserving. It is a love that moves the undeserving to a favorable position. It is a love that desires security and assurance bestowed on its objects.

God saw the inability of man to reach Him because of sin. And so, He reached down to man, and determined to pay the penalty for sin Himself. It is a fact of history that the Jesus was arrested at night, secretly tried, and publicly crucified on a cross. While Jesus was hanging on the cross, He cried out three words: "It is finished" (John 19:30). The penalty of sin has been paid once and for all by God Himself in Jesus Christ!

Do you see, beloved, how loved you are by God in Jesus Christ? Paul responds with these words in Romans 5:11. "We may hold our heads high in the light of God's love because of the reconciliation which Christ has made."

All we are going to see in Romans is a beautiful love story as your Lord has done everything that you may be saved and live with Him forever. Charles Wesley's hymn refrain becomes the cry of our hearts: "Amazing love! How can it be that thou, my God, should die for me!" Today will you, as the hymnwriter, Helen H. Lemmel, has encouraged, "Turn your eyes upon Jesus, look full in His wonderful face, and the things of earth will grow strangely dim, in the light of His glory and grace." Write a prayer to the Lord expressing all that is on your heart today.

READ AND STUDY GOD'S WORD

1. Today is a day to look at the love of God and how you are the object of His love. Take some time to look at each of these verses in and write what you learn about the great love of God and how you are saved.

Romans 5:5-9

Ephesians 1:3-6

Ephesians 2:4-10

2. Yours is a beautiful love story between you and your Lord. Oh how He loves you with an everlasting love (Jeremiah 31:3). He determined to save you Himself—the first prophecy of Christ's coming is seen in Genesis 3:15, then the blood necessary from the Passover lamb during the exodus (Exodus 12:1-13) points to Christ's shed blood for you, all parts of the tabernacle (Exodus 25-30) point to Christ, even the layout of the camps of the Israelites is in the shape of a cross (Numbers 2), the sacrifices in Leviticus necessary to atone for sin (Leviticus 1:1-4) point to Christ's shed blood as your atonement, the promise of a ruler born in Bethlehem (Micah 5:2) points to Jesus' birth in Bethlehem, and the promise of a son who would be Wonderful Counselor, Mighty God, Eternal Father, Prince of Peace (Isaiah 9:6) is fulfilled in Christ. We then move on to the New Testament and see that the Word became flesh and dwelt among men (John 1:14). God did indeed fulfill His promise in Isaiah 35:4 that He would save His people – the promise is fulfilled in Jesus, the Son who would "save His people from their sins" (Matthew 1:21). Even Abraham and his son Isaac are a picture of what the Lord has done for us when Abraham told Isaac, "God will provide for Himself the lamb for the burnt offering" (Genesis 22:8).

God loves you and is your Provider in the sacrifice and shed blood of Jesus Christ that you might be forgiven of your sins. As you think about the love story that is yours, read Hebrews 9:11-12 and write what is most significant to you today.

3. Jesus gave a dramatic picture of God's amazing love and His heart for you in His parable about the prodigal son in Luke 15:11-32. In His story, Jesus described a father with two sons. The younger son demanded his inheritance, left home, and eventually lost all his money with wild living. Finally, he came to his senses and returned home, hoping to be hired as a servant. But the prodigal underestimated his father's love. It was always there, but he never saw it or realized the depth of it until now. "And while he was still a long way off, his father saw him coming. Filled with love and compassion, he ran to his son, embraced him, and kissed him" (Luke 15:20). Do you see the depth of God's love for you? His love does not hold us at arm's length, but initiates a run towards us and a reconciliation with us, embracing us with His everlasting arms, and expressing deep affection. Kenneth Bailey, in his book, *The Cross and the Prodigal*, describes this event from a Middle Eastern context, and reveals that the father's cost in leaving the comfort and security of home, and going out to the prodigal is a clear picture of the incarnation and the atonement of Jesus Christ. He writes: "The father's actions are a drama of reconciliation that can restore the boy to his home and to his community. After this scene, no one in the village can reject or despise him."[12] How does the parable of the prodigal son help you see God's amazing love for you?

4. One of the most well-known summaries of the gospel is called "The Romans Road to Salvation." These powerful truths from Romans lay out the heart of the gospel—our need for the gospel, God's provision, how we may experience forgiveness of sins and eternal life, and the results. In these verses you see what is on the heart of God and His plan and purpose for you. Read these verses and underline your favorite and most significant words and phrases.

- We all need salvation because we have all sinned: "For all have sinned and fall short of the glory of God" (Romans 3:23).

- The penalty for sin is death: "For the wages of sin is death, but the free gift of God is eternal life in Christ Jesus our Lord" (Romans 6:23).

- Jesus Christ died for our sins; He paid the price that we might be forgiven: "But God demonstrates His own love toward us, in that while we were yet sinners, Christ died for us" (Romans 5:8).

- We receive salvation and eternal life through Jesus Christ: "If you confess with your mouth Jesus as Lord, and believe in your heart that God raised Him from the dead, you will be saved; for with the heart a person believes, resulting in righteousness, and with the mouth he confesses, resulting in salvation…for whoever will call on he name of the Lord will be saved" (Romans 10:9-10,13).

- Salvation through Christ brings us into an eternal relationship with God: ""Therefore, having been justified by faith, we have peace with God through Lord Jesus Christ" (Romans 5:1). "Therefore, there is now no condemnation for those who are in Christ Jesus" (Romans 8:1).

5. Today, as you have been studying God's love for you, have you underestimated His love for you or do you realize in a new way just how much He loves you?

ADORE GOD IN PRAYER

Pray the words of Psalm 18:1-2 NLT: "I love You, LORD, my strength. The LORD is my rock, my fortress, and my deliverer, my God, my rock where I seek refuge, my shield and the horn of my salvation, my stronghold."

YIELD YOURSELF TO GOD

Salvation is entirely and altogether of God, and is the result of the great and eternal love of God…Before the foundation of the world, before the world was ever made, before man was ever created, before time had ever come into existence, God planned this mighty and glorious way of salvation. He planned it in detail; He planned that at a given point in time His Son should come into the world in order to make the Atonement, whereby alone salvation would be made possible…Salvation is not an afterthought. Nothing is an afterthought where God is concerned. God sees the end from the beginning…God had planned it all before the foundation of the world…The very planning and purposing of it is a glorious manifestation of the love of God…There is no greater proof of the love of God towards us than the fact that He was aware of us, and had chosen us, before the foundation of the world. It was planned that Christ should die for us before we ever lived.[13]

D. MARTYN LLOYD-JONES IN ROMANS, EXPOSITION OF CHAPTER 5, ASSURANCE

ENJOY HIS PRESENCE

Think about all you've learned today about God's love for you. What is your favorite truth? What is your response to the love of God? Will you receive His love and forgiveness in Christ? Write your thoughts in your Journal in the back of this book, then close with a prayer to the Lord.

REST IN HIS LOVE

"He chose us in Him before the foundation of the world, that we would be holy and blameless before Him. In love He predestined us to adoption as sons through Jesus Christ to Himself, according to the kind intention of His will, to the praise of the glory of His grace, which He freely bestowed on us in the Beloved" (Ephesians 1:4-6).

BLOSSOM IN HIS PRESENCE

I will counsel you with My eye upon you. Psalm 32:8
Phoenix, Arizona, USA
Nikon D800E, ISO 250, f5.6, 1/2000sec, Adobe Photoshop, Nik Silver Efex Pro
MYPHOTOWALK.COM—CATHERINEMARTIN.SMUGMUG.COM

HOW THEN SHALL YOU LIVE

For in it [the gospel] the righteousness of God is revealed from faith to faith; as it is written, "But the righteous man shall live by faith."
ROMANS 1:17

PREPARE YOUR HEART

More than twenty-five years ago, Francis Schaeffer, a well known theologian, philosopher, pastor, and co-founder of the L'Abri community in Switzerland, filmed a series entitled, "How Should We Then Live?" In that series he showed the rise and decline of Western culture from a Christian perspective, and that the only hope was to return to God through Jesus Christ as revealed in the Scriptures. Francis Schaeffer, at the age of thirty-nine, came to a spiritual crisis in his life though he had walked with the Lord for many years and had seen much fruit in his ministry. He describes his experience in the introduction to his book, *True Spirituality*:

I faced a spiritual crisis in my own life. I had become a Christian from agnosticism many years before. After that I had become a pastor for ten years in the United States, and then for several years my wife Edith and I had been working in Europe. During this time I felt a strong burden to stand for the historical Christian position and for the purity of the visible Church. Gradually, however, a problem came to me—the problem of reality…it gradually grew on me that my own reality was less than it had been in the early days after I had become a Christian. I realized that in honesty I had to go back and rethink my whole position…I walked in the mountains when it was clear, and when it was rainy I walked backward and forward in the hayloft of the old chalet in which we lived. I walked, prayed, and thought through what the Scriptures taught, reviewing my own reasons for being a Christian…As I rethought my reasons for being a Christian, I saw again that there were totally sufficient reasons to know that the infinite-personal God does exist and that Christianity is true. In going further, I saw something else which made a profound difference in my life. I searched through what the Bible said concerning reality as a Christian. Gradually I saw that the problem was that with all the teaching I had received after I was a Christian, I had heard little about what the

Bible says about the meaning of the finished work of Christ for our present lives. Gradually the sun came out and the song came. Interestingly enough, although I had written no poetry for many years, in that time of joy and song I found poetry beginning to flow again—poetry of certainty, an affirmation of life, thanksgiving, and praise…it expressed a song in my heart that was wonderful to me.[14]

Francis Schaeffer basically discovered the need for faith in biblical truth, especially "the finished work of Christ" for his own life. And dear friend, this is what we learn from Paul. "The righteous man shall live by faith." And where does our faith rest? On all the Lord says in His Word. Just the facts are all we need. And we get those facts, i.e. the truth, in Romans. Get ready for what Francis Schaeffer describes as the poetry of certainty, an affirmation of life, thanksgiving, praise, and a song in your heart.

Today, dear friend, ask the Lord to speak to your heart as you draw near to Him.

READ AND STUDY GOD'S WORD

1. In this final day of study in Week 1, we are going to look at the important words of Romans 1:17 and what they mean for us today. Read Romans 1:17 and write out that verse word for word in the space provided.

2. The first big truth we see that is going to become most important in the weeks to come is that in the gospel, "the righteousness of God" is revealed. Why is this so important? Why is it a big deal? Because we need "the righteousness of God" to be saved. And there is only one way we can have it. In Christ. There is a great truth revealed in the name of God discovered in Jeremiah 23:6, "The Lord Our Righteousness" (Yahweh Tsidkenu). Paul gives us greater insight into this when he contrasts a righteousness that is derived from the law and the righteousness that comes from God by faith. He writes that he wants to be found in Christ, "not having a righteousness of my own derived from the Law, but that which is through faith in Christ, the righteousness which comes from God on the basis of faith" (Philippians 3:9). Let's take some time to look at the righteousness of God in greater detail. Read the following verses and write your favorite insights about the righteousness of God.

Isaiah 61:1-3, 10-11

Romans 3:21-26

Romans 9:30-32

2 Corinthians 5:21

3. The righteousness of God cannot be received by works. Works cannot save us and we cannot save ourselves. Titus 3:5-6 says "He saved us, not on the basis of deeds which we have done in righteousness, but according to His mercy, by the washing of regeneration and renewing by the Holy Spirit, whom He poured out upon us richly through Jesus Christ our Savior." The world often thinks, "I'm good enough. I'm better than this person or that person." We learn in Romans that "all have sinned and fall short of the glory of God" (Romans 3:23). We will see this truth in detail next week. There is a righteousness—the righteousness of God—that is a gift because of the finished work of Jesus Christ on the cross—"the righteous man shall live by faith" (Romans 1:17). Paul is quoting Habakkuk 2:4, demonstrating the principle of faith in the Old Testament. The righteousness of God is "his saving activity whereby he puts men in the right (as a judge declares a man innocent), and whereby he puts men in a right relationship to himself."[15] God's righteousness is the rightness of God and rightness with God. God's righteousness is received by faith.

Spurgeon writes: "Faith is the telegraphic wire which links earth to Heaven, on which God's messages of love fly so fast that before we call He answers, and while we are yet speaking He hears us." Always remember that faith is taking God at His Word. When you take God at His Word, you will discover that faith is, as Corrie ten Boom used to say, a fantastic adventure in trusting Him. Read the following verses and underline your favorite phrases about the need for faith in our relationship with Christ and how it is that we may be saved.

Therefore, having been justified by faith, we have peace with God through our Lord Jesus Christ, through whom also we have obtained our introduction by faith into this grace in which we stand; and we exult in hope of the glory of God. Romans 5:1-2

I have been crucified with Christ; and it is no longer I who live, but Christ lives in me; and the life which I now live in the flesh I live by faith in the Son of God, who loved me and gave Himself up for me. Galatians 2:20

For by grace you have been saved through faith; and that not of yourselves, it is the gift of God; not as a result of works, so that no one may boast. Ephesians 2:8-0

And without faith it is impossible to please Him, for he who comes to God must believe that He is and that He is a rewarder of those who seek Him. Hebrews 11:6

4. What is the most important truth you have learned today and how does it encourage you in your relationship with the Lord?

ADORE GOD IN PRAYER

Let me turn to you, O Lord, from the sweetest of earthly joys, to find that you are best of all, the fairest among ten thousand, and altogether lovely.

F.B. MEYER IN DAILY PRAYERS

YIELD YOURSELF TO GOD

According to the Bible, we are to be living a supernatural life now, in this present existence, in a way we shall never be able to do again through all eternity. We are called upon to live a supernatural life now, by faith…Christians are called upon to be a demonstration at our point of history that the supernatural, the normally unseen world, does exist and, beyond that, that God exists.[16]

FRANCIS SCHAEFFER IN TRUE SPIRITUALITY

God does not ask people to *behave* in order to be saved, but to *believe*. It is faith in Christ that saves the sinner…Romans 1:17 is the key verse of the letter. In it

Paul announces the theme: "the righteousness of God." The word *righteousness* is used in one way or another over sixty times in this letter (*righteous, just*, and *justified*). God's righteousness is revealed in the gospel; for in the death of Christ, God revealed His righteousness by punishing sin; and in the resurrection of Christ, He revealed His righteousness by making salvation available to the believing sinner. The problem "How can a holy God ever forgive sinners and still be holy?" is answered in the Gospel. Through the death and resurrection of Christ, God is seen to be both "just and the justifier" (Romans 3:26).[17]

Warren W. Wiersbe in Be Right

James McConkey wrote: "Faith is dependence upon God. And this God-dependence only begins when self-dependence ends. And self-dependence only comes to its end, with some of us, when sorrow, suffering, affliction, broken plans and hopes bring us to that place of self-helplessness and defeat. And only then do we find that we have learned the lesson of faith; to find our tiny craft of life rushing onward to a blessed victory of life and power and service undreamt of in the days of fleshly strength and self-reliance." J.B. Stoney agrees by saying, "It is a great thing to learn faith: that is, simple dependence upon God. It will comfort you much to be assured that the Lord is teaching you dependence upon Himself, and it is very remarkable that faith is necessary in everything. "The just shall live by faith," not only in your circumstances, but in everything.[18]

As quoted in The Complete Works of Miles J. Stanford

Your salvation comes, not because your faith saves you, but because it links you to the Savior who saves…Let your faith, then, "throw its arms around all God has told you."

Hannah Whitall Smith in The Christian's Secret of a Happy Life

ENJOY HIS PRESENCE

This week we have begun to see the beauty in the book of Romans and the amazing love of our Lord for us. You can see why Paul was absolutely captured by his Lord there on the Damascus road and never looked back. All things became new for him and he spent the rest of his life preaching the gospel of Jesus Christ. He called himself "a bondservant of Christ Jesus" (Romans 1:1). As you close your quiet time with the Lord, how has your understanding of God's love grown? How has your love for the Lord grown? How is your faith these days? Are you living in the truth of God's Word? Have you received Jesus into your life by faith? You can right now by opening the door of your heart to Him. He will come in and stay forever. He says, "Behold, I stand at the door and knock; if anyone hears My voice and opens the door, I will come in to him, and will dine with him, and he with Me" (Revelation 3:20). Talk with the Lord now about all you are learning.

REST IN HIS LOVE

"He made Him who knew no sin to be sin on our behalf, so that we might become the righteousness of God in Him" (2 Corinthians 5:21).

KNOWING AND TRUSTING GOD

The Word became flesh and dwelt among us, and we saw His glory. John 1:14
Coachella Valley Preserve, Palm Desert, California, USA
Nikon D7000, ISO 100, f11, AEB, Adobe Photoshop, Nik Silver Efex Pro
MYPHOTOWALK.COM—CATHERINEMARTIN.SMUGMUG.COM

DEVOTIONAL READING
BY WILLIAM R. NEWELL

Dear Friend,

The next two days are your opportunity to review what you have learned this week. You may wish to write your thoughts and insights in your Journal. As you think about all you've learned, write:

Your most significant insight:

Your favorite quote:

Your favorite verse:

od, who is love, though infinitely holy and sin-hating, has chosen to act toward us in righteousness, in a manner wherein all His holy and righteous claims against the sinner have been satisfied upon a Substitute, His own Son. Therefore, in this good news, (1) Christ died for our sins according to the Scriptures, (2) He was buried, (3) He hath been raised the third day according to the Scriptures, (4) He was manifested (1 Cor. 15:3 ff),—in this good news there is revealed, now openly for the first time, God's righteousness on the principle of faith. We simply hear and believe: and, as we shall find, God reckons us righteous; our guilt having been put away by the blood of Christ forever, and we ourselves declared to be the righteousness of God in Him![19]

WILLIAM R. NEWELL IN ROMANS VERSE BY VERSE

Meditate on the words of this hymn, "The Love of God," written by Frederick Martin Lehman.

The love of God is greater far
  Than tongue or pen can ever tell.
It goes beyond the highest star
  And reaches to the lowest hell.
The guilty pair, bowed down with care,
  God gave His Son to win;
His erring child He reconciled
  And pardoned from his sin.

Refrain: O love of God, how rich and pure!
  How measureless and strong!
It shall forevermore endure—
  The saints' and angels' song.

When hoary time shall pass away,
  And earthly thrones and kingdoms fall;
When men who here refuse to pray,
  On rocks and hills and mountains call;
God's love, so sure, shall still endure,
  All measureless and strong;
Redeeming grace to Adam's race—
  The saints' and angels' song.

Could we with ink the ocean fill,
  And were the skies of parchment made;
Were every stalk on earth a quill,
  And every man a scribe by trade;
To write the love of God above
  Would drain the ocean dry;
Nor could the scroll contain the whole,
  Though stretched from sky to sky.

❧ WEEK ONE ☙

Getting Back To Middle C

You have just completed the first week of study in *The Proof of God's Amazing Love.* Today we are going to share together an overview of Romans and powerful truths we will learn in our study of Romans. In our time together I want you to see the truths that Paul wanted the Romans and us to learn about Christ and the essentials of the Christian life.

"For I am not ashamed of the gospel, for it is the power of God for salvation to everyone who believes, to the Jew first and also to the Greek. For in it the righteousness of God is revealed from faith to faith; as it is written, but the righteous man shall live by faith" (Romans 1:16-17).

What we learn in Romans about Christ and the Essentials of the Christian Life

1. Romans shows us what _______________________________is all about. Romans 1:4ff

2. We are _____________________in need of a Savior and in need of the righteousness of God. Romans 1-3, 3:23

3. Jesus did everything necessary to secure our _______________________________ and give us God's righteousness. Romans 3:21-26

4. Romans shows us the _________________of the gospel for our salvation. Romans 1:16

5. We can be saved by grace through _____________________________. Romans 1:17

6. Romans shows us our new eternal, unchangeable, and unshakeable ______________ in life because of salvation. Romans 1-8

7. We are _____________________with Christ and identified with Him. Romans 5-8

8. We now live in the land of _________________where we can grow. Romans 5:1-2

9. Romans shows us the great _______________________________God has for us. Romans 5:8

10. Romans shows us all about the life of _________________________________. Romans 1, 4

11. Romans shows us the sunny side of _________________________________. Romans 5

12. Romans shows us what life in the _____________________ is all about. Romans 8

13. Romans shows us God's sovereignty and His _____________for our lives. Romans 9-11

14. Romans shows us the need for _________________________________ and commitment
in following Christ and serving Him during our brief stay on earth. Romans 12:1

15. Romans shows us how to live in the _____________________, but not be of the
world, as He uses us to touch a lost and hurting world. Romans 12-16

How to find middle C, know where middle C is, and get back to middle C

1. _______________________________ Christ and enter into a personal relationship with Him.
*Lord Jesus, I need You. Thank You for dying on the cross for my sins. I ask You now to come
into my life, forgive my sins, give me eternal life, and make me the person You want me to
be. In Jesus' name, Amen.*

2. _____________________in Christ and pursue knowing God in relationship with Him
through the Lord Jesus Christ.

3. Establish a regular, daily _______________________________where you spend time alone
with God in His Word and in prayer.

4. Set aside a special ____ with the Lord.

5. Study _________________________________ and always be part of a Bible study.

*Video messages are available on DVDs or as Digital M4V Video. Audio messages are
available as Digital MP3 Audio. Visit the Quiet Time Ministries Online Store at www.quiettime.org.*

THE NEED FOR GOD'S RIGHTEOUSNESS

Romans 1:18-3:31

Keep your eye steadily fixed on the infinite grandeur of Christ's finished work and righteousness. Look to Jesus and believe, look to Jesus and live! Nay, more; as you look to him, hoist your sails and buffet manfully the sea of life. Do not remain in the haven of distrust, or sleeping on your shadows in inactive repose, or suffering your frames and feelings to pitch and toss on one another like vessels idly moored in a harbor. The religious life is not a brooding over emotions, grazing the keel of faith in the shallows, or dragging the anchor of hope through the oozy tide mud as if afraid of encountering the healthy breeze. Away! With your canvas spread to the gale, trusting in Him, who rules the raging of the waters.

J. R. MACDUFF

GOD REVEALED

For since the creation of the world His invisible attributes, His eternal power and divine nature, have been clearly seen, being understood through what has been made, so that they are without excuse.

ROMANS 1:20

PREPARE YOUR HEART

Have you ever had someone tell you they don't believe in God? In fact, perhaps they identified themselves as an agnostic or atheist. It seems that sometimes this statement is said as though it doesn't matter if there is a God, because they don't believe. Always remember these words from Proverbs: "There is a way which seems right to a man, but its end is the way of death" (Proverbs 14:12, 16:25). Paul is intent on sharing the truth of the gospel.

In his comprehensive work, *The Existence and Attributes of God*, Puritan writer Stephen Charnock speaks of atheism as folly. He goes on to write: "For though God be so inaccessible that we cannot know him perfectly, yet he is so much in the light, that we cannot be totally ignorant of him; as he cannot be comprehended in his essence, he cannot be unknown in his existence; it is as easy by reason to understand that he is, as it is difficult to know what he is."[1]

Paul begins his explanation of the gospel with God as He has revealed Himself to man in His creation. Paul makes a point to talk about God and say His name at least 153 times in Romans. He says that any who suppress the truth of God are "without excuse" (Romans 1:20) because God has indeed revealed Himself to man in all He has made. Not only that, but Paul is saying that His eternal power and divine nature can be seen and understood in what He has made. As David wrote in Psalm 14:1, "The fool has said in his heart, 'There is no God.'"

As we consider the words of Paul at the outset, it seems what he is getting at is that all of us are accountable to God. Because of His existence, there are no excuses that can stand up against anything He asks or says. He is the measure of all that is true and He alone possesses the right to command one's beliefs and actions.

Dr. Viggo Olsen, during his early days, soon after receiving his medical degree, considered himself an agnostic, not 100% sure of God's existence, and certainly not believing a self-existent God could ever be known. He describes in his book, *Daktar: Diplomat In Bangladesh,* how he came to a deep realization of his own accountability to God when he realized His existence. He basically asked himself the question, "Could there be design in the universe without a designer?" He concluded that he "could not find a design without a designer, or a pattern without a pattern-maker. And there was unquestionable evidence of pattern and design in our universe and on our planet. The millions of stars and planets track their courses precisely...The marvelous design of plants and animals which fits them to their sometimes inhospitable environment is remarkable in the extreme. The human body whose design and function I had come to know so well, possess a million different patterns in its many organs, group of cells, and chemical systems."[2] Ultimately, Dr. Olsen and his wife believed, and gave their lives to Jesus Christ.

Begin your quiet time by read the words of Psalm 19:1-2 and then ask the Lord to quiet your heart and speak to you in His Word.

READ AND STUDY GOD'S WORD

1. Last week in our study of Romans 1:1-17, we looked at an overview of Romans, including Paul, the recipients, the believers in Rome, and the occasion, purpose, and overall theme of Romans as seen in Romans 1:16-17. In Romans 1:17, Paul wrote that in the gospel "the righteousness of God is revealed." That word "reveal" is *apokalupto* and means to "expose to open view what was before hidden." And now, in Romans, Paul does this by explaining:

- The Need For God's Righteousness—Sin: Romans 1:18-3:31

- The Way Of God's Righteousness—Salvation: Romans 4-5

- The Union, Power and Provision of God's Righteousness—Sanctification, Security, Spirit of God: Romans 6-8

- The Scope and Plan of God's Righteousness—Sovereignty: Romans 9-11

- The Practical Applications of God's Righteousness—Service: Romans 12-16

This week we are going to look at the need for God's righteousness in Romans 1:18-3:31. And today, you have the opportunity to explore and think about the fact that God has revealed Himself to all of mankind. Read Romans 1:18-23 and write out what you learn about God.

2. The Bible reveals more than one hero of the faith who discovered God by observing and meditating on His works. Asaph wrote: "I will meditate on all Your work and muse on Your deeds. Your way, O God, is holy; What god is great like our God? You are the God who works wonders; You have made known Your strength among the peoples" (Psalm 77:12-14). God invites you to know Him. He wants to be known. He says, "Be still and know that I am God" (Psalm 46:10). Today is your opportunity to meditate on the work of the Lord and to be still and know that He is God. God has magnificent truths He wants to show you. Read Psalm 104:1-13, 24-35 and write out your most significant and favorite insights about God, His existence and His attributes. Optional: Job 38:4-5, 12, Psalm 65:5-13, Psalm 77:16-20, Isaiah 40:21-26, 28-31

3. God is Triune. He is the Father, the Son, and the Holy Spirit, and all three Persons of the Trinity are seen throughout Romans and also in His creation. In Genesis 1:1-2, we discover "In the beginning God created the heavens and the earth. The earth was formless and void, and darkness was over the surface of the deep, and the Spirit of God was moving over the surface of the waters." Then, in Colossians 1:16, we discover Christ in creation. "For by Him [Christ] all things were created, both in the heavens and on earth, visible and invisible, whether thrones or dominions or rulers or authorities—all things have been created through Him and for Him." The Triune God is also seen in our salvation: God the Father loved us and chose us in Christ before the foundation of the world (Ephesians 1:4, Romans 5:8), God, the Son justified, saved, reconciled, and redeemed us (Romans 5), and God, the Holy Spirit, seals us in Christ as a pledge of our inheritance, and empowers us, making our salvation a present reality (Ephesians 1:13-14, Romans 8). How does this expand your view of your great God?

4. James 4:8 carries a huge promise for you today. "Draw near to God and He will draw near to you." What is your most significant insight about God today from your time in His Word as you studied many verses about His splendor and majesty in all He has created? Talk with God about all you have seen and draw near to Him.

5. We have just one more powerful truth to discover today in preparation for all that is to come. In Romans 1:18 we have begun to see and understand our need for God's righteousness. Paul writes that "the wrath of God is revealed from heaven against all ungodliness and unrighteousness of men who suppress the truth in unrighteousness." Wrath against sin results in the penalty of sin i.e. death (Romans 6:23). This death for those who are not saved and whose names are not written in the book of life (Revelation 3:5, 20:14-15) results in hell and the lake of fire. We have just looked at the truth of God's splendor and majesty in all He has created through many passages of Scripture. The question possibly comes to our mind, "How then can anyone be saved?" Now you are going to see the power of the gospel and why we need Jesus. God stepped in and did for us what we could never do for ourselves. And it shows you His great love for you. This is in effect a spoiler for all that is to come in Romans, but it will be encouragement for you especially when we look more intently at the sin of man seen in Romans 1:18-3:31 in the days to come. Read the words of Romans 5:8-10 and underline those phrases that help you see how and why you may experience salvation. Notice how we are saved from God's wrath by Christ. This is the good news of the gospel!

> But God demonstrates His own love toward us, in that while we were yet sinners, Christ died for us. Much more then, having now been justified by His blood, we shall be saved from the wrath of God through Him. For if while we were enemies we were reconciled to God through the death of His Son, much more, having been reconciled, we shall be saved by His life (Romans 5:8-10).

ADORE GOD IN PRAYER

Pray this prayer by Corrie ten Boom: "Open our eyes, dear Lord, that we may see the far vast reaches of eternity. Help us to look beyond life's little cares so prone to fret us and the grief that wears our courage thin. O may we tune our hearts to Thy great harmony, that all the parts may ever be in perfect, sweet accord. Give us Thine own clear vision, blessed Lord."[3]

YIELD YOURSELF TO GOD

"If we witness a magnetic cloud thirty million miles in diameter moving a million miles per hour—is God bigger than that? Can He move faster than that? If the center of the sun has temperatures of fifteen million degrees centigrade and pressures of seven trillion pounds per square inch—could God walk into the core of the sun, take a nap, and walk back out? Every impressive structure or event in the universe should remind us of a God who is greater than all His works. With a God this powerful, why do we doubt that He has the power to help us order our lives…What we need is a new vision of God. The real God. Not some vague image we fold up and stuff in the back drawer of life, but the kind of God who parts the Red Sea and shakes Mount Sinai. The kind of God who stuns the physicists with symmetry, the mathematicians with precision, the engineers with design, the politicians with power, and the poets with beauty…When we understand the sovereignty, power, design, majesty, precision, genius, intimacy, and caring of an Almighty God, it takes away our fear. It removes our frustration. It allows us to sleep at night and trust Him with the running of His own universe. It allows us to have margin. It allows us to resume our proper role in the order of things rather than taking over His role. It allows us to seek His will rather than follow our own mind. The more we understand about God's power, the less we worry about our weakness. The more we trust in God's sovereignty, the less we fret about our future.[4]

RICHARD A. SWENSON M.D. IN MORE THAN MEETS THE EYE

ENJOY HIS PRESENCE

Paul has now begun his incredible treatise on the gospel. And remember, he wants those believers in Rome to be established and encouraged. He is giving them (and us) Christ and the essentials of the Christian life. Now we have begun to focus on the greatness and glory of God. We have seen how He has revealed Himself and there are no excuses because God has made Himself evident even in His creation. His wrath is revealed against all who suppress the truth in ungodliness and unrighteousness. Stop now and think about God and His creation. Have you ever gone outside at night, looked at the stars, and wondered what their names are? God knows. He calls them all by name (Isaiah 40:26). Oh, how great is your God! In the days ahead, we are going to see more and more why we need God's righteousness and why Jesus is the answer.

Close your time with God by talking with God about all that is on your heart today. Pray the words of this first stanza of "And Can It Be That I Should Gain" written by Charles Wesley:

And can it be that I should gain an int'rest in the Savior's blood?
Died he for me, who caused His pain? For me, who Him to death pursued?
Amazing love! How can it be that Thou, my God, should die for me?
Refrain: Amazing love! How can it be that Thou, my God, should die for me!

REST IN HIS LOVE

"Your way, O God, is holy; what god is great like our God? You are the God who works wonders; You have made known Your strength among the peoples" (Psalm 77:13-14).

REEDS BY THE WATER

Through everything God made, they can clearly see His invisible qualities." Romans 1:20 NLT
Coachella Valley Preserve, Palm Desert, California, USA
Nikon D7000, ISO 100, f5, 1/160sec, Adobe Photoshop, Nik Silver Efex Pro
MYPHOTOWALK.COM—CATHERINEMARTIN.SMUGMUG.COM

SIN REVEALED

As it is written, THERE IS NONE RIGHTEOUS, NOT EVEN ONE…*For all have sinned and fall short of the glory of God.*
ROMANS 3:10, 23

PREPARE YOUR HEART

hat happens when people find themselves in the presence of God who is holy, righteous, just, pure, majestic and glorious? Isaiah had just such an experience. He describes it this way: "I saw the Lord sitting on a throne, lofty and exalted, with the train of His robe filling the temple" (Isaiah 6:1). After Isaiah saw the Lord with the seraphim hovering above Him crying out "Holy, Holy, Holy," Isaiah cried out, "Woe is me, for I am ruined! Because I am a man of unclean lips, And I live among a people of unclean lips; For my eyes have seen the King, the LORD of hosts" (Isaiah 6:5). In the presence of holy God, Isaiah became aware that he was sinful. And that is what happens in our lives when we become aware of God—who He is, what He does, and all that He says.

During the Lewis Revival in Scotland in 1949-1952, the presence of God was so profound that people were making their way to the church to find out how they could be forgiven. There was an awareness of God and a conviction of sin so great that one young girl came running to the front of the church asking, "Is there mercy for me, is there mercy for me?"

Robert Lowry, Baptist minister and educator in the 1800s, asked the questions arising from an awareness of sin, in his hymn, "Nothing But The Blood." "What can wash away my sin? Nothing but the blood of Jesus. What can make me whole again? Nothing but the blood of Jesus." In the days to come, we will learn just how precious the blood of Jesus is to wash away all our sin.

In the mid-1700s, John Newton became the captain of a slave ship. On one of his return voyages from Africa, he leafed through a book he discovered on board the ship, *The Imitation of Christ* by Thomas a Kempis. It scared him just to think what might happen to him if it was all true. He closed the book. That night, March 21, 1748, the ship was caught in a powerful storm. Newton was terrified and prayed for the first time in many years. He knew if he died he was in trouble and that he could never be forgiven by God. After the storm passed, Newton was convinced that it was God who had delivered them. Newton began to read the Bible. He identified especially with the prodigal son in Luke 15. He resolved to be a better person and even went to church. But in less than a year, he was back to his old ways. While in Africa, he contracted malaria. Desperate over his sin and many failures, he cast himself upon the Lord, and put his faith in his Savior, Jesus Christ. As he grew in his new relationship with the Lord, he gave up his involvement in the slave trade, and pastored for 23 years. His favorite theme was grace and he wrote the beloved hymn, "Amazing Grace." God's grace opened his eyes as he sang, "Amazing grace, how sweet the sound, that saved a wretch like me. I once was lost but now am found. Was blind but now I see."

Every person who has ever become a Christian has a unique story of how they came to Christ, and believed in Him by grace through faith. Every story is different and yet, there are aspects of those stories that are the same. And one common theme is the moment they became aware that they were sinners and in need of salvation. That is an important part of the gospel and Paul spends three chapters in Romans explaining it to the saints in Rome. Always remember that Romans is a message for sinners, for messy, imperfect people who ultimately say, after coming to Christ: "I am a sinner saved by grace!"

Begin your quiet time today reading the words of David, Psalm 51:1-12, written after his sin with Bathsheba. Ask the Lord to speak to you as you study His Word today.

READ AND STUDY GOD'S WORD

1. In this section of Romans about the Need for God's Righteousness, Paul takes time to look at the unrighteousness of all mankind, both the pagan world including unrighteous Gentiles (Romans 1:18-32) and the self-righteous Jews (Romans 2:1-3:8). All of mankind is declared guilty and unrighteous. What Paul is doing here is showing us that we need a righteousness from God apart from the Law that only He can give us. After he shows the unrighteousness of all mankind, he concludes by saying, "There is no one righteous, not even one" (Romans 3:10). "All have sinned and fall short of the glory of God" (Romans 3:23). A sinner is one who falls short of the mark and requirement of God.

Today as we look at the unrighteousness of man, read Romans 1:18-32 and summarize in 1-2 sentences what you discover about unrighteousness and its results.

2. In Romans 1:18-32, Paul lists at least twenty-four sins and lays out many ways sin runs it course in immorality, depravity, perversion, degrading passions, and unrighteous deeds. Keep in mind the culture of the day. According to Leon Morris in his Romans Commentary, Paul says "that

these sinners received the due penalty of their misdeeds in themselves. Paul is not so much calling for a penalty as thinking of sexual perversion as itself a penalty (being a sinner is the punishment of sin!). This is sharply different from the general attitude among Greeks and Romans of the day."[6] William Barclay in his commentary says that Roman "society from top to bottom was riddled with unnatural vice."[7] He goes on to point out that the majority of Roman emperors themselves demonstrated these same sins. It was, as Barclay calls it, an age of "unparalleled immorality." Paul was writing from Corinth, and according to Everett Harrison in his Romans Commentary, "the temple of Aphrodite housed hundreds of cult prostitutes."[8] Paul was obviously aware of the immorality in that city as well as in Rome.

One can't help but think back to the garden of Eden, and the original sin of Adam after being tempted by Satan. "Through one man sin entered the world, and death through sin, and so death spread to all men, because all sinned" (Romans 5:12). Donald Grey Barnhouse, in his book, *The Invisible War*, gives a descriptive commentary of thoughts and insights illustrating the devastating results of sin in the world following the original sin of Adam in the garden. Barnhouse writes:

> War has been declared. The great, governing cherub had become the malignant enemy. Our God was neither surprised nor astonished, for, of course, He knew before it happened that it would happen, and He had His perfect plan ready to be put into effect. Although the Lord had the power to destroy Satan with a breath, He did not do so. It was as though an edict had been proclaimed in heaven: "We shall give this rebellion a thorough trial. We shall permit it to run its full course. The universe shall see what a creature, though he be the highest creature ever to spring from God's Word, can do apart from Him. We shall watch this experiment, and permit the universe of creatures to watch it, during this brief interlude between eternity past and eternity future called time. In it the spirit of independence shall be allowed to expand to the utmost. And the wreck and ruin which shall result will demonstrate to the universe, and forever, that there is no life, no joy, no peace apart from a complete dependence upon the Most High God, Possessor of heaven and earth."[9]

How does this passage of Romans 1:18-32 help you understand what Barnhouse calls "the wreck and ruin" of sin and evil at work in the first century and in the world today?

3. One horrifying result is described in a phrase that Paul mentions more than once: "God gave them over." This phrase means that God "allowed sin to run its course as an act of judgment."[5] Certainly, in these verses we see the ugliness of sin and God's abhorrence of it. So here's the question, why did God give them over? And what happens when God allows people to go their own way? Note that the wrath of God is "a holy, just revulsion against what is contrary to and opposes God's holy nature and will."[10] Keep in mind the point is to show the need for God's righteousness, not man's righteousness—sinners need a Savior. This is leading to good news as the utter guilt of mankind is revealed. The best is soon to come as we see salvation for sinners by grace through faith. Read Romans 1:21-23, 25, 28, and 32 again and write out the reasons Paul lists in these verses about why the wrath is being revealed from heaven and why He gave them over.

Romans 1:21

Romans 1:25

Romans 1:28

Romans 1:32

4. Paul is showing that all mankind is guilty before just and holy God. The diagnosis is necessary to understand the remedy so one can be healed. There comes a moment when a person realizes they need the grace that both Paul and John Newton have written about. They become convicted of sin and realize they are sinners. Then, they can turn away from themselves and run to God, and cry out, "How can I be saved?" Always remember that God hates the sin, but loves the sinner. Sin breaks God's heart and has devastating consequences. The penalty of sin is death and the ultimate destination is hell (Matthew 25:46, Revelation 21:8). It is as though all mankind is on death row. Salvation is only possible through Christ. Christians in Rome have experienced this conviction of sin and have turned to Christ. Now, because of Paul's words, they are coming to a new and deeper understanding of the utter sinfulness of sin. Also, they are living in Rome, a worldly culture, and are witnessing ungodliness all around them. Just imagine what it must have meant to know they are forgiven though they were at one time in a hopeless, helpless state. Read the following verses and underline what is significant to you about the work of God convicting you of sin, forgiving you, and saving you. Optional: Ephesians 1:13-14, Colossians 1:3-6

And He [the Holy Spirit], when He comes, will convict the world concerning sin and righteousness and judgment. John 16:8

Remember that you were at that time separate from Christ, excluded from the commonwealth of Israel, and strangers to the covenants of promise, having no hope and without God in the world. But now in Christ Jesus you who formerly were far off have been brought near by the blood of Christ. Ephesians 2:12-13

If we confess our sins, He is faithful and righteous to forgive us our sins and to cleanse us from all unrighteousness. 1 John 1:9

ADORE GOD IN PRAYER

Heavenly Father, have mercy on those who do not know you, take from them all ignorance, hardness of heart, and contempt of your Word. So bring them home, blessed Lord, to your flock, that they may be saved and become one flock under the Great Shepherd and Bishop of souls.

F.B. MEYER IN DAILY PRAYERS

YIELD YOURSELF TO GOD

Why is Paul so proud of this gospel? Why is he so pleased with the fact that he has been called to be a herald and an announcer of this righteousness by faith, and with the fact that it is only the righteous that shall live? It is because something else has also been revealed; and what has been revealed is that nobody else shall live. That is why the gospel is so vital and so important, so unique and so glorious—it is the only way…Emperors and kings, consuls and proconsuls, prelates, senators, military men and captains—the whole world is guilty before God. He has the only message that can save anybody. It is the message about the righteousness that God Himself provides in Jesus Christ, and which is offered to Jew and Gentile alike.[11]

D. MARTYN LLOYD-JONES IN ROMANS, EXPOSITION OF CHAPTER 1, THE GOSPEL OF GOD

ENJOY HIS PRESENCE

How is God speaking to you in His Word today? Perhaps you are convicted of sin today, and are in need of the Savior. Perhaps you have indeed exchanged the truth of God for a lie (Romans 1:25). If you have never received God's forgiveness, draw near to Him now, confess your sin, and ask Him into your heart and life. Confession means to agree with God that you have sinned. Keep in mind God's love for you, His desire for your salvation, and eternal life. Write out your thoughts in your Journal and pour out your heart in prayer to the Lord.

REST IN HIS LOVE

"But when He, the Spirit of truth, comes, He will guide you into all the truth" (John 16:13).

REFUGE IN THE STORM

The life of every living thing is in His hand. Job 12:10 NLT
Coachella Valley Preserve, Palm Desert, California, USA
Nikon D7000, ISO 160, f4, 1/60sec, Adobe Photoshop, Nik Silver Efex Pro
MYPHOTOWALK.COM—CATHERINEMARTIN.SMUGMUG.COM

LAW REVEALED

By the works of the Law no flesh will be justified in His sight;
for through the Law comes the knowledge of sin.
ROMANS 3:20

PREPARE YOUR HEART

ola Levitt longed more than anything to be close to God. He wanted to experience the nearness of God. Growing up in an orthodox Jewish home, he regularly attended synagogue, learned Hebrew, and experienced his bar mitzvah ceremony at the age of thirteen. The more he did, the more he was hungry for God, and the less satisfied he was in experiencing God. He felt a thousand miles away from God. In graduate school at Indiana University, he met some Campus Crusade for Christ staff members who invited him to Bible study. He felt as though he had already studied the Bible, and told them so. However, he was curious and decided to go anyway. What he saw just astounded him. These people actually took verses in the Bible, talked about what they meant, and regarded the Bible as truth and authoritative to command their beliefs and actions. He had never seen such a high regard for the Bible in Hebrew School or anywhere else in his life.

Three weeks later, late one night in his dormitory room, he sensed the presence of God there with him. He was so impressed by God in those moments, that he said, "If You're there, show me." Oh that is one of the most powerful prayers anyone can pray. Paul writes about a veil that lies over the hearts of many who hear words of Moses, but "whenever a person turns to the Lord, the veil is taken away" (2 Corinthians 3:16).

It was not long until Zola Levitt surrendered his heart and life to Jesus Christ. Remarking on how the Lord worked in his life, he said, "The Word is very powerful and I was saved." Zola Levitt became a very well-known Messianic Jewish teacher in his day, hosted a popular television show, wrote more than 50 books, and composed at least 200 songs.

One of the things that Zola Levitt realized in the very beginning when he first came to know Christ is how he had never really known, read, or studied the Bible though he had attended Hebrew school. He felt it was such a tragedy that many Jewish people he knew did not read the Bible. He observed that so many carried it, revered it, touched it, but didn't read or study it as God's Word.

How many in the world today are religious, or consider themselves good people, and yet have no relationship with God through the Lord Jesus Christ? Today, as you continue your quiet times with the Lord in Romans, ask the Lord to speak to your heart from His Word.

READ AND STUDY GOD'S WORD

1. In Romans, Paul addresses not only the pagan world and Gentiles, but also the Jews who have the Law and are filled with self-righteousness. At the outset of Romans 2, Paul begins a dialogue with Jews. And who better to converse with Jews than Paul who had been trained by the great Gamaliel, the well-known teacher of the Law. Paul knew what they were thinking, and wrote, through inspiration of the Holy Spirit, the exact words to help them see they were not excluded from judgment, though they may have felt they were because they had the Law. What a way to begin his conversation by saying "Therefore, you have no excuse, everyone of you who passes judgment, for in that which you judge another, you condemn yourself; for you who judge practice the same things" (Romans 2:1). Read Romans 2:1-16 and write your most significant insights about God—His judgment (2:2-3), His kindness (2:4), and justification (2:13).

2. Read Romans 2:17-25 and write out your most significant insights about what Paul is saying about the Jews' attitudes and actions and their relationship with the Law. Pay attention to the main things that Paul is saying. Remember that the main thing being said here before revealing the work of Christ on the cross is that all are guilty and in need of God's righteousness. Write out any questions you have in your journal. Your questions may be answered in future study or even in a commentary or study Bible you consult. Just note here in one or two sentences your most significant insights.

3. So Paul has now pointed out the hypocrisy of those who judge others. They are guilty of the same things. They are boasting in the Law, but still break the Law (Romans 2:23). So now we must wonder about the purpose of the Law and we will see more in Romans 3. Read the following two verses and underline those words and phrases that help you understand more about the Law.

But before faith came, we were kept in custody under the law, being shut up to the faith which was later to be revealed. Therefore the Law has become our tutor to lead us to Christ, so that we may be justified by faith. Galatians 3:23-24

For whoever keeps the whole law and yet stumbles in one point, he has become guilty of all. James 2:10

4. Paul shares something very important with the Jews—the true sign of belonging to God is inward and the work of the Holy Spirit. Note: Paul spoke of this in Philippians 3:3, 9, "We are the true circumcision, who worship in the Spirit of God and glory in Christ Jesus and put no confidence in the flesh…not having a righteousness of my own derived from the Law, but that which is through faith in Christ, the righteousness which comes from God on the basis of faith." Read Romans 2:28-29 and write out what you learn.

5. And now, we come to the heart of what Paul has been getting at as he begins his explanation of the gospel in Romans 1-2. Read these verses in Romans 3 and write out who is righteous (Romans 3:9-12), who is accountable to God (Romans 3:19), and the purpose of the Law (Romans 3:20).

Who is righteous, who understands, and who seeks God? Romans 3:9-12

Who is accountable to God? Romans 3:19, 23

What is the purpose of the Law? Romans 3:20

6. When we think of the Law we think of the Old Covenant given to Moses on Mt. Sinai. The Law gives us knowledge of sin but doesn't justify us (Romans 3:20). As we prepare to learn more about the work of Christ on the cross, what does Jesus say about covenant, a most solemn, binding agreement with God? Jesus spoke of a New Covenant during the Passover meal He shared with His disciples the night He was betrayed and preparing to walk the road to the cross to pay the penalty for our sins. We learn in Hebrews 9:15 that Jesus "is the mediator of a new covenant, so that, since a death has taken place for the redemption of the transgressions that were committed under the first covenant, those who have been called may receive the promise of the eternal inheritance." The good new is that the New Covenant is ratified by the blood of Jesus and cannot be broken. Read His words, and underline those truths that mean the most to you today.

> And when He had taken some bread and given thanks, He broke it and gave it to them, saying, "This is My body which is given for you; do this in remembrance of Me." And in the same way He took the cup after they had eaten, saying, "This cup which is poured out for you is the new covenant in My blood." Luke 22:19-20

Adore God in Prayer

Beloved, you may be wondering who can ever be saved. That is what the disciples asked Jesus one day. Jesus responded, "With people it is impossible, but not with God; for all things are possible with God" (Mark 10:27). Oh yes, dear friend, we have looked at the diagnosis and seen that all have sinned and there is none righteous, not even one. We need the righteousness of God. And now we are going to begin looking in earnest at the proof of God's amazing love, beginning in the next two days. We will see that "apart from the Law, the righteousness of God has been manifested" (Romans 3:21). Draw near to the Lord, dear friend, and talk with Him about what you learned today, especially a verse or insight that He showed you in your study.

Yield Yourself to God

William Newell, in his commentary on Romans, shares the following quote: "It is astonishing that men, while they acknowledge that there is a God, should act without any fear of His displeasure. They fear a worm of dust like themselves, but disregard the Most High!" Then, Newell writes about what he believes we should do with these verses in Romans:

> This great passage then, needs to be pondered, prayed over, thoroughly believed, and preached continually, in these last days, when God-consciousness is dying

out. It is no kindness, but a terrible wrong, to hide from a criminal the sentence that must surely overtake him unless pardoned; for a physician to conceal from a patient a cancer that will destroy him unless quickly removed; for one acquainted with the hidden pitfalls of a path he beholds someone taking, not to warn him of his danger.[12]

WILLIAM NEWELL IN ROMANS, VERSE BY VERSE

ENJOY HIS PRESENCE

Those words of Newell are compelling in light of the life and times in every generation including our own day and culture. Imagine how powerful these three chapters in Romans were for the believers who lived in Rome in their day. Paul speaks of how "every mouth may be closed and all the world may become accountable to God" (Romans 3:19). These words offer an image of a defendant in court who is given the opportunity to speak, and yet remains silent because the evidence against him is overwhelming. There is an awareness of guilt in the face of a holy and righteous God. And perhaps that is how you felt reading much of Romans 1-3. Guilty. Panicked. In need of help outside of your own abilities. In need of a Savior. Now you are indeed ready to hear the good news, the best news, and it will be indeed the proof of God's amazing love. Turning to Jesus will revive your heart and establish you in your faith, just as it did the church at Rome.

In the 1700s, preacher and theologian Jonathan Edwards wrote a sermon entitled, "Sinners in the Hands of an Angry God." What a title! And the words of that sermon lived up to the title. The story is told that he gave that sermon by holding the paper in front of his face and reading it in the presence of the congregation. People in the church held on to the pews and were clinging to pillars because they were so overwhelmed with the presence of God, convicted of sin, and fearful of what might happen as a result. It is a wonderful and life-changing moment in anyone's life when they realize the presence and power of God. You are never the same. It's a moment like Jacob experienced when he said, "Surely the LORD is in this place, and I did not know it" (Genesis 28:16). He immediately became afraid and said, "How awesome is this place!"

Today was a powerful day of study with so many verses that were significant about who God is, what God does, and all that He says. One of the profound statements Paul made was in Romans 2:4 —"Or do you think lightly of the riches of His kindness and tolerance and patience, not knowing that the kindness of God leads you to repentance?" That word "lightly" in the Greek means to despise, overlook, not care about, or disregard. And we see this attitude sometimes in the world around us, don't we. But let it never be true of us. Let us all, beloved, have a high regard for our God and His Word. Give Him honor and respect for His greatness and glory. Always know that His kindness, tolerance, and patience leads us to repentance (a change of heart and mind). Oh how He loves us. May this be a time of deeper love, commitment, and openness with your Lord. Knowing your need of Christ is an essential in the Christian life. As you close your time alone with the Lord, what was most significant to you in your quiet time and what are you thinking about as a result? Write out your thoughts in your Journal and close by writing a prayer to the Lord.

REST IN HIS LOVE

"That I may gain Christ, and may be found in Him, not having a righteousness of my own derived from the Law, but that which is through faith in Christ, the righteousness which comes from God on the basis of faith, that I may know Him…" (Philippians 3:8-10).

THE MAJESTY OF GOD

O LORD, our Lord, Your majestic name fills the earth. Psalm 8:1 NLT
Indian Wells, California, USA
Nikon D800E, ISO 1250, f5.6, 1/800sec, Adobe Photoshop, Nik Silver Efex Pro
MYPHOTOWALK.COM—CATHERINEMARTIN.SMUGMUG.COM

SAVIOR REVEALED

The righteousness of God through faith in Jesus Christ for all those who believe.
ROMANS 3:22

PREPARE YOUR HEART

hilip Paul Bliss grew up with a love for music and a passion for singing. His father was dedicated to Christ, led daily family prayers, and took the entire family to church. At the age of twelve, Bliss made his first public confession of Christ. Between jobs he attended school and participated in revival meetings. At the age of seventeen, he fulfilled the requirements to obtain teaching credentials and became a schoolmaster in Hartsville, New York. In the next two years, Bliss began going in the direction of music, his great love. He received formal voice training and also met a noted composer of sacred music. Through these two musicians, he was led to surrender himself to serve the Lord and to be a music teacher. In the next few years, he married a woman named Lucy, who was his sister's dear friend. He and his wife moved to Chicago when he was 26 years old. In Chicago he began conducting musical institutes and became known as a singer and composer.

In 1869, he experienced a life-changing moment. He was walking past a revival meeting in a church where a man named D. L. Moody was preaching. He went inside to hear Mr. Moody. After the service, Moody asked Bliss to help in the singing whenever he could. Bliss also engaged in ministry with another evangelist of the day, Daniel Whittle, where he helped lead songs in gospel meetings. During this time he became a choir director at a church there in Chicago and wrote a number of popular hymns including "Hold the Fort" and "Jesus Loves Even Me." His fame as a songwriter was growing. One night was particularly important in his relationship with the Lord. He sang a song he had written, "Almost Persuaded," at an evangelistic meeting led by Whittle, and it is said that there was a powerful move of the Holy Spirit. Many people came to Christ that night. As a result, Bliss surrendered his life to Christ in a new and deeper way and he gave up everything so he could join Whittle in evangelistic crusades. He wrote more hymns including the music to the words of the beloved hymn written by Horatio Spafford, "It Is Well With My Soul." One of the most powerful hymns he ever wrote was written near the end of his life, "Hallelujah, What a Savior." A few weeks before Bliss went home to be with the Lord, he preached a message at the Indiana state prison on "Man of Sorrows," and followed it up with singing the hymn, "Hallelujah What A Savior." Many prisoners gave their lives to Christ that day.

As you prepare for your quiet time today all about your Savior, Jesus Christ, meditate on these words written by Philip Bliss, underline your favorite phrases in this hymn, and ask the Lord to speak to you today in His Word.

> Man of Sorrows! What a name
> For the Son of God, who came
> Ruined sinners to reclaim.
> Hallelujah! What a Savior!
>
> Bearing shame and scoffing rude,
> In my place condemned He stood;
> Sealed my pardon with His blood.
> Hallelujah! What a Savior!
>
> Guilty, vile, and helpless we;
> Spotless Lamb of God was He;
> "Full atonement!" Can it be?
> Hallelujah! What a Savior!
>
> Lifted up was He to die;
> "It is finished!" was His cry;
> Now in Heav'n exalted high.
> Hallelujah! What a Savior!
>
> When He comes, our glorious King,
> All His ransomed home to bring,
> Then anew His song we'll sing:
> Hallelujah! What a Savior!

READ AND STUDY GOD'S WORD

1. In our last two days of study, we have looked at why we need the righteousness of God. We have seen how the wrath of God is revealed against all ungodliness and unrighteousness. We have seen God as a righteous judge declaring the whole world guilty and accountable to God. "There

is none righteous, not even one" (Romans 3:10) and "by the works of the Law no flesh will be justified in His sight" (Romans 3:20). And now, just when we think all is lost, we are going to learn that the righteousness we need—the righteousness of God—His saving activity where He puts you in right standing with Himself—is made possible. The Lord Jesus was direct and clear about our need for God's righteousness when He said: "But seek first His kingdom and His righteousness, and all these things will be added to you" (Matthew 6:33). Read Romans 3:21-24 and write out what you learn about how the righteousness of God can be yours.

2. What a hallelujah moment to realize that apart from the law the righteousness of God comes through faith in Christ for all who believe (Romans 3:22)! Don't you love that little word "all." "All" means anyone who believes by faith in Jesus Christ. You'll notice that all the days of study this week have the word "revealed" in the titles. Augustine said that the New is in the Old concealed; the Old is in the New revealed. The truths that are made known and explained to us in the New Testament have sometimes been misunderstood from the Old Testament. Everything in the Old Testament points to Christ. We have a Savior and His name is Jesus. One of the best places to recognize Him as Savior in the Old Testament is in Isaiah 53. Read Isaiah 53:1-12 to learn more about your Savior. Record your favorite discovery about His work on your behalf, personalizing what you see i.e. He bore my griefs and carried my sorrows.

3. And now, let's hear from Jesus Himself in the New Testament. Read Luke 4:16-22 as He reads from Isaiah 61ff. What did Jesus say after He closed the book? How did people respond?

4. Don't you find it interesting that Jesus read those words from Isaiah 61? He was well aware of His mission and purpose on your behalf. Now read Isaiah 62:1-4 to understand the heart of your Lord for you. Oh how He loves you and me. These words describe what He has in His mind and in His heart for you. What is your favorite phrase in this short, but powerful passage of Scripture?

5. Just think about those words in Isaiah 62 and how you are a crown of beauty in His hand and His delight is in you. Jesus Christ is your Savior and you are His beloved. He died in your place that you might be set free. Hallelujah, what a Savior! Read the following words of Paul and underline your favorite phrases about the work of Jesus Christ and all that is ours because of Him.

"But by His doing you are in Christ Jesus, who became to us wisdom from God, and righteousness and sanctification, and redemption." 1 Corinthians 1:30

"For as in Adam all die, so also in Christ all will be made alive." 1 Corinthians 15:22

"For God saved us and called us to live a holy life. He did this, not because we deserved it, but because that was his plan from before the beginning of time—to show us his grace through Christ Jesus. And now he has made all of this plain to us by the appearing of Christ Jesus, our Savior. He broke the power of death and illuminated the way to life and immortality through the Good News." 2 Timothy 1:9-10 NLT

"Because of his grace he made us right in his sight and gave us confidence that we will inherit eternal life. Titus 3:7 NLT

6. What does knowing and believing in Jesus Christ mean to you today?

ADORE GOD IN PRAYER

Pray this prayer by Peter Marshall: "Lord Jesus, Thou knowest the things that are trembling upon our lips, stirring in our hearts and along the corridors of our souls, walking on tiptoe across the cloistered spaces of our consciousness, conforming to the distant pealing of an angelus [a tolling bell], looking expectantly upward, making prayers without words, breathing aspirations that have only wings. Hear us, we pray Thee, as we call upon Thee for help, for strength, for peace; for grace, for reassurance, for companionship, for love, for pardon, for health, for salvation—for joy. Hear us, Lord Jesus. Amen."[13]

YIELD YOURSELF TO GOD

If you are not lost, what do you want with a Savior? Should the shepherd go after those who never went astray? Why should the woman sweep her house for the pieces of money that were never out of her purse? No, the medicine is for the diseased; the quickening is for the dead. The pardon is for the guilty; liberation is for those who are bound. The opening of eyes is for those who are blind. How can the Savior and His death on the cross and the Gospel of pardon be accounted for unless it is true that men are guilty and worthy of condemnation? The sinner is the Gospel's reason for existence. If you are undeserving, ill-deserving, hell-deserving, you are the sort of man for whom the Gospel is ordained and arranged and proclaimed. God justifies the ungodly.[14]

CHARLES SPURGEON IN ALL OF GRACE

Christ has come, the Light of the world. Long ages may yet elapse before His beams have reduced the world to order and beauty, and clothed a purified humanity with light as with a garment. But He has come; the Revealer of the snares and chasms that lurk in darkness; the Rebuker of every evil thing that prowls by night; the Stiller of the storm winds of passion; the Quickener of all that is wholesome; the Adorner of all that is beautiful; the Reconciler of contradictions; the Harmoniser of discords; the Healer of diseases; the Saviour from sin. He has come: the Torch of truth, the Anchor of hope, the Pillar of faith, the Rock for strength, the Refuge for security, the Fountain for refreshment, the Vine for gladness, the Rose for beauty, the Lamb for tenderness, the Friend for counsel, the Brother for love. Jesus Christ has trod the world. The trace of the Divine footsteps will never be obliterated.[15]

PETER BAYNE IN THE TESTIMONY OF CHRIST TO CHRISTIANITY

ENJOY HIS PRESENCE

Meditate on the words of the hymn "Hallelujah, What a Savior" in Prepare Your Heart. Allow the words of this hymn and the Word of God to penetrate your heart and stir your soul. Who can know the moment when The Lord Jesus will touch your heart in a reviving and life-changing way through the power of the Holy Spirit. Perhaps it will be today. Write a prayer to the Lord in your Journal expressing all that is on your heart today. Tell the Lord what He means to you and why you love Him. Hallelujah, what a Savior!

REST IN HIS LOVE

"Who has saved us and called us with a holy calling, not according to our works, but according to His own purpose and grace which was granted us in Christ Jesus from all eternity, but now has been revealed by the appearing of our Savior Christ Jesus, who abolished death and brought life and immortality to light through the gospel" (2 Timothy 1:9-10).

SPARKLING GRACE

For of His fullness we have all received, and grace upon grace. John 1:16

Mauna Lani Terrace, Pauoa Bay, Waimea Bay, Island Of Hawaii, Hawaii, USA
Nikon D7000, ISO 160, f3.5, 1/1600sec, Adobe Photoshop, Nik Silver Efex Pro
MYPHOTOWALK.COM—CATHERINEMARTIN.SMUGMUG.COM

SALVATION REVEALED

Being justified as a gift by His grace through the redemption which is in Christ Jesus.
ROMANS 3:24

PREPARE YOUR HEART

he Lord has used the letter to the Romans to bring many to faith in Christ. Perhaps one of the greatest stories is that of Martin Luther. Luther was born in Eisleben, Germany in 1483. His father had high hopes for him to be a successful lawyer. However, it was never meant to be and his life turned in a whole new direction when he was twenty-one. He was almost struck by lightning in a severe thunderstorm. In sheer terror, he said that if he survived, he would become a monk. Well he made it through the storm and did indeed enter an Augustinian monastery. His father, of course, was furious. In the monastery, he pursued God his own way, attempting to be accepted by God through works. He tried prayer, fasting, vigils for at least 15 years. He became a priest in 1507 and then was sent to Rome in 1510. This marked a turning point for him. He thought going to Rome would be the height of spirituality and was so dismayed and disillusioned when he witnessed hypocrisy and corruption in the Roman church. He climbed a special set of stairs, the "Scala Sancta" (Holy Stairs), repeating the Lord's Prayer, kissing each step, hoping to attain the peace of God as a result. He discovered that he was no closer to God and felt no peace. One question haunted him: How is a sinful man made right before a holy God? He became obsessed with Romans 1:17—"For in it [the gospel] the righteousness of God is revealed from faith to faith, as it is written, 'The righteous shall live by faith.'" Meditating on those words day and night, finally "by the mercy of God," said Luther, he came to an eye-opening and life-changing moment understanding that the righteousness of God is a gift and that the righteous man lives by faith. He realized that righteousness is a gift of grace for sinners, not a reward for works. Salvation is given by grace as one trusts in the finished work of Christ. He realized he was justified by faith alone (*sola fide* in Latin). He put his faith in Christ and Christ alone. And thus, Luther was saved, and the Reformation began.

Today is one of the most important days of study in Romans as you are going to discover in great detail how much the Lord loves you and what He has done for you. Ask the Lord to speak to you from His Word today. Then, meditate on the words of this hymn, "My Savior's Love," written by Charles H. Gabriel (1905), author of more than 7000 hymns.

> I stand amazed in the presence of Jesus, the Nazarene
> And wonder how He could love me, a sinner, condemned, unclean.
>
> *Refrain* How marvelous, How wonderful! And my song shall ever be:
> How marvelous, How wonderful! Is my Savior's Love for me.
>
> He took my sins and my sorrows; He made them His very own
> He bore the burden to Calv'ry and suffered and died alone. *Refrain*
>
> When with the ransomed in glory His face I at last shall see,
> 'Twill be my joy thro' the ages to sing of His love for me. *Refrain*

READ AND STUDY GOD'S WORD

1. In the final verses in Romans 3 we learn we need God's righteousness "for all have sinned and fall short of the glory of God" (Romans 3:23). We need God's righteousness because we don't have any on our own and there is no way for us to get it on our own (Romans 3:10-12). There is, in fact, an uncrossable chasm between man and God because of sin. Because we fall short of the glory of God, on our own we cannot achieve God's righteous and holy requirement. There is such good news in this chapter because "Now apart from the Law the righteousness of God has been manifested, being witnessed by the Law and the Prophets, even the righteousness of God through faith in Jesus Christ for all those who believe" (Romans 3:21-22).

As you have already learned, one of the names of your Lord is "Yahweh Tsidkenu" (Jeremiah 23:6) meaning "The Lord Our Righteousness?" Once you put your faith in Him, He is indeed, your righteousness. So now, let's look at what Christ, who is your righteousness, accomplished for us as He bridged the great uncrossable chasm between our righteous and holy God and sinful man by dying on the cross. Read Romans 3:24-26 and write out those words and phrases that show you what Christ accomplished on your behalf.

2. There are some wonderful theological words that Paul uses in Romans to help us see just how powerful Christ's finished work on the cross really is. When we trust Christ by grace through faith, we experience salvation because "there is one God, and one mediator also between God and men, the man Christ Jesus, who gave Himself as a ransom for all" (1 Timothy 2:5-6). Jesus is the only way to God. As Jesus said in John 14:6, "I am the way, and the truth, and the life; no one comes to the Father but through Me."

And now we will learn more about our salvation. Read the definitions of each of these words, then read the verses and underline those words and phrases most significant to you about your salvation when you put your faith in Christ. Oh, how great is the work of Jesus Christ our Lord!

Justified (justification)—to acquit, declare righteous, and put in the right. "It is a legal act where God pronounces that the believing sinner has been credited with all the virtues of Jesus Christ."[16] Optional: Romans 3:20, 25-28, Galatians 3:24, Titus 3:3-7

> Being justified as a gift by His grace through the redemption which is in Christ Jesus. Romans 3:24

> A man is not justified by the works of the Law but through faith in Christ Jesus. Galatians 2:16

Grace—the unmerited favor of God. "A favor done without expectation of return; the absolutely free expression of the loving kindness of God to men finding its only motive in the bounty and benevolence of the Giver."[17] Optional: Romans 3:24

> Therefore, having been justified by faith, we have peace with God through our Lord Jesus Christ, through whom also we have obtained our introduction by faith into this grace in which we stand; and we exult in hope of the glory of God. Romans 5:1-2

> For you know the grace of our Lord Jesus Christ, that though He was rich, yet for your sake He became poor, so that you, through His poverty might become rich. 2 Corinthians 8:9

For by grace you have been saved through faith; and that not of yourselves, it is the gift of God. Ephesians 2:8

Redemption—Christ purchased believers out of the slave market of sin and set them free. Optional: Romans 3:24, 1 Corinthians 6:20

In Him we have redemption through His blood, the forgiveness of our trespasses, according to the riches of His grace which He lavished on us. Ephesians 1:7-8

…through His own blood, He entered the holy place once for all, having obtained eternal redemption. Hebrews 9:12

Propitiation (NASB), *Sacrifice of Atonement* (NIV)—the righteous demands of holy God are fully satisfied by Christ. Because Christ died for our sins, God's justice is satisfied and His wrath is placated and turned away. Man's sins may be forgiven, he is reconciled to God, and now is offered access and communion with God. Sins can be passed over because Christ has made the atoning sacrifice and paid the penalty for sin. Optional: Leviticus 17:11, Romans 3:25, Colossians 1:20, Revelation 1:5

Therefore, He had to be made like His brethren in all things, so that He might become a merciful and faithful high priest in things pertaining to God, to make propitiation for the sins of the people. Hebrews 2:17

By this the love of God was manifested in us, that God has sent His only begotten Son into the world so that we might live through Him. In this is love, not that we loved God, but that He loved us and sent His Son to be the propitiation for our sins. 1 John 4:9-10

3. We see in these verses the work of Jesus on the cross and the shedding of his blood that made it possible for sins to be passed over. There is that word "Passover" that is a Jewish celebration of God's rescue of them from Egypt and its oppression. This is a picture of a much greater rescue by God through Jesus. In Exodus 12 the people of Israel were instructed to take an unblemished lamb, kill it, and take some of the blood and put it on the doorposts and lintel of each of their houses. Then God said, "For I will go through the land of Egypt on that night, and will strike

down all the firstborn in the land of Egypt…the blood will be a sign for you on the houses where you live, and when I see the blood I will pass over you, and no plague will befall you to destroy you when I strike the land of Egypt" (Exodus 12:12-13).

How does this help you understand the sacrifice of Christ on your behalf and all He has done for you? No wonder Jesus is called our "Passover Lamb" (1 Corinthians 5:7)! Hallelujah, what a Savior!

4. Jesus died on the cross in our place and paid the penalty for our sins so that we might become the righteousness of God, justified by His grace, be forgiven, and inherit eternal life. We have just read many beautiful truths about the finished work of Christ. Paul was passionate about the cross and said, "May I never boast about anything except the cross of Jesus Christ" (Galatians 6:14).

Before we finish our time in God's Word today, we need to think about Jesus going to the cross to appreciate anew what He did for us. Jesus revealed that no one took His life, but that He gave His life when He said, "I lay it down on My own initiative" (John 10:18). He said to His Father in Gethsemane, "My Father, if this cannot pass away unless I drink it, Your will be done" (Matthew 26:42). Jesus knew what was to come. In fact, He told His disciples and the crowds, "I am the door; if anyone enters through Me, he will be saved…the thief comes only to steal and kill and destroy; I came that they may have life, and have it abundantly. I am the good shepherd; the good shepherd lays down His life for the sheep" (John 10:9-11). Do you hear His heart of love that beats passionately for you?

He went to the cross out of love for you dear friend. Paul tells us about Jesus in Philippians 2:8—"Being found in appearance as a man, He humbled Himself by becoming obedient to the point of death, even death on a cross." When He cried out, "It is finished," on the cross, the Greek word for "finished" is *tetelestai*, meaning the work is complete. According to Hebrews 1:3, Jesus is now sitting at the right hand of the Majesty on high, another proof that Jesus has completed everything so that you may be forgiven and inherit eternal life. He "canceled out the certificate of debt consisting of decrees against us, which was hostile to us; and He has taken it out of the way, having nailed it to the cross" (Colossians 2:14).

Read John 19:16-30 about His death on the cross. What touches your heart the most, dear friend? Use the words of John 19:16-30 as a meditation of what Jesus endured as a proof of His amazing love for you. No wonder one hymnwriter wrote in reflection on all Christ did out of love for us: "Were you there when they crucified my Lord. O sometimes it causes me to tremble! tremble! tremble!"

5. Do you see all that the Lord has done for you? An illustration that helps us understand involves a young man who was convicted of a capital offense. He stood before the judge to hear his sentence. The judge read the man's offenses, declared him guilty as charged, and then levied the death penalty. The man stood in front of the judge with great shame and despair. But then there was a shocking and unexpected turn of events. The judge stood, removed his robes, stepped down, and walked over to the prisoner. He turned to the bailiff and said, "I will take this man's place and pay his penalty." Then he told the young man he was free to go. Of course, in real life this would never happen. But for you, dear friend, this act of grace and mercy has happened. The Lord has stepped in and taken your place, atoned for your sins by dying on the cross, and has paid the penalty for you. He became a curse for you, and has set you free. You can't earn forgiveness of sins and eternal life, but you can receive it by grace through faith. He offers it all to you as a gift because of His amazing love for you. This is one of the most important essentials about Christ and the Christian life. What have you learned today that means the most to you? If someone asked you how to become a Christian and why they need to be saved, what would you say to them?

Adore God in Prayer

Talk with the Lord about all you have learned today. What has blessed you the most?

Yield Yourself to God

How does God touch our hearts? Our heavenly Father generally uses a soft, tender, gentle, quiet, calm, and peaceful—still, small—voice. Softly and gently, the Holy Spirit works like the breath of spring dissolving icebergs and melting glaciers. After winter has taken every stream by the throat and held it fast, spring sets it free. No hammer or file is heard as the icey bonds fall off; only the soft south wind blows, and all is life and liberty. So it is with the work of the Holy Spirit when He comes into the soul. He can be a mighty rushing wind (Acts 2:2), for He comes according to His own sovereign pleasure. Yet when He brings the peace of God, He usually descends as the dove (Matt. 3:16) or as the dew from heaven—all peace, all gentle, and all quiet. Satan can set the soul on fire with agony, doubt, fear, and terror. Then the Spirit comes in tender love and reveals Christ the Gentle One. He sets up the Savior's cross and speaks peace, pardon, and salvation. This is what we want and need: the work of the Spirit of God coming in His own manner of living love.[18]

Charles Haddon Spurgeon in Beside Still Waters

Charles Haddon Spurgeon, the Prince of Preachers, describes his moment of salvation and he entitles his description, "That Happy Day."

> "There and then the cloud was gone, the darkness had rolled away, and that moment I saw the sun; and I could have risen that instant, and sung with the most enthusiastic of them, of the precious blood of Christ, and the simple faith which looks alone to Him…That happy day, when I found the Saviour, and learned to cling to His dear feet, was a day never to be forgotten by me. An obscure child, unknown, unheard of, I listened to the Word of God; and that precious text led me to the cross of Christ. I can testify that the joy of that day was utterly indescribable. I could have leaped, I could have danced; there was no expression, however fanatical, which would have been out of keeping with the joy of my spirit at that hour…My spirit saw its chains broken to pieces, I felt that I was an emancipated soul, an heir of Heaven, a forgiven one, accepted in Christ Jesus, plucked out of the miry clay and out of the horrible pit, with my feet set upon a rock, and my goings established. I thought I could dance all the way home. I could understand what John Bunyan meant, when he declared he wanted to tell the crows on the ploughed land all about his conversion. He was too full to hold, he felt he must tell somebody."

Charles Haddon Spurgeon in The Autobiography of Spurgeon

Enjoy His Presence

Today you have been given a window into the salvation that is made possible by the work of your Lord Jesus Christ on the cross. Just think about the love of your great God and His heart for you. Just as He saw the desperate slavery of His people by the Egyptians (see Exodus 3:9) and determined to set them free, so He determined to set us free from the slavery of sin and death Himself. He did for us what we could never do for ourselves. Oh beloved, you have a Rescuer and a Redeemer, Jesus Christ your Lord. As you think of all you have studied, what stands out to you the most today? Close your quiet time by talking with God and expressing all that is on your heart. Thank the Lord for all He is teaching you and especially for His great love for you. And if you have never received Christ, forgiveness of sins, and the promise of eternal life, today is the day for you to respond to Jesus. The gospel is clear: God loves you and has a wonderful plan for your life. People are sinful and separated from God, therefore they cannot know or understand God's love or His plan for their lives. Jesus Christ is God's only provision for man's sin. Through Him, you can know God's love and plan for your life. We must individually receive Jesus Christ to know God's love and experience His plan for our lives. If you have never received Christ, you may pray a simple prayer: *Lord Jesus, I need You. Thank You for dying on the cross for my sins. I ask You now to come into my life, forgive my sins, and make me the person You want me to be. Amen.*

REST IN HIS LOVE

"In Him we have redemption through His blood, the forgiveness of our trespasses, according to the riches of His grace which He lavished on us" (Ephesians 1:7-8).

THE WAY OF THE CROSS

The message of the cross…is the very power of God. 1 Corinthians 1:18 NLT
El Santuario de Chimayo, Chimayo, New Mexico, USA
Sony A6000, ISO 100, f11, 1/125sec, Adobe Photoshop, Nik Silver Efex Pro
MYPHOTOWALK.COM—CATHERINEMARTIN.SMUGMUG.COM

DEVOTIONAL READING
BY D. MARTYN LLOYD-JONES

Dear Friend,

This week has been a deep time of study and learning about all about why we need God's righteousness. We have looked at a lot of doctrinal truths in Scripture that show us where to place our faith. Always remember that doctrine leads to devotion. Think about how you have grown in your love for the Lord and your intimate relationship with Him. And think also how you are seeing the proof of God's amazing love and the power of the gospel. Take some time now to write about all that you have learned this week. How is the Lord speaking to you in His Word? What have you learned about your Savior that blesses you the most? What has been most significant to you? Close by writing a prayer to the Lord in your journal.

What were your most meaningful discoveries this week as you spent time with the Lord?

Most meaningful insight:

Most meaningful devotional reading:

Most meaningful verse:

There is no more wonderful word than "grace." It means unmerited favour, or kindness shown to one who is utterly undeserving. Here again the purely gratuitous character of our salvation is brought out. It is something that results from the sole exercise of the spontaneous love of God. It is not merely a free gift, but a free gift to those who deserve the exact opposite, and it is given to us while we are "without hope and without God in the world"…Redemption means release as the result of the payment of a price. This is an essential part of the meaning of the word and it must never be omitted. The truth about us all is that we are not able to pay the adequate price, but, thank God, Another has come and paid the price for us. Here we have the great idea of substitution. The Lord Jesus Christ came to ransom us, to deliver us; He has paid the price, and so the prison in which we were held captive by the devil has been opened, and we who were slaves have been made free. This is the doctrine which is taught here so plainly by the Apostle. The Apostle is so deeply concerned that we should be clear about this that he describes it as "the redemption which is in Christ Jesus." All the glory must go to Christ. It is He who by His work has purchased us and set us at liberty. We are forgiven and delivered from the power of Satan by Him alone.[19]

D. MARTYN LLOYD-JONES IN ROMANS, EXPOSITION OF CHAPTER
3:20-4:25, ATONEMENT AND JUSTIFICATION

When I survey the wondrous cross on which the Prince of Glory died.
My richest gain I count but loss and pour contempt on all my pride.

Forbid it, Lord, that I should boast save in the death of Christ, my God!
All the vain things that charm me most, I sacrifice them through His blood.

See from His head His hands His feet sorrow and love flow mingled down.
Did e're such love and sorrow meet or thorns compose so rich a crown.

Were the whole realm of nature mine that were a tribute far too small.
Love so amazing so divine demands my soul my life my all.

ISAAC WATTS, 1707

The Proof Of God's Amazing Love

In Week Two of *The Proof of God's Amazing Love*, we have had the opportunity to study in great depth our need for God's righteousness in Romans 1-3. We have seen that we have a Savior, the Lord Jesus Christ. In Him and all He has done for us, we discover the proof of God's amazing love (Romans 5:8). We will explore this in greater detail next week. Today I want to survey the wondrous cross with you and look at God's love for us. So grab your Bible, and let's get into the Word of God together.

"Yet the proof of God's amazing love is this: that it was while we were sinners that Christ died for us" (Romans 5:8 Phillips)

The Theme of Romans—The Gospel and the Revelation of God's Righteousness
Romans 1:16-17
The Outline of Romans:
The Need For God's Righteousness Romans 1-3
The Way Of God's Righteousness Romans 4-5
The Union, Power and Provision of God's Righteousness Romans 6-8
The Scope and Plan Of God's Righteousness Romans 9-11
The Practical Applications of God's Righteousness Romans 12-16

The Divine Dilemma — Romans 5:5-8

1. The nature of divine justice, _________________________________, and righteousness.

2. The nature of divine ____.

The Act of Divine Love — Romans 5:5-10

Summed up in a Person — ____.

When We Survey the Wondrous Cross of Jesus Christ

1. Jesus accomplished ____for us. Romans 3:21-24

2. Jesus accomplished ____for us. Romans 3:25

3. Jesus accomplished ____for us. Romans 4:7, Ephesians 1:7

4. Jesus accomplished ____for us. Romans 5:18

5. Jesus accomplished ____for us. Romans 5:10

6. Jesus accomplished ____for us. Romans 6:22

7. Jesus accomplished our _____________________________ as sons and daughters. Romans 8:15

8. Jesus accomplished ____for us. Romans 8:30

The Result of Divine Love

We may be in an eternal ____with God.

Our Response to Divine Love

1. No more reason to ____the wrath of God.

2. We may hold our heads high in the light of God's _________________________________

Video messages are available on DVDs or as Digital M4V Video. Audio messages are available as Digital MP3 Audio. Visit the Quiet Time Ministries Online Store at www.quiettime.org.

THE WONDROUS CROSS OF CHRIST

Divine Justice <The Divine Dilemma> Divine Love

UNCROSSABLE CHASM BETWEEN GOD AND MAN —SIN BRINGS DEATH PENALTY

GLORIFICATION

ADOPTION

SANCTIFICATION

The Act of Divine Love
Jesus Christ

YET THE PROOF OF GOD'S AMAZING LOVE IS THIS: THAT IT WAS WHILE WE WERE SINNERS THAT CHRIST DIED FOR US — ROMANS 5:8

RECONCILIATION

JUSTIFICATION

FORGIVENESS

PROPITIATION

REDEMPTION

FOR GOD LOVED THE WORLD SO MUCH THAT HE GAVE HIS ONLY SON, SO THAT EVERYONE WHO BELIEVES IN HIM SHOULD NOT BE LOST, BUT SHOULD HAVE ETERNAL LIFE. — JOHN 3:16

WHILE WE WERE HIS ENEMIES, CHRIST RECONCILED US TO GOD BY DYING FOR US. —ROMANS 5:10

UNCROSSABLE CHASM BETWEEN GOD AND MAN —SIN BRINGS DEATH PENALTY

Depravity of Man <The Human Dilemma> Purpose of Man

THE WAY OF GOD'S RIGHTEOUSNESS

Romans 4-5

None can be lost who take Jesus as the door of faith to their souls. Entrance through Jesus into peace is the guarantee of entrance by the same door into heaven. Jesus is the only door, an open door, a wide door, a safe door; and blessed is he who rests all his hope of admission to glory upon the crucified Redeemer.[1]

CHARLES HADDON SPURGEON

GOD'S RIGHTEOUSNESS IN ABRAHAM

Abraham believed God and it was credited to him as righteousness.
Romans 4:3 NIV

PREPARE YOUR HEART

Have you discovered the secret of faith? It's not about how much faith you have, but where you place your faith. Ours is an objective faith in the Lord and His Word. Faith is not a feeling. A radio talk show host was talking about the whole idea of God and becoming a Christian. He said that his problem was that he had no faith. In fact, that was not his problem at all. He had plenty of faith. He just placed his faith in the wrong things; the temporal, untrue, and unreliable things of the world.

As we read and study Romans, we are discovering all that Christ has done for us. How can we experience salvation, forgiveness of sins, and eternal life? By grace through faith (Ephesians 2:8). We have the promises of God in Christ. We put our faith in Him and receive all He promises related to who He is, what He has done, and all that He says. And now, what we are going to see is that Abraham also lived by faith. All he received from God was on the same principle: "Abraham believed God and it was credited to him as righteousness" (Romans 4:3 NIV).

We have an exciting week of study ahead as we look at the way of righteousness. We will explore God's righteousness in Abraham along with his faith as a great example for us, our unshakeable position in Christ, the power that now is ours, the salvation we now enjoy, and the assurance and eternal security we have in Christ. Draw near to the Lord now and ask Him to speak to you in His Word.

READ AND STUDY GOD'S WORD

1. Today we are going to learn the best news and it is going to come from the example of Abraham. We are going to understand in a deeper way through Abraham the relationship of faith, works, and God's righteousness. If Paul felt the need to give an example of justification by faith, who would be his first choice? The one who would have the most credibility would obviously be Abraham. God called Abraham "my friend" (Isaiah 41:8) and Abraham "believed in the LORD and He reckoned it to him as righteousness" (Genesis 15:6).

Abraham has quite a history with God. God called Abraham to leave his home country and go to an unknown place that he would receive as an inheritance from God. And so, Abraham "went out, not knowing where he was going" (Hebrews 11:8). God loved Abraham's obedience and high regard for all He said. God even gave a testimony about Abraham—"Abraham obeyed me and kept My charge, My commandments, My statutes, and My laws" (Genesis 26:5). Abraham is a great hero of the faith. And now, Paul is going to teach a big truth about how faith is seen in the life of Abraham.

Read Romans 4:1-15 and write your most important insights about Abraham's faith and God's righteousness. How was Abraham credited as righteous? Was it by faith or by works?

2. As you read through Romans 4:1-15, you saw the word "credited," "counted," or "accounted." "Faith was credited to Abraham as righteousness" (Romans 4:9). That word "credited" in the Greek means to reckon something to a person, or put it in that person's account. A somewhat limited example would be looking in your bank account and finding unlimited funds put in there as a gift of grace. You did nothing to earn it. But you did have to receive it. Read Romans 4:4-8 and write out what you learn about works versus faith. Why was Abraham righteous by faith and not by works? In other words, what is the only way to God's righteousness?

3. Do you see the point that is being made here? God's righteousness is "by grace through faith, not as a result of works, so that no one may boast" (Ephesians 2:8-9). You might think about grace as God's love in action. It is a gift we receive, not something we earn. And when we put our faith in Christ, we are made righteous and justified. We are that person David described, "whose lawless deeds have been forgiven, and whose sins have been covered. Blessed is the man whose sin the LORD will not take into account" (Romans 4:7-8). Do you see, dear friend, this amazing truth for your own life today? Salvation through Christ is never earned, but given by grace as a gift by faith. Read Romans 4:16 and underline your favorite words and phrases.

> "So the promise is received by faith. It is given as a free gift. And we are all certain to receive it, whether or not we live according to the law of Moses, if we have faith like Abraham's. For Abraham is the father of all who believe." Romans 4:16 NLT

4. Sometimes the truth of God's Word is more than we can imagine, and almost too good to be true. We are only beginning to see "the proof of God's amazing love" (Romans 5:8). Read Romans 4:20-25 and write what you learn from Abraham's example of faith and how righteousness is credited to you. Do you see how you are included in the plan of God?

ADORE GOD IN PRAYER

What is your response to God today? Maybe you are feeling a bit uncomfortable receiving something you didn't earn. Get used to God's grace and His amazing love. You can't earn all God has for you. But you can receive it by grace through faith. Talk with Him about all you have learned and thank Him for His wondrous love, mercy and grace. Jeremiah found great comfort in God when he wrote, "This I recall to my mind, therefore I have hope. The LORD's lovingkindnesses indeed never cease, for His compassions never fail. They are new every morning; great is Your faithfulness" (Lamentations 3:21-23).

YIELD YOURSELF TO GOD

When Abraham believed God, he did the one thing that a man can do without doing anything! God made the statement, the promise; and God undertook to fulfill it. Abraham believed in his heart that God told the truth. There was no effort here. Abraham's faith was not an act, but an attitude. His heart was turned completely away from himself to God and His promise. This left God free to fulfill that promise. Faith was neither a meritorious act by Abraham, nor a change of character or nature, in Abraham: he simply believed God would accomplish what He promised: "In thee shall all the families of the earth be blessed."[2]

WILLIAM NEWELL IN ROMANS VERSE BY VERSE

The righteousness of God resulted not from his works but from his faith. "He believed God; and it was reckoned unto him for righteousness." Now it was not written for his sake alone, that it was reckoned unto him; but for our sake also, unto whom it shall be reckoned, who believe on Him that raised Jesus our Lord from the dead" (Gal. 3:6, Rom. 4:23-24, R.V.). Oh, miracle of grace! If we trust ever so simply in Jesus Christ our Lord, we shall be reckoned as righteous in the eye of the eternal God. We cannot realize all that is included in those marvelous words. This only is evident, that faith unites us so absolutely to the Son of God that we are One with Him for evermore; and all the glory of His character—not only what He was when He became obedient unto death, but what He is in the majesty of His risen nature – is reckoned unto us…In the counsels of eternity that which is true of the glorious Lord is accounted also true of us who, by a living faith, have become members of His body, of His flesh, and of His bones. Jesus Christ is made unto us Righteousness, and we are accepted in the Beloved. There is nothing in faith, considered in itself, which can account for this marvelous fact of imputation. Faith is only the link of union, but inasmuch as it unites us to the Son of God, it brings us into the enjoyment of all that He is as the Alpha and Omega, the Beginning and the End, the First and the Last.

F.B. MEYER IN ABRAHAM: THE OBEDIENCE OF FAITH

ENJOY HIS PRESENCE

How have you seen God's love in everything you studied today? Just think of God's love that holds out a gift for you to receive! How is His great love seen in the gift of grace discovered in the fact that we are justified by faith and our faith is credited as righteousness? Close your time alone with the Lord by praying the words from the second and third stanzas of "And Can It Be That I Should Gain" by Charles Wesley.

Tis mystery all! The Immortal dies! Who can explore His strange design?
In vain the firstborn seraph tries to sound the depths of love divine!
Tis mercy all! Let earth adore, let angel minds inquire no more.
Refrain: Amazing love! How can it be that Thou, my God, should die for me!

He left His Father's throne above, so free, so infinite His grace;
Emptied Himself of all but love, and bled for Adam's helpless race;
Tis mercy all, immense and free; For, O my God, it found out me.
Refrain: Amazing love! How can it be that Thou, my God, should die for me!

Rest in His Love

"Now not for his sake only was it written that it was credited to him, but for our sake also, to whom it will be credited, as those who believe in Him who raised Jesus our Lord from the dead, He who was delivered over because of our transgressions, and was raised because of our justification" (Romans 4:23-25).

Rooted And Grounded

You, being rooted and grounded in love. Ephesians 3:17
Muir Woods National Monument, Mill Valley, California, USA
Nikon D810, ISO 400, f8, 1/4sec, Adobe Photoshop, Nik Silver Efex Pro
MYPHOTOWALK.COM—CATHERINEMARTIN.SMUGMUG.COM

THE UNSHAKEABLE POSITION

*Therefore, having been justified by faith, we have peace
with God through our Lord Jesus Christ.*

ROMANS 5:1

PREPARE YOUR HEART

he story is told of a couple who saved up their money to go on a cruise. It was something they
had longed to do for many years and looked forward to once they had enough money to buy
the tickets. It was a luxurious cruise liner with the most lavish food spreads anyone could imagine.
In fact, the meals were the most talked-about part of the whole trip on that cruise. Many of the
travellers noticed, however, that this one couple never ate any of the wonderful food at any of the
meals. Instead that couple would take a brown bag lunch they had prepared before getting on the
ship, and would sit outside on the deck and eat sandwiches and other snacks they had packed. So
one day, near the end of the trip, someone was brave enough to walk up and ask them why they
never ate any of the wonderful and incredible meals laid out lavishly for the guests. The couple's
facial expression saddened just slightly, and they replied, "We only had enough money for the
tickets to sail on the cruise. We knew we couldn't afford more than that including all the meals, so
we brought our own food." Then they learned the truth of what they did not know and discovered
news that was just too good to be true. The food was included in the price of the ticket. They
had more than they knew or imagined with their tickets on that cruise. Well, guess what. They
ate to their heart's content for the rest of that trip once they knew that it was part of the ticket.

Now we are launching out into the best news you can imagine. When you are saved by grace
through faith, all that you receive in Christ and all that is true is something that will take a lifetime
to discover. The gift of God in Jesus Christ your Lord will take a lifetime to unwrap. As you begin
your quiet time with the Lord, ask the Lord to open your eyes to His Word and give you ears to
hear all that He is saying.

READ AND STUDY GOD'S WORD

1. Now you are stepping onto sacred ground as you discover all that is yours because of Christ.
D. Martyn Lloyd-Jones, the great pastor of Westminster Chapel in London, has written and

preached extensively on the book of Romans. His thoughts about Romans 5-8 are very helpful in understanding what the Lord wants us to see. He writes that Paul is "showing and demonstrating and asserting the certainty, fulness, and finality of this great salvation. He is giving us a picture of the utter, absolute security of the Christian man."[3] With that in mind, today you are going to see how the Lord has now placed you in an unshakeable position with Him. Read Romans 5:1-2 and write out all that is true of you because you are "justified by faith." Personalize all you learn i.e. I have peace with God.

2. You discovered in Romans 5:1 that, having been justified by faith (pardoned, acquitted, declared righteous), you now have "peace with God." This phrase has been described as sitting down in one's heart with God and experiencing gladness in being with Him.[4] What a beautiful picture of the relationship that is now ours with God because of Christ. Read the following verses that help you understand what Jesus accomplished to make peace with God possible. Note: To reconcile means to change the relationship from enmity to friendship, from hostility to peace and divine favor.

Romans 5:10-11

2 Corinthians 5:17-19

3. In Romans 5:2, you saw that "we have obtained our introduction by faith into this grace in which we stand." Standing in God's grace is an unshakeable position. Nothing can touch you and nothing can knock you down. You are held strong by God and God alone. Think again about that couple who had it all when they bought the cruise ticket. They just didn't know or realize it. Kenneth Wuest translates the phrase this way: "we have as a permanent possession into this

unmerited favor in which we have been placed permanently." Wuest in his Word Studies points out that "Grace here is seen as a haven or harbor, and the word is used of the landing-stages or approach of a ship to the harbor."[5] Wuest also points out that the verb tenses in this verse are perfect in tense meaning the result of standing in grace is permanent. Do you know what that means for all who are saved? They stand in His grace and experience His favor forever. Matthew Henry says, "The saints' happy state is a state of grace." What are your thoughts and insights about Romans 5:2 and your forever stance in God's grace today? What has God given you because of grace and what does it mean for you in your life? Let's get practical and personal. List as many truths as you can think of from all you have learned thus far in this study i.e. "I am forgiven, I am saved, I am justified…"

Adore God in Prayer

Use the words of this beloved hymn by John Newton, written in 1779, as your prayer to the Lord today:

> Amazing grace, how sweet the sound
> That saved a wretch like me
> I once was lost, but now I am found
> Was blind, but now I see
>
> 'Twas grace that taught my heart to fear
> And grace my fears relieved
> How precious did that grace appear
> The hour I first believed

Through many dangers, toils and snares
I have already come
'Twas grace has brought me safe thus far
And grace will lead me home

When we've been there ten thousand years
Bright, shining as the sun
We've no less days to sing God's praise
Than when we'd first begun

JOHN NEWTON 1779

YIELD YOURSELF TO GOD

When we are justified through faith, we have peace. Peace of conscience in the mercy of God; peace of heart in the love of God; peace of mind in the truth of God; peace of soul in the presence of God. [6]

W.H. GRIFFITH THOMAS IN ROMANS: A DEVOTIONAL COMMENTARY I-V

Every believer is accepted by the Father, in Christ…The peace is God's toward us, through His beloved Son—on this our peace is to be based. God is able to be at peace with us through our Lord Jesus Christ, "having made peace through the blood of his cross" (Colossians 1:20). And we must never forget that His peace is founded solely on the work of the cross, totally apart from anything whatsoever in or from us, since "God commendeth his love toward us, in that, while we were yet sinners, Christ died for us" (Romans 5:8). [7]

MILES J. STANFORD IN PRINCIPLES OF SPIRITUAL GROWTH

William Newell shares some profound thoughts about grace in his commentary on Romans. [8] Take some time to meditate on these insights as you think about your permanent, unshakeable position in grace. Underline your favorite phrases as you think about all he is saying.

The Nature of Grace: Grace is God acting freely, according to His own nature as Love; with no promises or obligations to fulfil; and acting of course, righteously— in view of the cross. Grace, therefore is *uncaused* in the recipient: its cause lies wholly in the GIVER, in GOD. Grace also is *sovereign*. Not having debts to pay, or fulfilled conditions on man's part to wait for, it can act toward whom, and how, it pleases. It can, and does, often, place the worst deservers in the highest favors.

The Place of Man Under Grace: He has been accepted *in Christ*, who is his standing! He is not "on probation." As to his life past, *it does not exist* before God: he *died* at the Cross, and *Christ is his life*. Grace, once bestowed, is *not withdrawn*: for God knew all the human exigencies beforehand: His action was independent of them, not dependent upon them. The failure of devotion does not cause the withdrawal of bestowed grace (as it would under the law).

The Proper Attitude of Man Under Grace: To *believe*, and to consent to be *loved while unworthy*, is the great secret. To refuse to make "resolutions" and "vows"; for that is to trust in the flesh. To expect to be blessed, though realizing more and more lack of worth. To testify of God's goodness, at all times. To be certain of God's future favor; yet to be even more tender in conscience toward Him. To rely on God's chastening hand as a mark of His kindness. A man under grace, if like Paul, has no burdens regarding himself; but many about others.

Things Which Gracious Souls Discover: To "hope to be better" is to fail to see yourself in Christ only. To be disappointed with yourself, is to have believed in yourself. To be discouraged is unbelief,—as to God's purpose and plan of blessing for you. To be proud, is to be blind! For we have no standing before God, in ourselves. The lack of Divine blessing, therefore, comes from unbelief, and not from failure of devotion. Real devotion to God arises, not from man's will to show it; but from the discovery that blessing has been received from God, while we were yet unworthy and undevoted. To preach devotion first, and blessing second, is to reverse God's order, and preach law, not grace. The Law made man's blessing depend on devotion; Grace confers undeserved unconditional blessing; our devotion may follow, but does not always so,—in proper measure.

ENJOY HIS PRESENCE

And now, you are entering into the land of God's grace and righteousness where you experience peace with God and the atmosphere and beauty of grace, all bestowed on you because of His amazing love demonstrated through Jesus Christ. Do you see how safe and secure you are? How do you need His peace today? No wonder Paul concluded Romans 5:1-2 by saying "we exult in hope of the glory of God." Oh yes, dear friend, you have a future and a hope. Close your quiet time with the Lord by writing out your favorite insight from today, then talk with God about all that is on your heart.

Rest in His Love

"Therefore, if anyone is in Christ, he is a new creature; the old things passed away; behold, new things have come" (2 Corinthians 5:17).

Strong And Steadfast

Like trees planted along a riverbank with roots that go deep. Jeremiah 17:8 NLT
Coachella Valley Preserve, Palm Desert, California, USA
Nikon D7000, ISO 100, f4, 1/40sec, Adobe Photoshop, Nik Silver Efex Pro
myPhotoWalk.com—catherinemartin.smugmug.com

POWER IN TRIALS

And not only this, but we also exult in our tribulations...
ROMANS 5:3

PREPARE YOUR HEART

Howard Hendricks, beloved professor at Dallas Seminary, told the story that one day he was walking down the hall and passed by one of his students. He called out to the student, "How are you doing?" The student, somewhat downhearted and frustrated, replied, "Fine, under the circumstances." Hendricks, in his inimitable style, shot right back, "Well what are you doing there, *under* the circumstances!" Howard Hendricks was known as Prof by his students and was especially remembered for his classes on how to study the Bible. He would assign a verse to his students and ask them to come back with 25 observations. That was difficult enough. But then he would ask for 25 more. He loved the Word of God and challenged his students to have a high view of the Bible, trusting all that was in it as the authority for their belief. So when he asked that student what he was doing under the circumstances, he was making more than a simple observation. He was encouraging that frustrated one to get into God's Word and find promises from God that would lift him up and out of the pit by the power of the Holy Spirit.

One of the great promises in Scripture that fuels our ability to make it through a trial is found in Matthew 19:26. "With God all things are possible." That is why Corrie ten Boom would always say, "God has no problems, only plans." Mrs. Charles Cowman encouraged believers in her devotional, *Streams in the Desert* with these words: "We love to see the impossible done. And so does God. Face it out to the end, cast away every shadow of hope on the human side as an absolute hindrance to the Divine, heap up all the difficulties together recklessly, and pile as many more on as you can find; you cannot get beyond the blessed climax of impossibility. Let faith swing out to Him. He is the God of the impossible."

No wonder Paul wrote, "We also exult in our tribulations" (Romans 5:3). Did you know that there is a sunny side to trials when you know Christ, have permanent peace with God, and stand forever in His beautiful and luxurious grace? Oh what a new discovery this is! Elisabeth Elliot, author and speaker, once described it this way: "Suffering is not for nothing." Today you are going to have the opportunity to discover more powerful truths about all that is yours because of Christ, and all you may trust even in the midst of difficult days. How do you need help and hope today? Quiet your heart before the Lord now, and pray these words from Psalm 119:18 NLT—"Open my eyes to see the wonderful truths in Your instructions."

READ AND STUDY GOD'S WORD

1. Paul takes you now from standing in grace to difficult times and is going to show you what you can count on whenever you face a trial in your life. These are the truths that enable you to handle trouble in your life differently than those who do not know Christ and are without God in the world. Power in trials is an essential truth in the Christian life. Read Romans 5:3-5 and write out all the reasons why he says, "We exult in our tribulations" (NASB) or "We rejoice in our sufferings" (ESV). That word "exult" has also been translated "rejoice" and means to boast, glory, and triumph over.

2. When you read Romans 5:3-5, you discover important and valuable results that are developed in you as a result of trials. You can know that God is always at work in the midst of any suffering you experience. First, tribulation brings about perseverance. "Perseverance" is *hupomone* in the Greek and is "the spirit which can bear things, not simply with resignation, but with blazing hope. It is not the patience which grimly waits for the end, but the patience which radiantly hopes for the dawn."[9] The writer of Hebrews confirms the importance of perseverance [also translated endurance]. "Patient endurance is what you need now, so that you will continue to do God's will. Then you will receive all that he has promised" (Hebrews 10:35). Then, you saw that perseverance brings about proven character. "Proven character" is *dokime* in the Greek and means that one is tested and tried to meet specification and to put one's approval on him. "Hope" is *elpis* and is a confident expectation. In the case of Romans 5:5, it is a confident expectation that does not disappoint. Finally, we see that the "love of God has been poured out within our hearts through the Holy Spirit who was given to us." This is God's *agape* love—it is unconditional and literally floods our hearts because of the indwelling Holy Spirit, given by the Lord and with us forever. In light of all you have learned here, what is your favorite truth, how will it help you in a trial, and why do you need it right now?

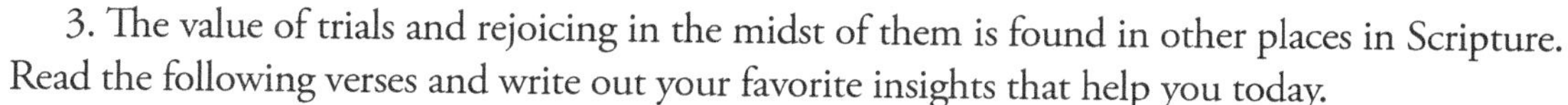

3. The value of trials and rejoicing in the midst of them is found in other places in Scripture. Read the following verses and write out your favorite insights that help you today.

John 16:33

Philippians 2:17-18, the example of Paul

James 1:2-4, 12

1 Peter 1:6-7

1 Peter 4:12-13

1 Peter 5:7-10

4. One of the truths Paul shares with the believers in Rome is that "the love of God has been poured out within our hearts through the Holy Spirit who was given to us." A permanent flood of God's love flows in us. The abiding presence of the Holy Spirit as a result of your salvation is an incomprehensible comfort for you. He is always with you and gives you what you need to face whatever circumstance you are experiencing in life. The Holy Spirit is your Comforter and the Helper. Jesus spoke of the promised Holy Spirit— Read His words in the following two

passages of Scripture in John and underline those phrases that help you understand more about the promised Holy Spirit.

> "I will ask the Father, and He will give you another Helper, that He may be with you forever; that is the Spirit of truth, whom the world cannot receive, because it does not see Him or know Him, but you know Him because He abides with you and will be in you. John 14:16-17

> "I tell you the truth, it is to your advantage that I go away; for if I do not go away, the Helper will not come to you; but if I go, I will send Him to you. And He, when He comes will convict the world concerning sin and righteousness and judgment…I have many more things to say to you, but you cannot bear them now. But when He, the Spirit of truth comes, He will guide you into all the truth; for He will not speak on His own initiative, but whatever He hears, He will speak; and He will disclose to you what is to come. He will glorify Me, for He will take of Mine and disclose it to you." John 16:7-8, 12-14

ADORE GOD IN PRAYER

> Give me, my Father, a loving and thankful heart. May your mercies, like cords, bind me to the horns of your altar. Let nothing be held back from you; but may my entire nature be surrendered to your indwelling and service, like a palace in which every room is freely open to its Lord.

> F.B. MEYER IN DAILY PRAYERS

YIELD YOURSELF TO GOD

Corrie ten Boom, who suffered the horrors of Ravensbruck, the notorious women's death camp during World War 2, was released on a clerical error, and went on to serve the Lord throughout the world. She would often share that if the worst happens, the best remains, and His light is brighter than the deepest darkness. Her words are credible because of all she suffered. She knew that when she walked through the gates of Ravensbruck, it was not the end, but the beginning of a new life with the Lord. She writes about her life following her time in Ravensbruck:

"After that time in prison, the entire world became my classroom. Since World War II, I have traveled around it twice, speaking in more than sixty countries on all continents. During these three decades I have become familiar with airports, bus stations, and passport offices. Under me have been wheels of every description: wheels of automobiles, trains, jinrikishas, horse-drawn wagons, and the landing gear of airplanes. Wheels, wheels, wheels! Even the wheels of wheelchairs. I have enjoyed the hospitality in a great number of homes and have slept in many times more than a thousand beds…Always in my travels, even now that I am in my ninth decade of life, I have carried in my hand and in my heart the Bible—the very Word of Life which is almost bursting with Good News. And there has been plenty for everyone…plenty for the dying ones in the concentration camps, plenty for the thousands gathered in universities, in town halls, and in churches all over the world…God has plans—not problems—for our lives. Before she died in the concentration camp in Ravensbruck, my sister Betsie said to me, 'Corrie, your whole life has been a training for the work you are doing here in prison—and for the work you will do afterward.' The life of a Christian is an education for higher service…Looking back across the years of my life, I can see the working of a divine pattern which is the way of God with His children."[10]

ENJOY HIS PRESENCE

Do you hear the heart in those words by Corrie ten Boom? Her love for God and His Word is unmistakable even in the face of great suffering. Not long after she was released from Ravensbruck Corrie spoke at a church in Munich. After her message, she saw a heavyset man in a gray overcoat making his way up to speak with her. And in that moment, she saw him not as he was now, but as he was then, back in Ravensbruck with blue uniform and visored cap. He was one of the cruelest guards there in that prison. And now, he stood in front of her and said, with his hand thrust out: "A fine message, Fraulein! How good it is to know that, as you say, all our sins are at the bottom of the sea!" He shared with her about how he had been a guard there in Ravensbruck. He then said, "I have become a Christian. I know that God has forgiven me for the cruel things I did there, but I would like to hear it from your lips as well? Will you forgive me?" And Corrie wrestled. She knew forgiveness was an act of the will, but struggled until she finally cried out to Jesus for help. She lifted her hand and said, "I forgive you brother, with all my heart." They grasped each others hands and Corrie said that it was the most intense experience of God's love she had ever known. And it was then she realized that it was the experience of Romans 5:5 where God promises to shed His love in our hearts through the Holy Spirit.[11] You have been studying such powerful truths today in how God works in your life even in trials that can be like a dark night of the soul. And perhaps, dear friend, you are experiencing a trial that has burdened your heart and soul. Take some time now to "give all your worries and cares to God, for he cares about you" (1 Peter 5:7 NLT). Focus on how God is giving you perseverance, proven character, hope, and His love through the Holy Spirit. God is sovereign and perhaps He has brought you to this day's quiet time "for such a time as this." Close your quiet time today by talking with the Lord about all that is on your heart.

REST IN HIS LOVE

"After you have suffered for a little while, the God of all grace, who called you to His eternal glory in Christ, will Himself perfect, confirm, strengthen, and establish you" (1 Peter 5:10)

BELIEVING GOD FOR THE IMPOSSIBLE

Nothing is too difficult for You. Jeremiah 32:17
Coachella Valley Preserve, Palm Desert, California, USA
Nikon D800E, ISO 100, f5.6, 1/1250sec, Adobe Photoshop, Nik Silver Efex Pro
MYPHOTOWALK.COM—CATHERINEMARTIN.SMUGMUG.COM

GOD'S LOVE IN SALVATION

*Yet the proof of God's amazing love is this: that it was
while we were sinners that Christ died for us.*
ROMANS 5:8 PHILLIPS

PREPARE YOUR HEART

George Matheson was born in Glasgow, Scotland in 1842. He had only partial vision as a boy and by the time he entered Glasgow University, he quickly lost his sight and was totally blind at 18 years of age. He was a brilliant scholar and received high honors in seminary. In 1886 he became the pastor of a church with 2,000 people in Edinburgh. He was known as one of the outstanding preachers in Scotland and drew large crowds with his eloquent preaching.

One night he wrote one of his best-loved hymns, "O Love That Will Not Let Me Go," and it was the fruit of deep suffering. Some have thought that it may have been written out of the trauma of his fiancee leaving him just before marriage when she discovered he would be totally blind. Matheson described the writing of this hymn with these words: "Something happened to me, which was known only to myself, and which caused me the most severe mental suffering. The hymn was the fruit of that suffering. It was the quickest bit of work I ever did in my life. I had the impression rather of having it dictated to me by some inward voice than of working it out myself. I am quite sure that the whole work was completed in five minutes, and equally sure it never received at my hands any retouching or correction. I have no natural gift of rhythm. All the other verses I have ever written are manufactured articles; this came like a dayspring from on high."[12] How gracious of the Lord to pour out His love on the broken and suffering heart of George Matheson and lead him to write a hymn that highlights His love that never lets us go.

Today is the day to think about that great truth set forth by Paul in Romans 5:8 that is behind the title of this study: "Yet the proof of God's amazing love is this: that it was while we were sinners that Christ died for us" (Romans 5:8 Phillips). God's love is greater than we will ever fully understand. In fact, you might describe it as unfathomable and incomprehensible. If you ask the question, "How much does God love me?," just look at the truths of Romans 5:8 and Jesus, nailed to the cross to die for our sins, and you can answer "That much!" Jesus said it Himself when He told Nicodemus, a teacher of Israel, who was inquiring how one could be born again: "For God so loved the world, that He gave His only begotten Son, that whoever believes in Him shall not perish, but have eternal life. For God did not send the Son into the world to judge the world, but that the world might be saved through Him" (John 3:16-16).

Open your quiet time with the Lord meditating on the words of this beautiful hymn written by George Matheson. Then write a simple prayer thanking the Lord for His love and for the time you will spend together with Him today.

O Love that will not let me go,
I rest my weary soul in thee.
I give thee back the life I owe,
that in thine ocean depths its flow
may richer, fuller be.

O Light that follows all my way,
I yield my flick'ring torch to thee.
My heart restores its borrowed ray,
that in thy sunshine's blaze its day
may brighter, fairer be.

O Joy that seekest me through pain,
I cannot close my heart to thee.
I trace the rainbow through the rain,
and feel the promise is not vain,
that morn shall tearless be.

O Cross that liftest up my head,
I dare not ask to fly from thee.
I lay in dust, life's glory dead,
and from the ground there blossoms red,
life that shall endless be.

GEORGE MATHESON

READ AND STUDY GOD'S WORD

1. You have discovered such assurance in the words of Paul in your study thus far in Romans 5. And now, you are going to think more deeply about the proof of His amazing love. Yes, His love is amazing. Take some time now and read Romans 5:5-11, 15-19 and write out all the ways the Lord has shown His love for you. What did He do and what has He accomplished on your behalf?

2. The love of the Lord is seen throughout God's Word. Read the following verses and underline those words and phrases that mean the most to you today. Optional Verses: 2 Corinthians 5:14-15, Galatians 2:20, Ephesians 5:2, Titus 3:4-5, 1 John 4:16-19

How precious is your unfailing love, O God! All humanity finds shelter in the shadow of your wings. Psalm 36:7 NLT

For the LORD your God is living among you. He is a mighty savior. He will take delight in you with gladness. With his love, he will calm all your fears. He will rejoice over you with joyful songs. Zephaniah 3:17 NLT

There is no greater love than to lay down one's life for one's friends. John 15:13 NLT

Overwhelming victory is ours through Christ, who loved us. And I am convinced that nothing can ever separate us from God's love. Neither death nor life, neither angels nor demons, neither our fears for today nor our worries about tomorrow—not even the powers of hell can separate us from God's love. No power in the sky above or in the earth below—indeed, nothing in all creation will ever be able to separate us from the love of God that is revealed in Christ Jesus our Lord. Romans 8:37-39 NLT

Even before he made the world, God loved us and chose us in Christ to be holy and without fault in his eyes. God decided in advance to adopt us into his own family by bringing us to himself through Jesus Christ. This is what he wanted to do, and it gave him great pleasure. Ephesians 1:4-5 NLT

But God is so rich in mercy, and he loved us so much, that even though we were dead because of our sins, he gave us life when he raised Christ from the dead. (It is only by God's grace that you have been saved!) For he raised us from the dead along with Christ and seated us with him in the heavenly realms because we are united with Christ Jesus. So God can point to us in all future ages as examples of the incredible wealth of his grace and kindness toward us, as shown in all he has done for us who are united with Christ Jesus. Ephesians 2:4-7 NLT

Then Christ will make his home in your hearts as you trust in him. Your roots will grow down into God's love and keep you strong. And may you have the power to understand, as all God's people should, how wide, how long, how high, and how deep his love is. May you experience the love of Christ, though it is too great to understand fully. Then you will be made complete with all the fullness of life and power that comes from God. Ephesians 3:17-19 NLT

See how very much the Father loves us, for he calls us his children, and that is what we are. 1 John 3:1 NLT

3. The Song of Solomon is considered by some commentators to be a picture of our relationship with Christ. H.A. Ironside, in his beautiful *Addresses on the Song of Solomon*, writes that the marriage relationship is used throughout Scripture "to set forth our union and communion with the Eternal Lover of our souls." Paul writes about the Church and Jesus Christ using the marriage relationship in Ephesians 5:22-33. Ironside speaks of our intimate relationship with Christ when he writes: "The more we get to know of Christ, the more we delight in His presence." He calls the banqueting house "the place of the soul's deep enjoyment when all else is shut out, and Christ's all-satisfying love fills the spirit's vision, and the entire being is taken up with Himself."[13] Meditate on these words from Song of Solomon today, and underline your favorite words and phrases.

> "Like an apple tree among the trees of the forest, so is my beloved among the young men. In his shade I took great delight and sat down, and his fruit was sweet to my taste. He has brought me to his banquet hall, and his banner over me is love… When I found him whom my soul loves; I held on to him and would not let him go." Song of Solomon 2:3-4, 3:4

ADORE GOD IN PRAYER

How do you respond to the amazing love of God? Pour out your heart to the Lord in prayer.

YIELD YOURSELF TO GOD

> In this section we have the foundation of the principle by which the Apostle proves that God's love is assured to us, making justification permanent…If Love can die for us when "we were in a repulsive state of impotence" much more now that we are reconciled will it cherish and keep us. If the death of Christ was the means of our reconciliation, the life of Christ will be the means of our preservation.[14]
>
> W. H. GRIFFITH THOMAS IN ROMANS: A DEVOTIONAL COMMENTARY I-V

ENJOY HIS PRESENCE

What does the love of God mean to you today? Oh, how He loves you. Have you ever doubted His love? What have you read today that helps you see and trust His amazing love for you in a new and deeper way? Paul says that "we may hold our heads high in the light of God's love because of the reconciliation which Christ has made" (Romans 5:11 Phillips). Oh dear friend, hold your head high today and rejoice in God's amazing love. Draw near to the Lord Jesus now and tell Him how you love Him and how much His love means to you. Reflect on the image below entitled "Heart Overflowing." Close your quiet time with the Lord by meditating on the words of that beautiful hymn, "O Love That Will Not Let Me Go" in the Prepare Your Heart section.

Rest in His Love

"See how very much our Father loves us, for He calls us His children, and that is what we are" (1 John 3:1 NLT).

A Heart Overflowing

I love You, Lord. You are my strength. Psalm 18:1
Oak Creek, Sedona, Arizona, USA
Nikon D800E, ISO 100, f22, 0.4sec, Adobe Photoshop, Nik Silver Efex Pro
MyPhotoWalk.com — catherinemartin.smugmug.com

ETERNAL ASSURANCE AND SECURITY

As sin reigned in death, even so grace would reign through righteousness to eternal life through Jesus Christ our Lord.

ROMANS 5:21

PREPARE YOUR HEART

The story is told of a very wealthy man who, with his devoted young son, shared a passion for art collecting. Together they traveled around the world, adding only the finest art treasures to their collection. Priceless works by Picasso, Van Gogh, Monet and many others adorned the walls of the family estate. The widowed, elderly man looked on with satisfaction as his only child became an experienced art collector. The son's trained eye and sharp business mind caused his father to beam with pride as they dealt with art collectors around the world.

As winter approached, war broke out, and the young man left to serve his country. After only a few short weeks, his father received a telegram. His beloved son was missing in action. The art collector anxiously awaited more news, fearing he would never see his son again. Within days, his fears were confirmed. The young man had died while rushing a fellow soldier to a medic.

Distraught and lonely, the old man faced the upcoming Christmas holidays with anguish and sadness. The joy of the season, a season that he and his son had so looked forward to, would visit his house no longer. On Christmas morning, a knock on the door awakened the depressed old man. As he walked to the door, the masterpieces of art on the walls only reminded him that his son was not coming home.

He opened the door, and was greeted by a soldier with a large package in his hand. He introduced himself to the man by saying, "I was a friend of your son. I was the one he was rescuing when he died. May I come in for a few moments? I have something to show you." As the two began to talk, the soldier told of how the man's son had told everyone of his and his father's, love of fine art. "I'm an artist," said the soldier, "and I want to give you this." The old man unwrapped the package, and discovered a portrait of his beloved son.

Though the world would never consider it the work of a master artist, the painting featured the young man's face in striking detail. Overcome with emotion, the man thanked the soldier, promising to hang the picture above his fireplace. True to his word, the painting was hung above the fireplace, pushing aside thousands of dollars of paintings. And then the man sat in his chair and spent Christmas gazing at the gift he had been given. During the days and weeks that followed, the man realized that even though his son was no longer with him, the boy's life would live on because of those he had touched. Later he learned that his son had rescued dozens of wounded soldiers before a bullet took his life.

As the stories of his son's gallantry continued to reach him, fatherly pride and satisfaction began to ease the grief. The painting of his son soon became his most prized possession, far eclipsing any interest in the pieces for which museums around the world clamored. He told his neighbors it was the greatest gift he had ever received.

The following spring, the old man became ill and passed away. The art world greatly anticipated the sale of the many masterpieces! Not knowing the story of the man's only son, but in his honor, those paintings would be sold at an auction. According to the will of the old man, all of the art works would be auctioned on Christmas day, the day he had received his greatest gift. The day soon arrived and art collectors from around the world gathered to bid on some of the world's most spectacular paintings. Dreams would be fulfilled this day; greatness would be achieved as many were hoping to claim "I have the greatest art collection." The auction began with a painting that was not on any museum's list. It was the painting of the man's son. The auctioneer asked for an opening bid. The room was silent.

"Who will open with a bid of $100?" he asked. Minutes passed. No one spoke. From the back of the room came, "Who cares about that painting? It's just a picture of his son. Let's forget it and go on to the good stuff."

More voices echoed in agreement. "No, we have to sell this one first," replied the auctioneer. "Now, who will take the son?" Finally, a friend of the old man spoke, "Will you take ten dollars for the painting? That's all I have. I knew the boy, so I'd like to have it."

"I have ten dollars. Will anyone go higher?" called the auctioneer. After more silence, the auctioneer said, "Going once, going twice. Gone." The gavel fell, cheers filled the room and someone exclaimed, "Now we can get on with it and we can bid on these treasures!"

The auctioneer looked at the audience and announced the auction was over. Stunned disbelief quieted the room. Someone spoke up and asked, "What do you mean it's over? We didn't come here for a picture of some old guy's son. What about all of these paintings? There are millions of dollars of art here! I demand that you explain what's going on here!" The auctioneer replied, "It's very simple. According to the will of the father, whoever takes the son…gets it all."[15]

Oh dear friend, do you understand the profound truth of all we have been studying? This is exactly what we are learning in Paul's letter to the Romans. Whoever has the Son of God because of the love of the Father, gets it all. You have everything and you have it forever. You are eternally secure. That is at the heart of what Paul understood when he first met Christ, all he has learned since that day, and all he is now passing on in the gospel.

So today, dear friend, as we are coming to the end of Week Three in our study of Romans, "The Way of God's Righteousness," draw near to the Lord and ask Him to quiet your heart and speak to you in His Word.

READ AND STUDY GOD'S WORD

1. You have been reading and studying all that you have because of Christ. Read Romans 5:1-21 again and list your favorite short phrases/words that give you eternal assurance and security in Him.

2. In Romans 5:9 we see that "Much more then, having now been justified by His blood, we shall be saved from the wrath of God through Him." In Hebrews 9:22 we see that "without shedding of blood there is no forgiveness." As you have already seen, when God rescued His people from slavery in Egypt, He required them to find an unblemished lamb, sacrifice it, and take the blood and put it on the doorposts of their houses. When He saw the blood, He passed over them (Exodus 12:13). It's no wonder that when John the Baptist saw Jesus coming to him, he said, "Behold, the Lamb of God who takes away the sin of the world! (John 1:29). In Revelation, Jesus is seen as "the Lamb." Read Revelation 5:11-12 and write out what you learn about Jesus, the Lamb.

3. The words of Romans 5:10 are so very powerful. "For if while we were enemies we were reconciled to God through the death of His Son, much more, having been reconciled, we shall be saved by His life." Oh this is such an important truth for you today.

Ian Thomas describes the truth of these words in his book, *The Saving Life Of Christ*: "If you will but trust Christ, not only for the death He died in order to redeem you, but also for the life that He lives and waits to live through you, the very next step you take will be a step taken in the very energy and power of God Himself. You will have begun to live a life which is essentially supernatural, yet still clothed with the common humanity of your physical body, and still worked out in the things that inevitably make up the lot of a man who, though his heart may be with Christ in heaven, still has his two feet firmly planted on the earth. You will have become totally dependent upon the life of Christ within you."[16]

In Romans 5:10 you have a promise for both the present and the future. Christ is with you now and forever in eternity. This verse uses a little phrase, "much more," and this is Paul's way of reasoning from the greater to the lesser. If the Lord did this, then surely He can and will do that. He uses the "much more" phrase four times in Romans 5 and its use gives you added assurance and security.

The Lord says in Hebrews 13:5, "Never will I leave you; never will I forsake you." And then, in Colossians 3:1-4, Paul shares: "Since you have been raised to new life with Christ, set your sights on the realities of heaven, where Christ sits in the place of honor at God's right hand. Think about the things of heaven, not the things of earth. For you died to this life, and your real life is hidden with Christ in God. And when Christ, who is your life, is revealed to the whole world, you will share in all his glory." Finally, think about the words of Paul in Galatians 2:20—"I have been crucified with Christ; and it is no longer I who live, but Christ lives in me; and the life which I now live in the flesh I live by faith in the Son of God, who loved me and gave Himself up for me."

How do these verses filled with truths about the life of Christ in you encourage you and give you hope and security today?

4. In Romans 5:21 you discover that grace and God's righteousness give you eternal life through Jesus Christ our Lord. "As sin reigned in death, even so grace would reign through righteousness to eternal life through Jesus Christ our Lord." GRACE is often remembered with the acronym, "Gods Riches At Christ's Expense." What a blessed assurance to know that all we have in Christ lasts forever, extending on into eternity! Oh how He loves you and me!

Paul has just shown in Romans 5:12-20 that through one man (Adam), sin and death and condemnation entered the world. And now, the gift of righteousness reigns in life through the One, Jesus Christ. Spurgeon says, "As we are lost in one, so we are saved in One."

Dear friend, you can rest your head on the pillow, take a deep breath, and know that because you are now in Christ by grace through faith, you will live forever in heaven with your Lord. You have a future and a hope. This life is not all there is. And it's not the best there is either. Read the following verses and write out what you learn about your hope of heaven and eternal life. Optional: John 3:14-16, Titus 1:2

Romans 6:23

1 Corinthians 2:9-10

1 John 2:25

1 John 5:11-13

Revelation 21:1-4

Adore God in Prayer

When I think of Your lavish goodness
The longings You've satisfied
The forgiveness You've granted
The promises You've kept
When I think of Your irresistible love
Your ceaseless care
Your unfailing protection…
O Lord God
I want to raise flags
And fly banners
And sound bugles.
I want to run with lighted torches
And praise You
From the mountaintop.
I want to write symphonies
And shout for joy.
I want to throw a festive party
For ten thousand guests.
I want to celebrate with streamers
And bright lights
And an elaborate banquet. *Fine dear child. I'm ready.*

Ruth Harms Calkin in Precious Thoughts From The Heart[17]

Yield Yourself to God

Think about these words that Charles Haddon Spurgeon preached in a sermon at The Metropolitan Tabernacle entitled "Much More": "Dear brothers and sisters, since Christ lives, let us live with him, let us make the Lord Jesus Christ our daily Companion. I know that there are some Christians who cannot understand this advice, or cannot believe that they may put it into practice. But you will never know the very juice and marrow of the gospel until you do understand it, and get to feel that Christ is not a mere historical Personage who was upon the earth hundreds of years ago, but a living, personal Christ who is even now accessible, who can be spoken to, and who can speak to us in reply, and with whom we may live even now. Oh, if you can get into personal contact with Jesus Christ, then have you learnt how to live! Then is the dying Saviour inexpressibly dear to you, but then also the living Christ is, if possible, even more dear, and you live through him,—with him,—for him,—and he lives in you. So may God make it to be, for our Lord Jesus Christ's sake! Amen."

ENJOY HIS PRESENCE

What a week of study in Romans! God wants you to know that when you place your faith in Christ, you are saved forever and have eternal life. Oh how God loves us. You have seen the proof of His amazing love this week, and Paul says "we may hold our heads high in the light of God's love" (Romans 5:11 Phillips). What have you learned today that means the most to you? Today is the day to draw near to the Lord and think about your love relationship with Him. Do you walk and talk with Him daily? Close by meditating on the photography highlighting God's creation and on the words of this wonderful hymn written by Alfred H. Ackley (1887-1960). Think about how Jesus walks with you and talks with you day by day and moment by moment.

> I serve a risen Saviour, He's in the world today
> I know that He is living, whatever men may say
> I see His hand of mercy, I hear His voice of cheer
> And just the time I need Him He's always near.
>
> *Refrain*: He lives (He lives), He lives (He lives), Christ Jesus lives today
> He walks with me and talks with me
> Along life's narrow way
> He lives (He lives), He lives (He lives), Salvation to impart
> You ask me how I know He lives?
> He lives within my heart
>
> In all the world around me I see His loving care
> And though my heart grows weary I never will despair
> I know that He is leading, through all the stormy blast
> The day of His appearing will come at last. *Refrain*
>
> Rejoice, rejoice, O Christian Lift up your voice and sing
> Eternal hallelujahs to Jesus Christ, the King
> The Hope of all who seek Him, the Help of all who find
> None other is so loving, so good and kind. *Refrain*

REST IN HIS LOVE

"Since you have been raised to new life with Christ, set your sights on the realities of heaven, where Christ sits in the place of honor at God's right hand. Think about the things of heaven, not the things of earth. For you died to this life, and your real life is hidden with Christ in God. And when Christ, who is your life, is revealed to the whole world, you will share in all his glory" (Colossians 3:1-4 NLT).

ACROSS THE RIVER

Then we will be at home with the Lord. 2 Corinthians 5:8 NLT
Falls Highway, Klamath Falls, Oregon, USA
Nikon D7000, ISO 100, f11, 1/8sec, Adobe Photoshop, Nik Silver Efex Pro
MYPHOTOWALK.COM—CATHERINEMARTIN.SMUGMUG.COM

DEVOTIONAL READING
BY HANNAH WHITALL SMITH

DEAR FRIEND,

The next two days are your opportunity to review what you have learned this week. Thank the Lord for all you have seen that shows you the proof His amazing love and the power of the gospel of Christ. As you think about your study in Romans this week, record your:

Most meaningful insight:

Most meaningful devotional reading:

Most meaningful verse:

Read the following words of Hannah Whitall Smith as she talks about the language of faith found in the "much mores" in Scripture, especially in Romans 5. May you be encouraged to hold by faith to the "much mores," often unseen yet nevertheless true and a rock and a refuge for you no matter what you face today.

f our Lord is to be believed, His "*much mores*" of grace are abundantly equal to the worst emergency that can befall us…Let us settle it then that the language of our souls must henceforth be not the "much less" of unbelief, but the "*much more*" of faith. And I feel sure we shall find that God's "*much mores*" will be enough to cover the whole range of our needs, both temporal and spiritual. One of the deepest needs of our souls is the need for being saved. Is there a "*much more*" to meet this need? What does the apostle say? "But God commendeth his love toward us, in that, while we were yet sinners, Christ died for us. Much more then, being now justified by his blood, we shall be saved from wrath through him. For if, when we were enemies, we were reconciled to God by the death of his Son, much more, being reconciled, we shall be saved by his life" (Romans 5:8-10). The question of salvation seems to me to be absolutely settled by these "*much mores.*" Since Christ has died for us, and has thereby reconciled us to God (not God to us, He did not need reconciling), of course "much more," if only we will let Him, will He now save us. There can be no question as to whether He will save us. There can be no question as to whether He will or will not, for the greater must necessarily include the lesser, and, having done the greater, "*much more*" will He do the lesser. None of us doubt that He did the greater, and, in the face of these "much mores," we dare not doubt He will do the lesser. None of us doubt the greatness of salvation, and we dare not doubt that He will take care of us daily as well. We have only touched upon the wonders of grace hidden in these *much mores* of God. We can never exhaust their meaning in this life. But let us at least resolve to lay aside every "much less" of unbelief concerning salvation. Then out of the depths of our utter weakness, sinfulness and need, let us assert with a conquering faith, always and everywhere, the mighty "*much more*" of the grace of God.

HANNAH WHITALL SMITH IN THE GOD OF ALL COMFORT

❧ **WEEK THREE** ❧

Living In The Land Of Grace

This week we studied Romans 4-5 and learned about the way of God's righteousness. And today in our time together, we are going to enter into the marvelous and wonderful land of grace. So grab your Bible, and let's get into the Word of God together.

"Therefore having been justified by faith, we have peace with God through our Lord Jesus Christ, through whom also we have obtained our introduction by faith into this grace in which we stand; and we exult in hope of the glory of God" (Romans 5:1-2).

What is grace?

Grace is God's _______________________________________ in action. When you think of grace, think of God's arms open wide to you, regardless of what you have done. Grace opens the floodgates and allows God's endless love to pour into our lives, moment by moment, on into eternity.

What we learn about the land of grace in Romans 5

1. We enter into this land of grace at a _____________________________________ by faith. Romans 5:1

2. We have _______________________________ with God in the land of grace. Romans 5:1

3. We live in the land of grace by _____________________________, not by sight. Romans 5:2

4. The land of grace is like a _____________________________ where we thrive and grow. Romans 5:2, 2 Peter 3:18

5. We can rejoice in _____________________________ in the land of grace. Romans 5:3-5

6. We always have _____________________________ in the land of grace. Romans 5:5

7. We experience God's ________________________________ in the land of grace. Romans 5:5,8

8. We have the power of the ________________________________ in the land of grace. Romans 5:5

9. We walk and talk with Jesus and experience His ________________________________ in the land of grace. Romans 5:10, John 14:23

10. In the land of grace, there is always ________________________________ grace for whatever you face today. Romans 5:17, 2 Corinthians 9:8

11. We are in an unshakeable ________________________________ in the land of grace. Romans 5:17, Revelation 22:5

12. We have ________________________________ in the land of grace. Romans 5:21

Video messages are available on DVDs or as Digital M4V Video. Audio messages are available as Digital MP3 Audio. Visit the Quiet Time Ministries Online Store at www.quiettime.org.

THE UNION IN GOD'S RIGHTEOUSNESS

Romans 6-8:1-4

To be joined in life with the Risen Christ, and thus daily, hourly, to walk, is a wonder not conceived of by many of us. But it is the blessed portion of all true Christians. They shared Christ's death, and now are "saved by [or in] His life…But not only saved: we walk here on earth by appropriating faith, in the blessedness of His heavenly "newness" of resurrection life![1]

WILLIAM R. NEWELL

THE GREAT UNION

For if we have become united with Him in the likeness of His death,
certainly we shall also be in the likeness of His resurrection.

ROMANS 6:5

PREPARE YOUR HEART

Have you ever traveled to a foreign country that was new to you? The language was different to you and unfamiliar. The terrain was completely unknown. You always discover that a guidebook is very helpful in understanding the roads and the sites to see. But even more helpful is if you have a personal tour guide who has traveled the road, describes the area from personal experience, and shows you the way.

Paul does this very thing in Romans as he unfolds the gospel and takes all of us into the land of grace, teaches us the language of faith, shows us the multi-faceted character of Christ, and reveals the beauty and wonder of God's righteousness. And now, in Romans 6-8, Paul is calling back to us by sharing all that he has learned about this new life in Christ and his own relationship and walk with Jesus Christ.

As you begin your quiet time, draw near to the Lord and ask Him to speak to you as you study these important chapters in the Bible. Think about how Paul is calling back to you with his grand truth about union with Christ and all that it means for you now and forever. Who knows, the Lord may, in the days ahead, use you to call back to someone else with these powerful truths.

> If you have gone a little way ahead of me, call back—
> 'Twill cheer my heart and help my feet along the stony track;
> And if, perchance, Faith's light is dim, because the oil is low,
> Your call will guide my lagging course as wearily I go.
>
> Call back, and tell me that He went with you into the storm;
> Call back, and say He kept you when the forest's roots were torn;
> That, when the heavens thunder and the earthquake shook the hill,
> He bore you up and held you where the very air was still.

Oh, friend, call back, and tell me for I cannot see your face;
They say it glows with triumph, and your feet bound in the race;
But there are mists between us and my spirit eyes are dim,
And I cannot see the glory, though I long for word of Him.

But if you'll say He heard you when your prayer was but a cry,
And if you'll say He saw you through the night's sin-darkened sky—
If you have gone a little way ahead, oh, friend, call back—
'Twill cheer my heart and help my feet along the stony track.

Mr. Charles Cowman in Streams in the Desert

Read and Study God's Word

1. Paul is taking the believers there in Rome (and us) on quite the journey. And now, he is going to deal with the gospel life and something we are most likely questioning. What about sin? How does my relationship with Christ change my character and how does it impact the sin I still find present in my life at times? In Romans 6:5 we learn that we are "united" with Christ. Because of our union with Christ, we have a whole new identity. These are positional truths about us that cannot be touched or changed because we are united with Christ forever. Your firsthand experience of these truths will grow throughout your life as Christ works in you through the Holy Spirit conforming you to His image. Read Romans 6:1-14 and write out all that is true because of our union with Christ.

2. Your union with Christ means you have been "freed from sin." You are acquitted because you died with Christ, you were raised to new life with Christ, and now you live forever with Him. You have been brought into a vital saving relationship and are incorporated into Christ, united with Him forever. It is interesting to note that water baptism following salvation is practiced in obedience to Jesus' command in Matthew 28:18-20. The immersion in water following salvation is a sacrament or ordinance signifying our union with Christ that has already occurred—life, death, burial, resurrection described in Romans 6:3-4. So now, what is true of you and your new life with Christ? Read Galatians 2:20 and describe what happens when you have been "crucified with Christ" i.e. died with Christ. This is often called the crucified life.

3. And now, dear friend, you live in the land of grace. Paul says it this way: "For sin shall not be master over you, for you are not under law, but under grace" (Romans 6:14). You are no longer a slave to sin and now you are "under grace." This means that now you actually can say "no" to sin and "yes" to God and His righteousness in the power of the Holy Spirit. Being set free from the tyranny of sin's rule makes a life of godliness possible. And when and if you sin now, because you are still in the body here on earth, there is forgiveness in Christ—you are under grace. John says, "If we confess our sins, He is rightful and righteous to forgive our sins and to cleans us from all unrighteousness" (1 John 1:9). What is this land of grace like? Joseph Cooke, in his book, *Celebration of Grace,* describes grace as "nothing more or less than the face that love wears when it meets imperfection, weakness, failure, sin. Grace is what love is and does when it meets the sinful and the undeserving."[2] Grace is God's love in action. When you think of grace, think of God's arms open wide to you, regardless of what you have done. Grace opens the floodgates and allows God's endless love to pour into our lives, moment by moment, on into eternity. You have grace for today, grace for tomorrow, and grace forever. Now that's an extravagant, outrageous grace. Look at the following verses and write out your favorite insights about grace:

2 Corinthians 9:8

2 Corinthians 12:7-10

2 Thessalonians 2:16-17

4. As you think about your new identity, united with Christ, and living in the land of grace, just imagine the intimacy that is possible with Christ. You can walk and talk with Him in the garden of grace and grow daily in your relationship with Him. Peter encourages you with these words, "But grow in the grace and knowledge of our Lord and Savior Jesus Christ" (2 Peter 3:18).

As you grow, you will affirm who you are in Christ, and you will be able to say, "Because of God's grace I am secure, forgiven, accepted, and loved forever by God. I am always in God's audience, united with Christ, and indwelt by the Holy Spirit. I stand in extravagant grace, the perfect environment for spiritual growth. I am blessed with every spiritual blessing and have everything I need. I am God's beautiful masterpiece, designed for His purposes and plans. I have the hope of heaven where I will live with Christ forever."[3] Believe it, receive it, and live it.

ADORE GOD IN PRAYER

Talk with the Lord today about what you have learned about your relationship with Him. He is with you now and loves conversing with you. Always remember that He loves you with an everlasting love and delights in you (Jeremiah 31:3). His banner over you is love, dear friend (Song of Solomon 2:4).

YIELD YOURSELF TO GOD

When we place our trust in Jesus Christ for salvation from sin, we are said to be enveloped by Him in a spiritual sense. In a very real way, our identity becomes united with His, such that His experience becomes ours. He died and we died with Him. He rose from the dead to a new kind of life, and so shall we. By virtue of our identification with Jesus Christ, His death, and His resurrection, we have been emancipated from bondage to sin. Identity with Christ began with belief, but it has ongoing consequences.[4]

CHARLES R. SWINDOLL IN SWINDOLL'S NEW TESTAMENT INSIGHTS: ROMANS

Soul, thou and Jesus are standing face to face. Give thy whole self to Him and He gives His whole self to you. Go to your bare garret, go to your dying child, go to scenes of trouble and sorrow and pain. He goes too. You have got the fountain beside you. You do not need to take your pitcher and go to draw in some external well. You have Jesus in your heart, a fountain springing up to everlasting life.[5]

F.B. MEYER IN THE CHRIST LIFE FOR YOUR LIFE

ENJOY HIS PRESENCE

If you know Christ, then He now lives in you. Paul calls this truth "the riches of the glory of this mystery among the Gentiles. which is Christ in you, the hope of glory" (Colossians 1:27). Think about how knowing Christ and being united with Him in your life impacts and influences your perspective and attitude regarding sin and right living. Paul shared his overall goal in life when he said, "I want to know Christ and experience the mighty power that raised him from the dead" (Philippians 3:10 NLT). One of his conclusions as a result of knowing Christ was, "I can do all things through Christ who strengthens me" (Philippians 4:13).

This week you are learning about your union with Christ and your privilege to walk and talk with Him intimately, moment by moment and day by day. Over time, you will know Him more and more. And the more you know Him and spend time with Him, the more you will become like Him. How has knowing Christ changed your life? And how do you need His grace today? Write out your thoughts in your Journal or in the margin below. Then talk with the Lord and meditate on these wonderful words about the land of grace written by Annie Johnson Flint.

He giveth more grace when the burdens grow greater,
He sendeth more strength when the labors increase;
To added afflictions He addeth His mercy,
To multiplied trials, His multiplied peace.

When we have exhausted our store of endurance,
When our strength has failed ere the day is half done,
When we reach the end of our hoarded resources
Our Father's full giving is only begun.

Fear not that thy need shall exceed His provision,
Our God ever yearns His resources to share;
Lean hard on the arm everlasting, availing;
The Father both thee and thy load will upbear.

His love has no limits, His grace has no measure,
His power no boundary known unto men;
For out of His infinite riches in Jesus
He giveth, and giveth, and giveth again.

REST IN HIS LOVE

"'And God is able to make all grace abound to you, so that always having all sufficiency in everything, you may have an abundance for every good deed" (2 Corinthians 9:8).

THE FIRST GLEAM OF DAWN

The way of the righteous is like the first gleam of dawn. Proverbs 4:18
Coachella Valley Preserve, Palm Desert, California, USA
Nikon D800E, ISO 100, f22, 1/30sec, Adobe Photoshop, Nik Silver Efex Pro
MYPHOTOWALK.COM—CATHERINEMARTIN.SMUGMUG.COM

THE GREAT FREEDOM

*But now having been freed from sin and enslaved to God, you derive your
benefit, resulting in sanctification, and the outcome, eternal life.*

Romans 6:22

PREPARE YOUR HEART

Texas rancher, hunting in the mountains, came upon an eagle's nest, and took one of the eggs back home with him, and placed it under a setting hen. The eagle was hatched and cared for by the mother hen. For some period of time, the eagle seemed perfectly content to remain in the barnyard and feed along with the chickens. That is, until it heard the harsh scream of a mature eagle, swooping down in search of prey. In the blink of an eye, the young eagle ascended into the sky and was never seen again. It had found its new home in the mountainside cliffs, for that young eagle was not made for the barnyard dirt but meant to soar in the heights above.

Oh dear friend, today as you live in Romans 6, you are going to see a great change that has taken place in who you are and Whose you are. You are not meant for the barnyard dirt of this world, but you are like an eagle, set free to soar the heights with your Lord. And you can know this: "If the Son makes you free, you will be free indeed" (John 8:36).

As you begin your quiet time, ask the Lord to speak to you from His Word today.

READ AND STUDY GOD'S WORD

1. Today you are going to look at the change that has taken place in you as a result of your relationship with Christ. Record your insights about the following questions as you read these verses in Romans 6. Also, be sure to write out your own questions in your journal that may arise as you study these powerful verses in your quiet time. They may be answered as you continue to study.

What was your previous relationship to sin—Romans 6:6, 14, 17, 19-20

What is your relationship to sin and righteousness now that you know Christ—
Romans 6:2, 4, 6-7,10-11, 14, 18, 22-23

How then should we live—Romans 6:11-14, 19

2. Notice that Paul admits that he "is speaking in human terms" (Romans 6:19), and he is not saying we will not ever sin again. He is talking about our experience in the body vs. positional truths that can never change. Note in Romans 6:6-7 that "our old self was crucified with Him, in order that our body of sin might be done away with, so that we would no longer be slaves to sin, for he who has died is freed from sin." Being "freed from sin" means we are acquitted. There is a difference that has now taken place because of Christ. We're now slaves of righteousness (Romans 6:18) and we live "to God" because of our union with Christ and our identification with Him (Romans 6:10). There has been a change of masters. As you think about all Paul is saying here and his encouragement to "now present your members as slaves to righteousness" (Romans 6:19), what kind of life and attitude and action do you think he is encouraging that is now made possible because of Christ?

3. In Romans 6:22 we see that the benefit of being freed from sin and enslaved to God is sanctification and the outcome is eternal life. Now Paul is showing the wonderful change that takes place. *Sanctification* is *hagiasmos* and means holiness, and implies here that we are set aside to God for His holy purposes. In the New Testament we discover that we are sanctified (our unchangeable position in Hebrews 10:10) and we are being sanctified (the ongoing process of growing spiritually and becoming more like Christ seen in Hebrews 10:14). Sanctification is a great benefit because in it we see progressive spiritual growth that occurs in the life of a believer. Paul tells us in 2 Corinthians 5:17 that "if anyone is in Christ, he is a new creature; the old things pass away; behold, new things have come." You can live a holy life that brings glory to God as you become more and more like Christ. Read the following passages of Scripture and underline your most significant insights about how to live now that you are enslaved to God and freed from sin.

> Since you have been raised to new life with Christ, set your sights on the realities of heaven, where Christ sits in the place of honor at God's right hand. Think about the things of heaven, not the things of earth. For you died to this life, and your real life is hidden with Christ in God. And when Christ, who is your life, is revealed to the whole world, you will share in all his glory. Colossians 3:1-4 NLT

> For this is the will of God, your sanctification; that is, that you abstain from sexual immorality; that each of you know how to possess his own vessel in sanctification and honor. 1 Thessalonians 4:3-4

4. Think about all you have learned from Paul in the last few chapters of Romans including the unshakeable and eternally secure position of a believer in Romans 5, and then what you have studied in Romans 6. Write out in 1-2 sentences a summary of what Paul seems to be saying here in chapter 6 to the Christians in Rome. Pay attention especially to the questions he asks at the very beginning of Romans 6. Here are some questions to help you with your summary: Does living in the land of grace promote holiness or a life of sin? What does Paul want these believers (and you) to know and experience? How does our union with Christ make a difference in how we live?

Adore God in Prayer

Holy Spirit, teach me to put away anger, wrath, malice, and evil communications, loveless words and loveless acts, and may I put on a heart of compassion, kindness, humility, meekness, longsuffering. May I forbear with and forgive others as you bear with and forgive me.

F. B. Meyer in *Daily Prayers*

Yield Yourself to God

In chapter 6 he [Paul] deals with it in a very practical manner in regard to our daily life and our falling into sin. It is as if he imagined someone saying, "Look here, Paul, you have overpainted the picture. The fact is that men still fall into sin, and you are not telling them to live according to the law in order that they may overcome sin." "The answer," says Paul, "is that we are joined to Christ. We have been crucified with Him, we have died with Him, we have been buried with Him, we have risen again with Him. We, as beings, are no longer in Adam, we are in Christ, and in Christ we are absolutely safe." "Well, why do we sin?" asks someone. "Sin," replies the Apostle, "remains in the body in our mortal members, and the way to deal with that problem is to realize your standing in Christ and to reckon yourselves to be dead unto sin but alive unto God" — and he works it out in detail. That is the general argument in chapter six…he is explaining how sin still remains in the believer, and he shows how it is only by understanding the truth about ourselves in union with Christ that we overcome it.[6]

D. Martyn Lloyd-Jones in *Romans, Exposition of Chapter 1, The Gospel of God*

We are not only identified with Jesus in His death, but we are one with Him in His resurrection, and we are one with Him in His ascension. We all died with Him, we all went down into the grave with Him, we all rose with Him that first Easter morning, we ascended with Him into heavenly places, and we are there today, far above all principalities and powers.…"We wait," says Paul, "for the redemption of our bodies" (Romans 8:23). We wait for it; we live here in the flesh, in the body which is under the stroke and effect of man's original fall from sin. So long as we are in this world we will be very conscious that we inhabit a body of corruption and death…When Christ died, the self-life died, and He took a new life up to the throne of God when He ascended into heaven, and He poured out into the hearts of believers a life that is far above principality and power, a life that is seated with Him in heavenly places. In the flesh I am on the earth, but in the spirit I am in heaven…By faith am I going to take my place where I am in spirit with the Lord Jesus…Get onto the victory side again; you have been placed there![7]

Alan Redpath in Victorious Christian Living

Enjoy His Presence

We have seen in Romans 6 that once we know Christ, we are no longer slaves to sin and we are now enslaved to God (Romans 6:22). The power of sin in our lives is broken because Christ has set us free. We are now united with Christ. We are no longer under the Law but under grace. Yours is an unchangeable and unshakeable position in Christ. You are forever secure in Christ. It means that presenting ourselves to the Law and making resolutions and vows doesn't help us live to God and righteousness. What it does mean is that united with Christ, and living in His power, we now are set free to actually resist sin and say "no" to sin as we present our members to God in the power of the Holy Spirit. Liberty and freedom are never a license to sin. Experientially, as we walk in newness of life, we will grow spiritually and our lives will display the life of Christ at work in us as we become more and more like Him. As you think about all these deep things from Romans 6, what have you learned and how have you experienced the life of Christ at work in your own life? Is there sin in your life you need to confess and repent of today? The Holy Spirit is faithful to convict us of sin. Always remember 1 John 1:9—"If we confess our sins, He is faithful and righteous to forgive us our sins, and to cleanse us from all unrighteousness." Write your thoughts in your Journal.

Take some time to look at the image of the flower at the end of this quiet time and think about the newness of life and the growth the Lord is causing in your life. Write your thoughts in your Journal, and then close by praying the words of the fourth stanza of "And Can It Be That I Should Gain" written by Charles Wesley.

> Long my imprisoned spirit lay fast bound in sin and nature's night
> Thine eye diffused a quick'ning ray, I woke, the dungeon flamed with light;
> My chains fell off, my heart was free; I rose, went forth and followed Thee.
> *Refrain*: Amazing love! How can it be that Thou, my God, should die for me!

Rest in His Love

"God has called us to live holy lives, not impure lives" (1 Thessalonians 4:7 NLT).

Grow In Grace

Grow in grace. 2 Peter 3:18 AMP
Palazzo Pitti, Florence, Tuscany Italy
Nikon D7000, ISO 250, f5.6, 1/1250sec, Adobe Photoshop, Nik Silver Efex Pro
myPhotoWalk.com—catherinemartin.smugmug.com

THE GREAT CRY

But now we have been released from the Law, having died to that by which we were bound, so that we serve in newness of the Spirit and not in oldness of the letter."
ROMANS 7:6

PREPARE YOUR HEART

lisabeth Elliot has been a beloved author and speaker over the years. Her first husband was Jim Elliot, and they ministered together in the jungle of Ecuador. In 1956, the Auca Indians killed five missionaries, including her husband. She wrote the story in her book, *Through Gates of Splendor*. A number of years later, she and their daughter Valerie traveled back into the jungle and lived with the very Aucas who had killed her husband. She saw many of those Aucas give their lives to Christ. When she wrote her first book, her ministry of writing and speaking worldwide began. After some years of ministry, in 1966 she met and married Addison Leitch, a theologian and professor. A number of years later, he was diagnosed with cancer, and died in 1973. A year after his death, Elisabeth became a visiting professor at Gordon-Conwell Seminary in Wenham, Massachusetts. Three years later she married Lars Gren, a seminary student at Gordon-Conwell. He traveled with her when she spoke and they enjoyed a long and happy marriage. He cared for Elisabeth in later years, and after 37 years of marriage, she went home to be with the Lord in 2015.

Elisabeth Elliot's life was quite the adventure and she was married to three wonderful Christian men, with two of them suffering tragic deaths, and the third with her for many years until she stepped into heaven. Her life is such an example and she is a great hero of the faith who loved and served the Lord Jesus Christ.

Paul is now going to take us into two examples to help us understand our union with Christ and how our relationship with Him impacts our lives. Today we will look at the first example involving marriage and the death of one husband and marriage to another, to the Lord Jesus Christ. In the next day we will look at the second example found in the life of Paul himself. So now, as you begin your time alone with the Lord, ask Him to speak to you. Write a short prayer, expressing your heart to Him today.

READ AND STUDY GOD'S WORD

1. In Romans 5 we saw that because our faith is in Christ, we are now in an unshakeable position as we are no longer under the law, but under grace. We are forgiven of all our sins and now have the hope of eternal life. In Romans 6 we saw that we are no longer slaves of sin, but now we live to God and are slaves of righteousness. We learned that we are united with Christ in His death and in His resurrection, so that now we can walk in newness of life. And yet, we still live in the body while here on earth until we step into heaven. Paul is going to explain truths we need to begin to understand related to the Law and our ongoing spiritual experience. These truths take a lifetime to grasp. Don't be afraid if you have questions. Just write them down and ask the Holy Spirit to open your eyes as you study God's Word.

Now Paul, in Romans 7 is going to give two examples, or illustrations, to help us see how a new life in Christ is possible. The first is an example involving marriage. Read Romans 7:1-6 and write your insights about what Paul is saying about marriage to teach believers in Rome (and us) about how it is that we can be joined to Christ and how it impacts our life.

2. So Paul has pointed out that if a husband dies, then the wife is free from the law, so she can be joined to another man. Elisabeth Elliot is a great example, for when each of her first two husbands had died, she was joined to another. But why is Paul using this example? Read Romans 7:4-6 and write out why you think Paul chose this example and how it impacts our daily life now.

3. And now Paul clarifies the Law and its purpose. He begins by asking the question, "Is the Law sin? May it never be! On the contrary, I would not have come to know sin except through the Law" (Romans 7:7). Read Romans 7:7-13 and write out what you learn about the Law and sin.

4. Describe now in you own words, why it is significant that, according to Romans 7:4-6, you died to the Law through the body of Christ and you have been released from the Law, having died to that which you were bound? What can now happen in your life because of those truths in Romans 7:4-6?

5. When you are joined to Jesus Christ, you are, in fact, part of the church, the body of Christ (see Ephesians 5:23-32). You are His Bride. In the first century, when a man and woman wanted to marry, the fathers would establish a price for the bride as compensation for the bride's family. The man would pay the bride price, and then go to his family's home to prepare a place for he and his bride to live. Jesus has paid the price for His Bride by dying for her. And now, He has gone "to prepare a place for you" (John 14:3). Oh how the Lord loves you, nourishes and cherishes you, and will one day present you to Himself as part of His church, as His Bride, without spot or wrinkle, and holy and blameless (Ephesians 5:27). One day there is going to be the marriage of the Lamb and you will be seen as the Bride who has "made herself ready" and is clothed in fine linen (Revelation 19:7-8). To Him be all the glory! What does it mean to you to be the Bride of your Lord Jesus Christ and joined to Him forever?

Adore God in Prayer

Fanny Crosby wrote at least 5000 hymns in her lifetime. Take some time now and meditate on the words of "To God Be The Glory," written by Fanny Crosby, as a response to all that the Lord has done for you. These hymns mean so much more with the truths we are learning in Romans.

To God be the glory, great things He hath done,
So loved He the world that He gave us His Son,
Who yielded His life an atonement for sin,
And opened the life gate that all may go in.

Refrain: Praise the Lord, praise the Lord, let the earth hear His voice!
Praise the Lord, praise the Lord, let the people rejoice!
Oh, come to the Father, through Jesus the Son,
And give Him the glory, great things He hath done.

Oh, perfect redemption, the purchase of blood,
To every believer the promise of God;
The vilest offender who truly believes,
That moment from Jesus a pardon receives. *Refrain*.

Great things He hath taught us, great things He hath done,
And great our rejoicing through Jesus the Son;
But purer, and higher, and greater will be
Our wonder, our transport, when Jesus we see. *Refrain*.

Yield Yourself to God

In our study today, we learned that in Christ we "have been released from the Law, having died to that by which we were bound, so that we serve in newness of the Spirit and not in oldness of the letter" (Romans 7:6). We were "made to die to the Law through the body of Christ, so that you might be joined to another, to Him who was raised from the dead, in order that we might bear fruit for God" (Romans 7:4). Oh what a powerful truth this is for us.

Watchman Nee, a Chinese church leader and Christian teacher in the 20th Century, wrote an insightful book, *The Normal Christian Life*, where he teaches many of the truths found in Romans. One experience he shares is especially powerful. It's all about the day he realized his union with Christ, and that when Christ died, he died in Him. Here's how he describes it: "I remember one morning—that morning was a real morning and one I can never forget—I was upstairs sitting at my desk reading the Word and praying, and I said, "Lord, open my eyes!" And then in a flash I saw it. I saw my oneness with Christ. I saw that I was in Him, and that when He died I died. I saw that the question of my death was a matter of the past and not of the future, and that I was just as truly dead as He was because I was in Him when He died. The whole thing had dawned upon me. I was carried away with such joy at this great discovery that I jumped from my chair and cried, "Praise the Lord, I am dead!" I ran downstairs and met one of the brothers helping in the kitchen and I laid hold of him. "Brother," I said, "do you know that I have died?" I must admit he looked puzzled. "What do you mean?" he said, so I went on: "Do you not know that Christ has died? Do you not know that I died with Him? Do you not know that my death is no less truly a fact than His?" Oh it was so real to me! I longed to go through the streets of Shanghai shouting the news of my discovery. From that day to this I have never for one moment doubted the finality of that word: "I have been crucified with Christ."[8]

> The Apostle teaches in the fullest form what union with Christ really means. As marriage is the highest form of earthly union, so the spiritual union suggested here transcends every other aspect. Let us ponder this wonderful thought of the believer's union with the Lord Jesus Christ. The penalty of the law has been paid. He has been crucified with Christ, his former connection with the law has gone forever and a new Bridegroom claims his heart as He betroths him to Himself forever. [9]
>
> W.H. Griffith Thomas in Romans: A Devotional Commentary VI-XI

> Let faith ring these bells of heaven for our joy. Married to Christ. Himself the measure of our responsibilities; Himself the fulness of our capabilities; Himself the possessor of our hearts' affections; Himself the security of our hopes; Himself the well-spring of our fruitfulness; Himself the law of our hearts, our glory, and our crown.
>
> Marcus Rainsford in Lectures on Romans

Enjoy His Presence

W. H. Griffith Thomas invites us to "ponder this wonderful thought of the believer's union with the Lord Jesus Christ." Think about it, dear friend. When you put your faith in Christ, you are joined with Him forever. He is your Bridegroom, Shepherd, Savior, Lord, Rock, Redeemer,

Provider, and so much more. How well do you know Him? And how do these truths motivate you to love Him and be faithful to Him? Write your thoughts about your love relationship with Jesus, then close with a prayer to your Lord.

REST IN HIS LOVE

"Therefore, my brethren, you also were made to die to the Law through the body of Christ, so that you might be joined to another, to Him who was raised from the dead, in order that we might bear fruit for God" (Romans 7:4).

WITH HIM IN THE GARDEN

Walk with me and work with me—watch how I do it. Matthew 11:29 MSG
South Grand Avenue, Los Angeles, California, USA
Nikon D810, ISO 3200, f11, 1/400sec, Adobe Photoshop, Nik Silver Efex Pro
MYPHOTOWALK.COM—CATHERINEMARTIN.SMUGMUG.COM

THE GREAT QUESTION

Wretched man that I am! Who will set me free from the body of this death?
Romans 7:24

PREPARE YOUR HEART

here are so many benefits to a good question. And our beloved friend, the Apostle Paul, seems to have the gift of asking not just good questions, but great ones. And now, in Romans 7, Paul is going to share his own testimony in relation to all he has been sharing here in Romans, especially in Romans 6 and 7. He will end his personal experience with a great question. And aren't you glad he is going to share his story, because these are heavy and deep truths that the Lord is giving us in these chapters. Only the Lord, through the power of the Holy Spirit, can give us understanding and help us apply these truths to our lives. Let's remember the promise from Jesus to His disciples (and to us): "I have many more things to say to you, but you cannot bear them now. But when He, the Spirit of truth comes, He will guide you into all the truth; for He will not speak on His own initiative, but whatever He hears, He will speak; and He will disclose to you what is to come. He will glorify Me, for He will take of Mine and will disclose it to you" (John 16:12-14). Don't you love those words for our study in Romans!

Draw near to the Lord now, remembering the great promise that when you draw near to Him, He will draw near to you (James 4:8). Tell Him how much you love Him and the study of His Word. Thank Him for giving you the Holy Spirit who will guide you into all truth. Ask Him now to speak to you as spend quiet time with Him today. Remember He is always with you.

> Tho the path be dark and dangerous
> And I cannot see ahead,
> Tho my heart be sore and heavy
> And so often full of dread
> Tho the storm clouds
> darkly gather
> And His face they hide from view,
> Tho the path is steep and thorny
> It is wide enough for two.

For my Savior walks beside me,
I am never left alone.
I know He'll not forsake me,
He is mindful of His own.
He will share the heavy burdens
And the trials I must pass thru,
Tho the path is ofttimes narrow
It is wide enough for two,
The Things of earth are tinsel—
His glory all I see,
To know He's my companion—
That is enough for me.
He will guide my faltering footsteps
And will bring me safely thru.
Tho the path is dark before me
It is wide enough for two.[10]

RETA BELLE LYLE IN *QUOTES FROM THE QUIET HOUR*

READ AND STUDY GOD'S WORD

1. And now, we're going to hear from Paul as he shares in the first person related to all he has been talking about, especially in Romans 6 and 7. Keep in mind that he is writing to the saints in Rome. These are believers who are in an eternally secure relationship with Christ and living in the land of grace. What Paul is now going to describe is the conflict that takes place being in union with Christ, and yet still living in our body here on earth. In other words, though we are saved, we still sin and we struggle with sin, the world, the flesh, and the devil. And it seems that in Paul's sharing, there is strong conviction of sin taking place. Read Romans 7:14-25, then describe in 1-2 sentences the conflict he shares in these verses.

2. One of the big questions debated among commentators relates to Romans 7. Was Paul describing his experience as a Christian or as a non-Christian? It is the very words of Paul that give the answer here. What does he say about how he really wants to live? Write your insights about Paul's inner desires from the following verses:

Romans 7:15

Romans 7:18-19

Romans 7:20-21

Romans 7:22

3. The words of Paul show that he indeed loves God and wants to do good. His words also show that he is being convicted of sin. And perhaps you have felt the same way at times. Understand that those who don't know Christ, as described in Romans 3:10-18, do not love the Lord and there is no fear of God in them. In Paul's description of his struggle, he wants to do good, but doesn't always do the good that he longs to practice. In fact, according to Romans 7:22 he joyfully concurs with the Law of God in the inner man (see 2 Corinthians 4:16). There's obviously a struggle. Paul has what commentator William Newell calls a "holy self-despair." It is a great discovery to realize that there is no power in self and that now we are joined to Jesus Christ. Now we live daily in the power of the Holy Spirit and are renewed day by day. Read Romans 7:24-25. What is his great question and what is the answer?

4. Paul wrote another letter to the church at Corinth who needed to be reminded of who they were in Christ. These words shed light on who we are now in Christ. Read 2 Corinthians 5:14-17 and write your favorite truth from this passage of Scripture.

Adore God in Prayer

Dear friend, have you experienced the same struggle that Paul described? Perhaps you are challenged with temptation to sin in an area of your life even now. You are forgiven and set free. When you sin, count on God's promise, "If we confess our sins, He is faithful and righteous to forgive us our sins and to cleanse us from all unrighteousness" (1 John 1:9). Do you see that your union with Christ is the real story and that He is at work in you so that you might walk in newness of life? Talk with the Lord now about all you have learned, and ask Him for His strength and power in the Holy Spirit. Remember that you live and walk by faith in Christ, one step at a time.

Yield Yourself to God

Read these helpful comments by Chuck Swindoll in his book, *Insights on Romans*.

> Paul describes the fleshly pull toward sin as the "dwelling-within-me sin." While he received a new nature when he believed in Jesus Christ, his body seems to have a mind of its own. It's as though he were conjoined to a person who loves the very things he hates most. And the same is true for every believer. Every Christian receives a new nature, one that wants nothing more than to behave as Jesus Christ behaves. Meanwhile the flesh, the old human nature, wants life to continue as it was…All of us are chronically addicted to sin. Long after we are saved, our bodies crave that which gave us short-term pleasure and caused long-term anguish. And the pull to indulge craving for sin will always be a part of our lives…at least until we are freed from "the body of this death" (v.24)
>
> So, what is our duty now as believers saved by grace? Our primary purpose is to know Jesus Christ personally with ever-deepening intimacy (Phil. 3:8–11). If we read Scripture, pray, meditate, journal, or fast, let us do it for the sole purpose of knowing His mind. If we worship, serve, partake of communion, or spend time in the company of believers, let us learn about Him through His transforming work

in others. If we feed the poor, defend the weak, comfort the lonely, or proclaim the gospel to a broken and needy world, let our walking in His sandals give us firsthand knowledge of His character. Let every trial or triumph bring us closer to knowing Christ's nature and to understanding His purposes.[11]

Chuck Swindoll in Insights On Romans: Swindoll's New Testament Insights

"The old man" is no longer supreme. This does not mean that the believer lives untroubled by the possibility of sinning. There is a sense in which a death has taken place once and for all in the believer, but there is another in which he dies every day (1 Cor. 15:31). It is believers, not the unregenerate, who are urged to put off the old man (Eph. 4:22, cf. Col. 3:9). But it is another vivid way of saying that the power of sin is broken in the believer. To come to Christ means the complete end of a whole way of life. There may be slips, but they are uncharacteristic...Sin no longer has dominion.[12]

Leon Morris in The Epistle to the Romans

Paul had cried, Who shall deliver me? The answer is,—the discovery to his soul of that glorious deliverance at the cross! of death to sin and Law with Him! So it is said, "Through Jesus Christ our Lord." The word of the cross—of what Christ did there, is the power of God—whether to save sinners or deliver saints! But ah, what a relief to Paul's soul—probably out yonder alone in Arabia, struggling more and more in vain to compel the flesh to obey the Law, to have revealed to his weary soul the second glorious truth of the Gospel—that he had died with Christ—to sin, and to Law which sin had used as its power...He saw it at last, and bowed to it,—that all he was by the flesh, by Nature, was irrevocably committed to sin. So he gave up—to see himself wholly in Christ (who now lived in Him) and to walk not by the Law, even in the supposed powers of the quickened life—but by the Spirit only: in whose power alone the Christian life is to be lived.

William Newell in Romans, Verse-By-Verse

ENJOY HIS PRESENCE

Dear friend, what is the Lord teaching you in Romans right now? What is your favorite insight, maybe an *aha* moment of something you had never seen before? Close your time with the Lord by writing your thoughts and a prayer expressing all that is on your heart today. Thank the Lord for loving you and for all He has done for you.

REST IN HIS LOVE

"Thanks be to God through Jesus Christ our Lord" (Romans 7:25).

THE QUIET PLACE WITH GOD

Call to Me and I will answer you. Jeremiah 33:3
Pauoa Bay, Waimea, Island Of Hawaii, Hawaii, USA
Nikon D7000, ISO 250, f5, 1/60sec, Adobe Photoshop, Nik Silver Efex Pro
MYPHOTOWALK.COM—CATHERINEMARTIN.SMUGMUG.COM

THE GREAT PROMISE

Therefore there is now no condemnation for those who are in Christ Jesus.
ROMANS 8:1

PREPARE YOUR HEART

ctavius Winslow was a well-known preacher in the 19th century. He was a Baptist pastor and a contemporary of Charles Haddon Spurgeon and J.C. Ryle. In fact, he was so loved and respected that he delivered the keynote message at the opening of Spurgeon's church, the Metropolitan Tabernacle in London. During his lifetime, Winslow wrote many books, and one of the favorites was a much-loved study on Romans 8 entitled, *No Condemnation in Christ Jesus.* In the preface, Winslow writes: "It would, perhaps, be impossible to select from the Bible a single chapter in which were crowded so much sublime, evangelical, and sanctifying truth as this eighth of Romans. It is not only all gospel, but it may be said to contain the whole gospel."

Dr. Donald Grey Barnhouse, American pastor in the mid-1900s, asked a group of 20 Christian leaders this question: "If you were shipwrecked on a desert island, and could not take any book with you except the Bible and you could only take with you one chapter of the Bible, what chapter would you choose?" Five of those leaders named Romans 8 as their choice. Many Christians regard Romans 8 as the greatest chapter in the Bible. It has been called "the mountain peak" of the Bible and "the chapter of chapters for the Christian believer." A German author named Spener many years ago described it this way: "If Holy Scripture was a ring, and the Epistle to the Romans a precious stone, Chapter 8 would be the sparkling point of the jewel."

Dear friend, get ready to step onto the holy and sacred ground of God's Word in Romans 8. Today we are going to look at the great promise, and one of the magnificent truths that Paul has been leading up to all along. We have looked at many doctrinal truths—these are given to us by God in His Word—and these are the facts we believe and the fuel for our faith. Let's always remember that God's Word is not intended to make us more academic and intellectual, but instead to give us a deeper and more intimate relationship with God. Doctrine always leads to devotion and that is what this study is all about. We want to discover God's amazing love and embrace and experience the power of the gospel in our own lives.

So today, dear friend, ask the Lord to quiet your heart and give you eyes to see and ears to hear all that He is saying in His Word. Take some time to focus on the words of this beloved hymn by Fanny Crosby as a preparation of heart for your study in God's Word today.

> Blessed assurance, Jesus is mine!
> Oh, what a foretaste of glory divine!
> Heir of salvation, purchase of God,
> born of his Spirit, washed in his blood.
>
> *Refrain:* This is my story, this is my song,
> praising my Savior all the day long.
> This is my story, this is my song,
> praising my Savior all the day long.
>
> Perfect communion, perfect delight,
> visions of rapture now burst on my sight.
> Angels descending bring from above
> echoes of mercy, whispers of love. *Refrain*
>
> Perfect submission, all is at rest.
> I in my Savior am happy and bless'd,
> watching and waiting, looking above,
> filled with his goodness, lost in his love. *Refrain*

READ AND STUDY GOD'S WORD

1. And now, Paul continues to the great promise flowing out of all he has previously shared. And just think of all you have learned over these last few weeks of study. You have seen the need for the righteousness of God. And you have studied the way of God's righteousness and thought deeply about what it means to walk and live by faith, even looking at the example of Abraham. Then, we studied Romans 5 and learned about our relationship with Christ and how we have the assurance of our unshakeable position in Him and the eternal security that nothing can touch. We then looked at Romans 6-7 and the undeniable fact of our union with Christ. We saw how sin, the law, and God's righteousness relate to the truth that we are united with Christ. But now, we are going to see the grand conclusion and the great promise for you to stand on no matter what you face in life. Read Romans 8:1-4 and write your first impressions of these four verses.

2. What is the conclusion here? What are we to discover as the grand climax? It is this, dear friend. Paul is confidently declaring that the believer is no longer under condemnation because of Christ's finished work. This is your unchangeable, unshakeable position in Christ. You are eternally secure and assured of your salvation forever. Read Romans 8:1-4 and write out why "therefore, there is now no condemnation for those who are in Christ Jesus."

4. You are set free, dear friend. In fact, every believer would do well to memorize these four verses in Romans. And how are we set free? Because we are now "in Christ Jesus," the requirement of the Law is fulfilled in us, the law of the Spirit of life in Christ Jesus has set us free from the law of sin and death, and we walk according to the Spirit. Next week we are going to study all of Romans 8 and learn about the power of the Holy Spirit. But today, as we close this week of study, let's look at that little phrase "in Christ Jesus," for it is an important truth about us that is found throughout the New Testament. Read the following verses, underline "in Christ" in each, and personalize your significant discoveries as you write out what is true because you are "in Christ." Oh, you are in for such a blessing as you discover these beautiful truths! Circle or put a star next to your favorite truth.

1 Corinthians 1:30

1 Corinthians 15:22

2 Corinthians 2:14

2 Corinthians 5:17

Ephesians 1:3-8

Ephesians 2:6-7

Ephesians 2:10

Philippians 4:6-7

Philippians 4:19

5. You are "in Christ" and united with Him forever. What blesses you the most from your study today about Christ and all He has done for you and has promised you in your life?

ADORE GOD IN PRAYER

Pray the words of Charles Wesley in the fifth stanza of "And Can It Be That I Should Gain."

No condemnation now I dread; Jesus, and all in Him is mine!
Alive in Him, my living Head, and clothed in righteousness divine,
Bold I approach the eternal throne, and claim the crown through Christ my own.
Refrain: Amazing love! How can it be that Thou, my God, should die for me!

YIELD YOURSELF TO GOD

Those who are in Christ are not exposed to condemnation. Again, this does not only describe their present state but their permanent position. They are placed beyond the reach of condemnation. They will never be condemned. The meaning of a preposition is often best understood by the arguments by which it is sustained. It is so in this case. The whole chapter is a proof of the safety of believers, of their security not only from present condemnation but from future perdition. That nothing will ever separate them from the love of God is Paul's triumphant conclusion (Romans 8:35-39).[13]

CHARLES HODGE IN ROMANS

There is "no condemnation" since the indwelling Holy Spirit fulfills the righteousness of the Law in us. The Law cannot condemn us because we are dead to the Law. God cannot condemn us, for the Holy Spirit enables the believer to "walk in the Spirit" and thereby meet God's holy demands. It is a glorious day in the life of the Christian when he or she realizes that God's children are not under the Law, that God does not expect them to do "good works" in the power of the old nature. When the Christian understands that "there is no condemnation," then he realizes that the indwelling Spirit pleases God and helps the believer to please Him. What a glorious salvation we have![14]

WARREN WIERSBE IN WIERSBE'S EXPOSITORY OUTLINES ON THE NEW TESTAMENT

The Christian life, the life of a justified believer, is seen as being essentially life in the Spirit, that is to say, a life which is animated, sustained, directed, and enriched by the Holy Spirit.[15]

JOHN R.W. STOTT IN MAN MADE NEW

ENJOY HIS PRESENCE

As you think about these wonderful words in Romans 8:1-4, write out in 1-2 sentences what the great promise is here. Then, how does this promise impact you in your own life? Close by writing a prayer to the Lord thanking Him for all He has done for you.

Rest in His Love

"For we are His workmanship, created in Christ Jesus for good works, which God prepared beforehand so that we would walk in them" (Ephesians 2:10).

The Sedona Sunflower

Those who live at the ends of the earth stand in awe of Your wonders. Psalm 65:8 NLT
Cathedral Rock, Sedona, Arizona, USA
Sony A6000, ISO 100, f11, 1/160sec, Adobe Photoshop, Nik Silver Efex Pro
MyPhotoWalk.com—CatherineMartin.smugmug.com

DEVOTIONAL READING
BY W.H. GRIFFITH THOMAS

DEAR FRIEND,

This week you have studied in depth your union with the Lord Jesus Christ. Look back over your week of study and summarize your favorite truths.

What were your most meaningful discoveries this week as you spent time with the Lord?

Most meaningful insight:

Most meaningful devotional reading:

Most meaningful verse:

alvation emanating from God's righteousness is based upon justification, built up in sanctification, and crowned in glorification. And it is received at each point by *faith*. From God's side, Salvation is Righteousness by Grace *for* Faith. From man's side, it is Righteousness by Grace *through* Faith. *The one practical point* of all this is, whether these great doctrinal themes have become part of our personal experience. Doctrine separated from life is dry, abstract, unprofitable, and even dangerous; but doctrine received into, experienced by, and manifested through life is the secret of clearness of perception, and vigor of activity. St. Paul ever kept doctrine and life closely associated, for they were inextricably bound up in his experience and service. The life of truth and the life of obedience are both necessary, and it is the characteristic feature of these chapters that doctrine is set forth as the root and foundation of life, and life is set forth as the fruit and expression of doctrine. This is true Christianity, and for a genuine, balanced, Christ life there are few passages more essential, more valuable, and more powerful than these eight chapters (Romans 1-8).[16]

W.H. GRIFFITH THOMAS IN ROMANS: A DEVOTIONAL COMMENTARY VI-XI

Praise to the Lord, the Almighty, the King of creation!
O my soul, praise him, for he is your health and salvation!
Come, all who hear; now to his temple draw near,
join me in glad adoration.

Praise to the Lord, above all things so wondrously reigning;
sheltering you under his wings, and so gently sustaining!
Have you not seen all that is needful has been
sent by his gracious ordaining?

Praise to the Lord, who will prosper your work and defend you;
surely his goodness and mercy shall daily attend you.
Ponder anew what the Almighty can do,
if with his love he befriends you.

Praise to the Lord! O let all that is in me adore him!
All that has life and breath, come now with praises before him.
Let the Amen sound from his people again;
gladly forever adore him.

JOACHIM NEANDER

❧ WEEK FOUR ❧

Your Life In Jesus Christ

In Week Four of *The Proof of God's Amazing Love*, you had the opportunity to study Romans 6-8:1 and learn about your union with Jesus Christ and all that God has given you in Him. Today we are going to talk about your life in Jesus Christ and all that it means for you. So, grab your Bibles, and let's talk about your Lord and Savior Jesus Christ.

"For if we have become united with Him in the likeness of His death, certainly we shall also be in the likeness of His resurrection…Now if we have died with Christ, we believe that we shall also live with Him…Even so consider yourselves to be dead to sin, but alive to God in Christ Jesus" Romans 6:5,8,11

You are united with Christ. In this we see a ____.
You are in Christ. In this we see an ____.

Some insights from Romans 6:5-11

1. You have died with Him, have been buried with Him, and are raised to new life with Him.
2. The debt you owed because of your sin has been paid by Christ on the cross.
3. You have died to the Law and are now joined to Christ.
4. You are no longer under law, but under grace.
5. You are now enslaved to God and His righteousness with the result of abundant life.
6. There is a new law at work in you, the law of the Spirit of life in Christ Jesus.

Who is Jesus, the One with whom we are now joined?

1. He is your Lord. Romans 6:23, Isaiah 43:1-3
2. He is your Bridegroom. Ephesians 5:22-23
3. He is your Savior, Rescuer, and Redeemer. Philippians 3:20
4. He is your Shepherd. John 10:11
5. He is your Beloved. Ephesians 1:6

What is life in Jesus Christ really like?

1. Life in Christ is an ____.

2. Life in Christ is ____.

3. Life in Christ is a ____.

4. Life in Christ is ____.

5. Life in Christ is a ____ reality.

6. Life in Christ is a ____ life.

7. Life in Christ is ____.

8. Life in Christ is a knowing and _______________________________ life.

9. Life in Christ is a ____ life.

10. Life in Christ is a ____life.

11. Life in Christ is a ____ life.

12. Life in Christ is ____.

13. Life in Christ is an ____ life.

14. Life in Christ is a ____ life.

15. Life in Christ is a ____ life.

16. Life in Christ is ____.

Video messages are available on DVDs or as Digital M4V Video. Audio messages are available as Digital MP3 Audio. Visit the Quiet Time Ministries Online Store at www.quiettime.org.

THE POWER OF GOD'S RIGHTEOUSNESS

Romans 8:5-39

One meaning of the word "power" is "ability to do." There precisely is the wonder of the Spirit's work in the Church and in the hearts of Christians. His sure ability to make spiritual things real to the soul. This power can go straight to its object with piercing directness…Reality is its subject matter, reality in heaven and upon earth. It does not create objects which are not there but reveals objects already present and hidden from the soul. In actual human experience this is likely to be first felt in a heightened sense of the Presence of Christ. He is felt to be a real Person and to be intimately, ravishingly near.[1]

A.W. TOZER

POWER IN THE SPIRIT

However, you are not in the flesh, but in the Spirit, if indeed the Spirit of God dwells in you…if Christ is in you, though the body is dead because of sin, yet the spirit is alive because of righteousness.

ROMANS 8:9-10

PREPARE YOUR HEART

How is it that simple and sometimes untrained people can do what they never thought they could do? How could D.L. Moody and Billy Graham preach to thousands? How could Amy Carmichael lead a ministry in India rescuing children from temple prostitution? How could Lilias Trotter spend forty years bringing the love of Christ to Arab people in North Africa? How could Elisabeth Elliot take her young daughter, Valerie, and go back to the jungle in Ecuador and live with the very Auca Indians who killed her husband? Only one way—through the power of the indwelling Holy Spirit, given at the very moment of salvation when a man or woman places their faith in Jesus Christ.

Now, we are truly going to get to the heart of Paul's statement at the very beginning of Romans: "For I am not ashamed of the gospel, for it is the power of God for salvation to everyone who believes, to the Jew first and also to the Greek. For in it the righteousness of God is revealed from faith to faith; as it is written, 'But the righteous man shall live by faith'" (Romans 1:16-17). Once people are saved, they are indwelt by the Holy Spirit and the power of God is now present and working in them.

Romans 8 is all about the work of the Holy Spirit in the believer and the Power and Provision of Righteousness— this week we will see many aspects of the power of the Holy Spirit at work in your life. And you will see in a new way why Godet said in his commentary that "the probability is that every great spiritual revival in the church will be connected as effect and cause with a deeper understanding" of the book of Romans. God wants to start a revival and He does it beginning with you through the power of the Holy Spirit. Personal spiritual revival is "a quickening of heart and soul by God, imparting whatever is necessary to sustain one's spiritual life and enable a return to the experience of one's true purpose as ordained by God."[2] And how are we revived? By God, through His Word, in the power of the Holy Spirit. The psalmist discovered personal revival when he said: "Your promise revives me; it comforts me in all my troubles" (Psalm 119:50 NLT). This week you are going to discover many promises that are yours because you know Christ. The One who makes these promises come alive in your heart is the Holy Spirit. Jesus said, "When He, the Spirit of truth, comes, He will guide you into all the truth…He will glorify Me, for He will take of Mine and will disclose it to you" (John 16:13-14). As the Holy Spirit works in your life, and makes God's Word come alive to you, your heart is going to be set on fire. You will say, along with the two men on the road to Emmaus, the day they walked with Jesus, "Were not our hearts burning within us while He was speaking to us on the road, while He was explaining the Scriptures to us" (Luke 24:32). Jesus invites us to experience the reviving power of the Holy Spirit in John 7:37-38, "If anyone is thirsty, let him come to Me and drink. He who believes in Me, as the Scripture said, 'From his innermost being will flow rivers of living water.'" You have already seen that you are united with Jesus Christ. And now you are going to learn more about how you experience the Lord Jesus Christ, moment by moment and day by day through the power of the Holy Spirit. This is another essential of the Christian life.

As you begin your quiet time with the Lord today, use these words by Annie Johnson Flint as a prayer for your own life.

> Give me Thy strength for my day, Lord
> That whereso'er I go,
> There shall no danger daunt me
> And I shall fear no foe;
> So shall no task o'ercome me,
> So shall not trial fret,
> So shall I walk unwearied
> The path where my feet are set;
> So shall I find no burden
> Greater than I can bear,
> So shall I have a courage
> Equal to all my care;
> So shall no grief o'erwhelm me,
> So shall no wave o'erflow;
> Give me Thy strength for my day, Lord,
> Cover my weakness so.

ANNIE JOHNSON FLINT

READ AND STUDY GOD'S WORD

1. Today we begin living in Romans 8 and we are thinking about the power of God at work in our lives through the Holy Spirit. We have just learned there is a new law at work in us in our salvation, and it is "the law of the Spirit of life in Christ Jesus" (Romans 8:2). And how does it happen? Through the Holy Spirit who is in us and with us forever. Did you know that "Spirit" occurs at least 20 times in Romans 8 (ESV translation)? Let's take some time and see it for ourselves. Read Romans 8 and note all the occurrences of the Spirit. You might even want to underline "Spirit" throughout Romans 8. What was your favorite verse in Romans 8, this chapter of chapters for the Christian believer?

2. Jesus promised the Holy Spirit when He taught Nicodemus, a Pharisee what it meant to become a Christian. Read John 3:5-8 and underline those phrases that help you understand how a person is born again and how the Holy Spirit is involved in your salvation.

> Jesus answered, "Truly, truly, I say to you, unless one is born of water and the Spirit he cannot enter into the kingdom of God. That which is born of the flesh is flesh, and that which is born of the Spirit is spirit. Do not be amazed that I said to you, 'You must be born again.' The wind blows where it wishes and you hear the sound of it, but do not know where it comes from and where it is going; so is everyone who is born of the Spirit."

3. And now, Paul is going to talk about what is true because you have been born again and the Spirit of God dwells in you. Read Romans 8:5-11 and write your most significant insights about what is true of you because the Spirit of God dwells in you. Personalize your discoveries.

4. There is power from the Holy Spirit at work in you for your life. Read Romans 8:12-13 and write out how His power helps you in life.

5. Paul encourages believers in Ephesians 5:18 to "be filled with the Spirit." That word "filled" means to be controlled and empowered by Christ through the Holy Spirit. There are so many wonderful truths in Scripture about the work of the Holy Spirit in your life. Read Galatians 5:16-25, a powerful passage about the Holy Spirit and the flesh. Write out your most significant insights.

6. Read Acts 1:8 and underline the phrases that help you understand why you need the power of the Holy Spirit. The word "power" in the Greek is *dunamis* and means strength and power that makes you able and capable.

> But you will receive power when the Holy Spirit has come upon you; and you shall be My witnesses both in Jerusalem, and in all Judea and Samaria, and even to the remotest part of the earth.

ADORE GOD IN PRAYER

In what ways do you need the power of the Holy Spirit today? Talk with God, pour out your heart, and ask Him to fill you with His Holy Spirit.

YIELD YOURSELF TO GOD

To be filled with the Spirit is to have the Spirit fulfilling in us all that God intended Him to do when He placed Him there. To be filled is not the problem of getting more of the Spirit: it is rather the problem of the Spirit getting more of us. We shall never have more of the Spirit than the anointing which every true Christian has received. On the other hand, the Spirit may have all of the believer and thus be able to manifest in him the life and character of Christ. A spiritual person, then, is one who experiences the divine purpose and plan in his daily life through the power of the indwelling Spirit. The character of that life will be the out-lived Christ. The cause of that life will be the unhindered indwelling Spirit (Ephesians 3:16-21, 2 Corinthians 3:18).[3]

LEWIS SPERRY CHAFER IN HE THAT IS SPIRITUAL

Revival commences with those who in bad times remain good, in godless days remain Christian, in careless years remain constant and who have eternity in their hearts. Revival begins with those who stand firm, like Hezekiah, in an age of godless rejection, in an age when the people do what is right in their own eyes. It begins with the man who stands for that which is true and right and good; but it also requires a man who can see what the state of the church and the nation really is…Revival is always a personal thing, and no one is used in revival who is not himself revived first. That is very important to understand. Those whom God uses in leadership in revival are always men who have met with God in a powerfully personal way and have a burning passion for the glory of God and a life of holiness.[4]

BRIAN H. EDWARDS IN REVIVAL: A PEOPLE SATURATED WITH GOD

ENJOY HIS PRESENCE

What is your most significant insight about the power of the Holy Spirit? Do you realize just how present Christ is with you and in you through the Holy Spirit? Have you ever discovered compassion welling up in you for another person? That, dear friend, is the work of the Holy Spirit in you. Have you ever experienced strength for an impossible task? Again, that power is from the Holy Spirit at work in you. How do you need His power today? What difference do you think being filled with the Holy Spirit can make in reviving our hearts and spilling out into revival all around us? Write your thoughts and a prayer expressing all that is on your heart today.

REST IN HIS LOVE

"But I say, walk by the Spirit, and you will not carry out the desire of the flesh" (Galatians 5:16).

GOD'S SPIRIT RESTING ON YOU

The Spirit of glory and of God rests on you. 1 Peter 4:14
Pauoa Bay, Waimea, Island Of Hawaii, Hawaii, USA
Nikon D7000, ISO 200, f7.1, 1/200sec, Adobe Photoshop, Nik Silver Efex Pro
MYPHOTOWALK.COM—CATHERINEMARTIN.SMUGMUG.COM

POWER AS CHILDREN OF GOD

The Spirit Himself testifies with our spirit that we are children of God.
ROMANS 8:16

PREPARE YOUR HEART

In the book, *A Little Princess* by Frances Hodgson Burnett, Captain Ralph Crew is a wealthy English widower who has been raising his only child, a little girl named Sara, in India where he is serving with the British Army. He enrolled Sara in an all-girls boarding school in London, and even paid the arrogant headmistress Miss Minchin for special treatment and luxuries. Four years later, her father became ill and died, and also lost his entire fortune in a diamond mine venture. So Sara was made to become a servant at the boarding school and was treated with cruelty and contempt. Things looked bleak for Sara until a wealthy man, Mr. Carrisford, moved in near the boarding school. It turned out that he was a friend and partner with Captain Crewe in the diamond mine venture. The diamond mines were a reality, Mr. Carrisford became very wealthy, and returned to look for Sara, Captain Crewe's daughter. Finally he found Sara, adopted her, and she became an heiress to the diamond mines. *A Little Princess* is one of those stories with a great ending, the kind where you say, "and they lived happily ever after."

Yours is a story with a happy ending as well. We've seen it again and again throughout Romans with words like salvation and eternal life. And today, you are going to see that your union with Christ gives you a whole new identity. You are a child of God.

Today, ask the Lord to quiet your heart and speak to you in your quiet time alone with Him.

READ AND STUDY GOD'S WORD

1. Read Romans 8:14-17 and write out what is true of you because of the Holy Spirit.

2. A wonderful promise in Romans 8:14 is that the Spirit of God leads you. Oswald Chambers writes in his classic devotional, *My Utmost For His Highest*, "Faith never knows where it is being led, but it loves and knows the One Who is leading. It is a life of faith, not of intellect and reason, but a life of knowing Who makes us 'go'. The root of faith is the knowledge of a Person."[5]

How does the fact that He leads you encourage you? In what way do you need to know Him more, step out in faith, and trust Him to lead you today?

3. One of the important discoveries in Romans 8:17 is that you are not only a child of God, but an heir of God and a fellow heir with Christ. Read the following verses and write out what you learn about being an heir and all you inherit.

Galatians 3:28-29

Galatians 4:6-7

Ephesians 1:13-14

Titus 3:5-7

Hebrews 6:17-19

James 2:5

ADORE GOD IN PRAYER

Today, pray this beautiful prayer by Ruth Harms Calkin entitled, "Lord, You Love to Say Yes."

Lord, I asked You for abundant life
Rich, challenging, full of adventure
And You said Yes.
I asked You for an undisturbable joy
Independent of transitory change
And You said Yes.
I asked You to thread my tears into a song
When I was shattered and torn with grief
And You said Yes.
I asked You to steady me when I staggered—
To hold me when I struggled
To seize me when I resisted
And You said Yes.
I asked You to forgive my vain grasping
My foolish fears, my willful pride
And You said Yes.
I asked You to be my Helper, my Friend
My light in the darkness
And You said Yes.
I asked You to guide me all my life
With Your wisdom, Your counsel
Your captivating love
And You said Yes.

Sometimes, Lord
I feel like a spoiled child
Who gets whatever he asks for.
You overwhelm me with joy
For *You love to say Yes!*[6]

RUTH HARMS CALKIN IN PRECIOUS THOUGHTS FROM THE HEART

YIELD YOURSELF TO GOD

The term "heir," clearly suggests something additional to and higher than sonship…
It is for us to accept, to enter upon, and to enjoy this marvelous wealth of privilege.
No wonder that the Apostle is so certain, in view of this great prospect, that we
shall be saved and kept to the very end. This is how the Christian life will be
completed.[7]

W.H. GRIFFITH THOMAS IN ROMANS: A DEVOTIONAL COMMENTARY VI-XI

Is this your habitual way of thinking of yourself? Do you live rejoicing day by day
in the fact that you are a child of God, and because a child, then an heir? What
is your heart set upon? At what are you looking? Is it only at this present life
and world? Are you like the heroes of the faith in Hebrews 11? Are you like the
patriarchs and the saints? Are you looking forward? Are you like the believers in the
New Testament? They were all looking forward. We are only given "the earnest of
our inheritance" here; the great inheritance itself is to come…So we look forward,
and are waiting and looking unto and hasting unto the coming of this blessed,
glorious day of God, the day of glory, the day of our glorification, the day of our
ultimate, final, full salvation.[8]

D. MARTYN LLOYD-JONES IN ROMANS, CHAPTER 8:5-17, THE SONS OF GOD

ENJOY HIS PRESENCE

And now, what about you? Do you realize that you are a child of God, and an heir? Are you
looking forward, as D. Martyn Lloyd-Jones encourages? How do these truths from God's Word
revive your heart today? Close your time with the Lord by writing a prayer expressing all that is
on your heart.

REST IN HIS LOVE

"You were sealed in Him with the Holy Spirit of promise" (Ephesians 1:13).

THE STORY OF YOUR LIFE

I know the plans I have for you. Jeremiah 29:11
Coachella Valley Preserve, Palm Desert, California, USA
Nikon D800E, ISO 100, f11, AEB, Adobe Photoshop, Nik Silver Efex Pro
MYPHOTOWALK.COM—CATHERINEMARTIN.SMUGMUG.COM

POWER IN SUFFERING

*For I consider that the sufferings of this present time are not worthy
to be compared with the glory that is to be revealed to us.*

Romans 8:18

PREPARE YOUR HEART

omething Jesus taught us, and we know it to be true, is that "in the world you have tribulation, but take courage; I have overcome the world" (John 16:33). All of us have experienced suffering in some degree. And some know the agony of excruciating pain, whether it is physical, spiritual, or emotional. How can we make it through? Today we are going to look at power in suffering as we continue our journey in Romans 8 all about the power of the Holy Spirit in our lives. We need revival, renewal, and restoration especially in times of suffering. We are going to discover that God gives us the power we need even in the times of suffering, and in excruciating times when we don't see how we can make it. How does He give us this power? Through the Holy Spirit.

Annie Johnson Flint had the dream in her younger years of being a composer and concert pianist. She was forced to relinquish that dream as she became shut in as an invalid due to crippling arthritis early on in life. She loved the Lord and discovered she could write poetry. She dedicated her life, while bedridden and confined to one room, to writing verses of blessing that touched the hearts of thousands. One author said of her: "Here is one who wrote from her heart, who, in pain and suffering, endured heroically and triumphantly throughout a long life, wrote, like Milton, 'of things unseen by mortal sight,' and showed to the world how God could be glorified in the midst of physical trials and tribulations that few of us are called upon to bear."[9]

Today, as you begin your quiet time, meditate on these words written by Annie Johnson Flint:

> I know not, but God knows;
> Oh, blessed rest from fear!
> All my unfolding days
> To Him are plain and clear.
> Each anxious, puzzled "why?"
> From doubt or dread that grows,

Finds answer in this thought;
I know not, but He knows.

I cannot, but God can;
Oh, balm for all my care!
The burden that I drop
His hand will lift and bear.
Though eagle pinions tire,
I walk where once I ran,
This is my strength to know
I cannot, but He can.

I see not, but God sees;
Oh, all sufficient light!
My dark and hidden way
To Him is always bright.
My strained and peering eyes
May close in restful ease,
And I in peace may sleep;
I see not, but He sees.

ANNIE JOHNSON FLINT IN BEST-LOVED POEMS

READ AND STUDY GOD'S WORD

1. As we have been studying Romans 8, we are learning the Power and Provision of God's Righteousness in the Holy Spirit who lives in us forever when we place our trust in Christ, and we are born again. We just learned that we are children of God. And in Romans 8:17 we see that as a fellow-heir with Christ, "we suffer with Him so that we may also be glorified with Him." Now we are going to see the fact of suffering during our brief stay on earth until we step into heaven. You will notice the word "groan" used more than once. What a descriptive word for pain in suffering. Read Romans 8:18-25 and write out all you learn about suffering.

2. The Spirit gives us help in our suffering. Read Romans 8:23-25 and write out what you see that the Holy Spirit enables you to do in the midst of suffering.

3. In these verses we see two important qualities: hope and perseverance. We have hope as we eagerly wait for a future promise: "our adoption as sons, the redemption of our body" (Romans 5:23-24). Perseverance is seen in that "eagerly waiting" phrase in Romans 8:25. Sometimes the Greek word for perseverance is translated "endurance." These two qualities, given by the Holy Spirit, will help you through your suffering, even in dark nights of the soul. Read and meditate on the following verses, and underline those truths in each verse that help you the most.

> For whatever was written in earlier times was written for our instruction, so that through perseverance and the encouragement of the Scriptures we might have hope. Romans 15:4

> I pray that God, the source of hope, will fill you completely with joy and peace because you trust in him. Then you will overflow with confident hope through the power of the Holy Spirit. Romans 15:13 NLT

> This hope is a strong and trustworthy anchor for our souls. Hebrews 6:19 NLT

> Therefore, since we are surrounded by such a huge crowd of witnesses to the life of faith, let us strip off every weight that slows us down, especially the sin that so easily trips us up. And let us run with endurance the race God has set before us. We do this by keeping our eyes on Jesus, the champion who initiates and perfects our faith. Because of the joy awaiting him, he endured the cross, disregarding its shame. Now he is seated in the place of honor beside God's throne. Hebrews 12:1-2 NLT

Blessed is the man who perseveres under trial; for once he has been approved, he will receive the crown of life which the Lord has promised to those who love Him. James 1:12

After you have suffered for a little while, the God of all grace, who called you to His eternal glory in Christ, will Himself perfect, confirm, strengthen, and establish you. 1 Peter 5:10

Optional Verses: 1 Peter 5:6-9, 2 Peter 1:3-8

4. In Romans 8:18 we see the promise of future glory for us— "For I consider that the sufferings of this present time are not worthy to be compared with the glory that is to be revealed to us." Leon Morris, in his wonderful commentary on Romans, points out that believers do not have an easy road and will share in Christ's sufferings. The encouragement for all of us is that "the path of suffering is the path to glory."[10] Read the following verses and underline those words and phrases that give you hope today that the best is yet to come.

For those whom He foreknew, He also predestined to become conformed to the image of His Son, so that He would be the firstborn among many brethren; and these whom He predestined, He also called; and these whom He called, He also justified; and these whom He justified, He also glorified. Romans 8:29-30

Now to Him who is able to keep you from stumbling, and to make you stand in the presence of His glory blameless with great joy, to the only God our Savior, through Jesus Christ our Lord, be glory, majesty, dominion and authority, before all time and now and forever. Amen. Jude 24-25

ADORE GOD IN PRAYER

Pray these words by F.B. Meyer: "Make me, O blessed Master, strong in heart, full of courage, fearless of danger, holding pain and peril cheap when they lie in the path of duty. May I be strengthened with all might by your Spirit in my inner being."

YIELD YOURSELF TO GOD

Expose yourself to the circumstances of His choice,
for that is perfect acquiescence in the will of God.
Make me Thy mountaineer;
I would not linger on the lower slope.
Fill me afresh with hope, O God of hope,
That undefeated I may climb the hill
As seeing Him who is invisible,
Whom having not seen I love.
O my Redeemer, when this little while
Lies far behind me and the last defile
I all alight, and in that light I see
My Saviour and My Lord, what will it be?[11]

AMY CARMIACHAEL IN GOLD BY MOONLIGHT

"Trust" is elsewhere in the Old Testament translated "careless." "Be careless in the Lord!" Instead of carrying a load of care, let care be absent! It is the carelessness of little children running about the house in the assurance of their father's providence and love. It is the singing disposition that leaves something for the parent to do. Assume that He is working as well as thyself, and working even when things appear to be adverse.

JOHN HENRY JOWETT IN THE SILVER LINING

ENJOY HIS PRESENCE

Always remember that your God is the "God of all comfort" and promises to comfort you in all your affliction abundantly in Christ (2 Corinthians 1:3-5). One of the ways He does this is by giving you hope and perseverance through the Holy Spirit, so that miraculously, you can hold on with patient expectation. The power of the Holy Spirit flows from the power of the gospel of Jesus Christ at work in you. Embrace His power and cast all your care on the Lord today, for He cares for you (1 Peter 5:7). Oh dear friend, may the Lord give you a great trust in Him in whatever you are facing today. How do you need hope and endurance today? How does what you have learned minister to your heart? How do these truths revive your heart today? What is God teaching you?

Close your quiet time by reflecting on the image below, then write your thoughts and a prayer, expressing all that is on your heart today.

REST IN HIS LOVE

"Blessed is a man who perseveres under trial; for once he has been approved, he will receive the crown of life which the Lord has promised to those who love Him" (James 1:12).

WHEN GOD REVIVES

Though I walk in the midst of trouble, You will revive me. Psalm 138:7
Hagiwara Tea Gardens, DeYoung Museum, Golden Gate Park, San Francisco, California, USA
Nikon D810, ISO 400, f8, 1/800sec, Adobe Photoshop, Nik Silver Efex Pro
MYPHOTOWALK.COM—CATHERINEMARTIN.SMUGMUG.COM

POWER IN PRAYER

*In the same way the Spirit also helps our weakness; for we do not know how to pray
as we should, but the Spirit Himself intercedes with groanings too deep for words...*

ROMANS 8:26

PREPARE YOUR HEART

atherine Marshall was an American author and the wife of Peter Marshall, a well known
Presbyterian minister and Chaplain of the U.S. Senate. In her book, *Beyond Ourselves*, she
shares the story of how the Lord worked in her life during a time of suffering. She had been ill for
six months with a lung infection. In spite of evaluations by many specialists, nothing seemed to
help, and she was bedridden full-time. She came to a place where she surrendered to the will of
God in a new and deeper way and prayed: "I'm beaten, God. You decide what You want for me."
She sensed Christ with her and experienced revitalized faith and trust in Him, no matter what
happened. Her recovery began from that moment. She called it the Prayer of Relinquishment
where she voluntarily gave up her self-will to God, with no demands of Him, only trust for His
will, His way. And in time, Catherine fully recovered from her illness.

Oh how powerful God was in answering the prayers of Catherine Marshall. And prayer is a
journey, isn't it. And now, we are going to see how the Holy Spirit powerfully works even in prayer.
Ask the Lord now to quiet your heart and speak to you as you draw near to Him in your quiet time.

READ AND STUDY GOD'S WORD

1. Our first response in any kind of trial or suffering should be prayer. Paul encourages his
disciple, Timothy, "The first thing I want you to do is pray" (1 Timothy 2:1 NLT). Now you are
going to learn the power of the Holy Spirit in prayer. Read Romans 8:26-27 and write out how
the Holy Spirit helps even in our prayers.

2. Paul follows up this great truth about the prayers of the Holy Spirit for us according to the will of God with powerful promises. These promises will support you in your prayers. John writes: "This is the confidence which we have before Him, that, if we ask anything according to His will, He hears us. And if we know that He hears us in whatever we ask, we know that we have the requests which we have asked from Him" (1 John 5:14-15). The promises of God are a sure foundation for they reveal to us God's will and God's ways. Read Romans 8:28-34 and write out all the promises of God that you discover here.

3. What is your favorite promise in Romans 8:28-34 and why? You might want to write it on an index card and carry it with you today. And may you join in the affirmation of hymnwriter Russel Kelso Carter, as he wrote in his wonderful hymn: "I'm standing on the promises of God."

4. Romans 8:28 was called by R.A. Torrey "a soft pillow for a tired heart." Don't you love that description! What is God saying in this verse? How have you seen God weave together some difficult times into something that worked together for good according to His plan and purpose?

5. Another wonderful promise is found in Romans 8:29-30 where we discover that as believers we are predestined to be conformed to the image of Christ. William Newell writes in his Romans commentary what it means to be like Christ. We are "conformed to His image: in glory, in love, in holiness, in beauty, in grace, in humility, in tenderness, in patience!" A big word in this Romans 8:29 verse is "predestined." It means that God decided and determined and planned in advance for us to be conformed to the image of Christ. Take a step back and think about the plans that God has had for you a long time before you came to know Him!

James Montgomery Boice, in his Romans commentary, writes these words about Romans 8:29-30— "These verses introduce us to five great doctrines regarding believers in Jesus Christ: (1) foreknowledge, (2) predestination, (3) effectual calling, (4) justification, and (5) glorification. These five doctrines are so closely connected that they have rightly and accurately been described as 'a golden chain of five links.' Each link is forged in heaven. That is, each describes something God does and does not waver in doing."[12] Here we see the finished work of our salvation from God's view. Note the past tense of each word. These promises are so powerful for you, as a believer in Jesus Christ, to see and understand. God's foreknowledge means that God knew you intimately beforehand and fixed His love on you. Then, God predestined or appointed you in advance to be in the likeness of His Son. He has effectually called you, justified you, and glorified you. The work is finished and nothing can rob you of it. Oh beloved, swim in the assurance and eternal security God is revealing to you today. God knows you by name and loves you. Read Romans 8:29-30 again with these thoughts in mind. How do you see God's amazing love for you in these wonderful promises? How does it fill your heart with love for Him?

6. Let's look more closely at just one more wonderful promise in Romans 8:33 where we discover that we are "God's elect" and no one can bring a charge against us. God is the One who justifies. What does it mean to be "God's elect?" It means we are chosen by God. You, beloved, are chosen by God. You have placed your faith in Christ. God is the One who has declared you "not guilty" because Jesus paid the penalty for your sins even while you were yet a sinner. He loves you. Think on this promise today, dear friend. Read Romans 8:33-34 once again and thank the Lord for His amazing love.

ADORE GOD IN PRAYER

Pray these words written by Peter Marshall: "Lord, teach us to pray. Some of us are not skilled in the art of prayer. As we draw near to Thee in thought, our spirits long for Thy Spirit, and reach out for Thee, longing to feel Thee near. We know not how to express the deepest emotions that lie hidden in our hearts…We know, our Father, that we are praying most when we are saying least. We know that we are closest to Thee when we have left behind the things that held us captive so long. We would not be ignorant in prayer and, like children, make want lists for Thee. Rather, we pray that Thou wilt give unto us only what we really need. We would not make our prayers the importuning of Thee, an omnipotent God, to do what we want Thee to do. Rather, give us the vision, the courage, that shall enlarge our horizons and stretch our faith to the adventure of seeking Thy loving will for our lives. We thank Thee that Thou art hearing us even now. We thank Thee for the grace of prayer. We thank Thee for Thyself. Amen."[13]

YIELD YOURSELF TO GOD

Sooner or later God meets every trusting child who is following Him up the mountain and says, "Now prove that you believe this that you have told Me you believe, and that you have taught others to believe." Then is your opportunity. God knows, and you know, that there was always a hope in your heart that a certain way would not be yours. "Anything but that, Lord," had been your earnest prayer. And then, perhaps quite suddenly, you found your feet set on that way, that and no other. Do you still hold fast to your faith that He maketh your way perfect? It does not look perfect. It looks like a road that has lost its sense of direction; a broken road, a wandering road, a strange mistake. And yet, either it is perfect, or all that you have believed crumbles like a rope of sand in your hands. There is no middle choice between faith and despair.[14]

AMY CARMICHAEL IN GOLD BY MOONLIGHT

ENJOY HIS PRESENCE

Amy Carmichael surely knew the truth of the words she wrote about the importance of relying on God working out His will even though it looked like a broken road and a strange mistake. After an accident walking on the property of her mission at Dohnavur Fellowship in India, she was in severe pain and bedridden for the rest of her life. And yet, it was during that time she wrote most of her books. Corrie ten Boom often quoted a poem entitled "The Weaver" to encourage others to trust the Lord and pray to Him in the dark times of life. Spurgeon always said, "God is too good to be unkind and He is too wise to be mistaken. And when we cannot trace His hand, we must trust His heart." Close your time by meditating on the words of "The Weaving," then talk with God about all you have learned today.

My life is but a weaving
Between my God and me.
I cannot choose the colors
He weaveth steadily.

Oft' times He weaveth sorrow;
And I in foolish pride
Forget He sees the upper
And I the underside.

Not 'til the loom is silent
And the shuttles cease to fly
Will God unroll the canvas
And reveal the reason why.

The dark threads are as needful
In the weaver's skillful hand
As the threads of gold and silver
In the pattern He has planned.

He knows, He loves, He cares;
Nothing this truth can dim.
He gives the very best to those
Who leave the choice to Him.

REST IN HIS LOVE

"And we know that God causes all things to work together for good to those who love God, to those are called according to His purpose" (Romans 8:28).

THE HOPE OF A PROMISE

Your promise revives me. Psalm 119:50 NLT
The Rose Garden, Newport Beach, California, USA
Nikon D810, ISO 1250, f7.1, 1/200sec, Adobe Photoshop, Nik Silver Efex Pro
MYPHOTOWALK.COM—CATHERINEMARTIN.SMUGMUG.COM

POWER IN CHRIST'S LOVE

Who will separate us from the love of Christ?
ROMANS 8:35

PREPARE YOUR HEART

aul made it his practice to ask questions, especially in his letter to the Romans. These questions help us focus on particular themes and discover truth in God's Word. And now, we are going to discover the great promise offering us security in Christ forever. Oh, how we need this truth, especially during our brief stay on earth, when times can be tough and we feel as though our lives are greatly challenged or even falling apart. We have already discovered the proof of God's amazing love in Romans 5:8—"that it was while we were sinners that Christ died for us." And now, Paul is going to lead us into a great promise about this love by asking the question, "Who will separate us from the love of Christ?" (Romans 8:35). What an answer he writes and we are going to study it today.

Today, dear friend, is the day for you to not only dip your toes in the ocean of God's love, but do a deep dive and discover the wonderful bliss and joy you have searched for all your life. His love is unfathomable, and according to Romans 8:31-39, nothing can separate you from it.

Joseph Scriven, a preacher in the 1800s, wrote words of comfort to his mother upon learning of her serious illness. He included the text of "What A Friend We have In Jesus," written only for her and never intended for publication. Some time later it was included in a book, *Hymns and other Verses*, and finally made its way into hymnbooks where it has become a favorite of many. When you discover the power of Christ's love, you too will realize what a friend you have in Jesus. Ask the Lord now to speak to you in His Word as you spend quiet time alone with Him.

READ AND STUDY GOD'S WORD

1. And now, how does Paul answer that question, "Who will separate us from the love of Christ?" Read Romans 8:35-39 and summarize in 1-2 sentences write out what you learn.

2. There is a great promise in Romans 8:37 for you today. "But in all these things we overwhelmingly conquer through Him who loved us." The word that is "overwhelmingly conquer" in the Greek means that we are more than victorious. We gain a surpassing victory. According to this verse, how do we have such a surpassing victory and are more than conquerors?

3. Yes, we are victorious and overwhelmingly conquer through Him who loved us—the Lord Jesus Christ. So today, dear friend, swim in the ocean of His love. He always loves you and nothing "will be able to separate us from the love of God which is in Christ Jesus our Lord" (Romans 8:39). You are bound forever to His love and He makes you victorious in all things. Read the following verses enhancing the truth of your victory and the love of Christ.

John 10:27-29

1 Corinthians 15:57

2 Corinthians 2:14

Ephesians 3:20-21

4. In Romans 8:35-39, many different experiences in life are listed including death, life, angels, principalities, things present, things to come, powers, height, depth, and created things. Newell writes that "life is so much more difficult than death—life with its burdens, its bitternesses, its disappointments, its uncertainties; often with its physical mysteries."

Of all those circumstances listed in Roman 8:35-39, which one seems the most difficult to you, and how does knowing that it can't separate you from the love of God in Christ Jesus your Lord encourage you today?

ADORE GOD IN PRAYER

Use the words of Joseph Scriven in "What A Friend We Have In Jesus" as your prayer today.

> What a friend we have in Jesus,
> All our sins and griefs to bear!
> What a privilege to carry
> Everything to God in prayer!
>
> Oh, what peace we often forfeit,
> Oh, what needless pain we bear,
> All because we do not carry
> Everything to God in prayer!
>
> Have we trials and temptations?
> Is there trouble anywhere?
> We should never be discouraged—
> Take it to the Lord in prayer.

Can we find a friend so faithful,
Who will all our sorrows share?
Jesus knows our every weakness;
Take it to the Lord in prayer.

Are we weak and heavy-laden,
Cumbered with a load of care?
Precious Savior, still our refuge—
Take it to the Lord in prayer.

Do thy friends despise, forsake thee?
Take it to the Lord in prayer!
In His arms He'll take and shield thee,
Thou wilt find a solace there.

Blessed Savior, Thou hast promised
Thou wilt all our burdens bear;
May we ever, Lord, be bringing
All to Thee in earnest prayer.

Soon in glory bright, unclouded,
There will be no need for prayer—
Rapture, praise, and endless worship
Will be our sweet portion there.

YIELD YOURSELF TO GOD

"Through Him that loved us." Here is the great secret of our victory, the source of our triumph. Behold the mystery explained, how a weak, timid believer, often starting at his own shadow, is yet "more than a conqueror" over his many and mighty foes. To Christ who loved him, who gave himself for him, who died in his stead, and lives to intercede on his behalf, the glory of the triumph is ascribed. And this is the song he chants, "Thanks be to God which giveth us the victory through our Lord Jesus Christ." Through the conquest which he himself obtained, through the grace which he imparts, through the strength which he inspires, through the intercession which he presents, in all our "tribulation, and distress, and persecution, and famine, and nakedness, and peril, and sword" we are "more than conquerors." Accounted though we are as "sheep for the slaughter," yet our Great Shepherd, Himself slain for the sheep, guides his flock, and has declared that no one shall pluck them out of his hand. We are more than conquerors through his grace who loved us in the very circumstances that threaten to overwhelm. Fear not, then, the darkest cloud, nor the proudest waves, nor the deepest wants—in these very things you shall, through Christ, prove triumphant.

Octavius Winslow in No Condemnation In Christ Jesus

ENJOY HIS PRESENCE

Spurgeon concludes from the promises in Romans 8:35-39 that "therefore, no trouble or trial can prevent our progress toward heaven. Through divine grace we will walk through the fire." There is much value in thinking long and hard about all that is true because we know Christ and are now indwelt by the Holy Spirit and blessed with the presence of the Lord and a relationship with Him forever. Yes, it's true. We will never, not ever, be separated from Him. This means you can never get so far away that God can't reach you. Hallelujah! We are recipients of His powerful and amazing love forever. It is the love that sent His Son to die in our place. Even if you feel alone and unloved, He is with you and loves you with an everlasting love. As you close your quiet time with the Lord, and after studying Romans 8 this week, why are you thankful for the Holy Spirit? And what is most powerful to you in the promises of Romans 8:35-39 and why do you think they are so powerful for you especially today? May these closing promises in Romans 8 set your heart on fire with passionate love for Jesus Christ. Write your thoughts in the space provided, then write a prayer to the Lord, expressing all that is on your heart.

REST IN HIS LOVE

"Now to him who by his power within us is able to do infinitely more than we ever dare to ask or imagine" (Ephesians 3:20 Phillips).

FAR MORE ABUNDANTLY

Now to Him who is able to do far more abundantly beyond all that we ask or think. Ephesians 3:20
Golden Pebble Habitat, Palm Desert, California, USA
Nikon D810, ISO 3200, f11, 1/250sec, Adobe Photoshop, Nik Silver Efex Pro
MYPHOTOWALK.COM—CATHERINEMARTIN.SMUGMUG.COM

DEVOTIONAL READING
BY OCTAVIUS WINSLOW

Dear Friend,

You have walked on the blessed path of Romans 8, one of the jewels in Scripture. Octavius Winslow calls Romans 8 a precious portion in God's Word. And so it is. What has Romans 8 meant to you this week? How has your heart been revived and set on fire? How do you see God's amazing love in a new and deeper way? Take some time to think about all you have learned and write a prayer to the Lord expressing all that is on your heart.

What were your most meaningful discoveries this week as you spent time with the Lord?

Most meaningful insight:

Most meaningful devotional reading:

Most meaningful verse:

n this brief but luminous space [Romans 8] is embraced an epitome of all the privileges and duties, trials and consolations, discouragements and hopes of the

Christian. Commencing with his elevated position of "no condemnation from God," it conducts him along a path where flowers bloom, and honey drops, and fragrance breathes, and music floats, and light and shade blend in beautiful and exquisite harmony to the radiant point of "no separation from Christ." And amidst the beauties and sweets, the melodies and sunshine of this glorious landscape of truth, thus spread out in all its panoramic extent and magnificence before his eye, the believer in Jesus is invited to roam, to revel, and delight himself. May the Holy and Eternal Spirit impart to the reader, and, through his prayers, increasingly to the writer, the personal possession and heart-sanctifying experience of the Divine treasure of this precious portion of God's Word.

OCTAVIUS WINSLOW IN *NO CONDEMNATION IN CHRIST JESUS*

୬୬ **WEEK FIVE** ୬୬

When God Starts A Revival

In Week Five of *The Proof of God's Amazing Love,* you had the opportunity study Romans 8, the jewel in Romans, and discover the power of God's righteousness. Today we are going to learn about the reviving power of the Holy Spirit from Romans 8. So, grab your Bibles, and let's discover what happens when God starts a revival.

"However, you are not in the flesh but in the Spirit, if indeed the Spirit of God dwells in you… But if the Spirit of Him who raised Jesus from the dead dwells in you, He who raised Christ Jesus from the dead will also give life to your mortal bodies through His Spirit who dwells in you" (Romans 8:9,11).

When God starts a revival, He begins with one person who knows revival in their own lives.

Revival is a quickening of heart and soul imparting whatever is necessary to sustain one's spiritual life and enable a return to the experience of one's true_______________________ as ordained by God.

Paul is now taking us into life in the _______________________ of the Holy Spirit. Because you are indwelt by the Holy Spirit you are going to experience _______________________. You will experience the power of the Holy Spirit. Acts 1:8

What can we learn from Romans 8 about the reviving power of the Holy Spirit in our lives?

1. The Holy Spirit confirms our salvation and the eternal_______________________ of our position in Christ. Romans 8:1-4, 9

2. The Holy Spirit convicts you of _____________and helps you live for Christ. Romans 8:13

3. The Holy Spirit gives you assurance of your _______________________ as a child of God. Romans 8:14-16

4. The Holy Spirit _________________________us into God's plans and purposes for our lives. Romans 8:14

5. The Holy Spirit informs us of our _______________________________. We have an inheritance. We are going to be glorified with Christ. Romans 8:17-18

6. The Holy Spirit gives us power in our ______________________________. Romans 8:17-23

7. The Holy Spirit gives us power to make it through ____________________. He gives us hope and perseverance. Romans 8:24-25

8. The Holy Spirit helps our _______________________________by interceding for us in prayer and by praying according to the will of God. Romans 8:26-27

9. The Holy Spirit helps us know that nothing can thwart God's ____________________ in our life. Romans 8:28

10. The Holy Spirit reminds us that God has ______________________________from the beginning that we would be His, conformed to the image of Christ, and we have a bright future and hope of being glorified with Christ. You are here by God's design. Romans 8:29-30

11. The Holy Spirit is our strength and ________________________________in every obstacle, challenge and need in life. Romans 8:31-32

12. The Holy Spirit reminds us that we overwehelmingly _______________________________ through Him who loved us. He reminds us to never give up. Romans 8:37

13. The Holy Spirit reminds us that nothing can separate us from the ___________________ of God which is in Christ Jesus our Lord. Romans 8:39

THE PLAN OF GOD'S RIGHTEOUSNESS

Romans 9-11

God's "plan of salvation" is a mighty river of destiny into which a believer plunges. This river of righteousness will eventually flood the world, washing away the old order to make room for the new…Paul's letter to the Romans is not about our salvation. His primary subject is the righteousness of God, of which our salvation is a part. The Lord is pursuing His own agenda, remember. It is to remove death from the throne of creation and give it to His Son so that the righteousness of God will rule over all things… By the time of Paul's writing the church in Rome, the majority of Jews had rejected Jesus as their Messiah…Paul takes this opportunity to address the thorny question of the Jews and their rejection of the gospel.[1]

CHARLES R. SWINDOLL IN INSIGHTS ON ROMANS

SOVEREIGNTY IN GOD'S RIGHTEOUSNESS

So then it does not depend on the man who wills or the man who runs, but on God who has mercy.

ROMANS 9:16

PREPARE YOUR HEART

Imagine trying to wrap your mind around the incomprehensible and the unfathomable ways of God. Chuck Swindoll says that one of his beloved and well-respected seminary professors often warned in studying biblical theological truths: "Let's not try to make these truths 'walk on all fours.'" Another seminary professor encouraged his students to make room in their theology for "mystery." Even Paul uses the word "mystery" in this next section of his letter to the saints in Rome—Romans 9-11. And what this means for any of us studying God's Word is that we will always have questions along the way, and some may not be answered until we get to heaven.

There is something Paul has been thinking about, probably for a long time. Now Paul is going to deal with the questions, "Why have the Jewish people rejected the gospel?" "And what about their destiny as a people?" These are especially important questions for the church in Rome and Paul is sensitive to his audience. The original believers in Rome were most likely Jews, but now it seems there are more Gentiles than Jews in the church at Rome. There could be friction and even animosity between these two groups; one thinking themselves better than the other; when, in fact, "there is no partiality with God" (Romans 2:11). The Scope and Plan of God's Righteousness is "for all who believe" (Romans 3:22), and "there is no distinction between Jew and Greek" (Romans 10:12). So now, in Romans 9-11, Paul takes us into the unfathomable ways of God, how He acts in mercy not condemnation, and always brings His plans to fruition. In Romans 9, Paul talks about the fact that God is absolutely sovereign and chooses whomever He will. His sovereignty means He rules over all things, is absolute in authority, all-powerful, and controls all things. In Romans 10, Paul shows Israel's need to believe and not work, and that Israel has insisted on trying establish her own righteousness her own way. God's righteousness is by faith, not works. Finally, in Romans 11 we see God's mercy and faithfulness and the fact that there is a future and a hope for Israel and a remnant that will believe.

What we want to do in our study this week is keep in mind all that we learn about our God—who He is, what He does, and all that He says. Think about His great invitation in Psalm 46:10—"Be still, and know that I am God." As we study this section of Scripture, remember that the theme of Romans is the gospel and the revelation of God's righteousness and the fact that "the righteous man shall live by faith" (Romans 1:17). Discovering truth about God will strengthen your faith in Him. Oh, how great is your God! You can always trust Him. As you begin your quiet time today, ask the Lord to give you a heart to draw near to Him in love and worship.

Take some time to meditate on these words from Psalm 77:12-20. "I will meditate on all Your work and muse on Your deeds. Your way, O God, is holy; What god is great like our God? You are the God who works wonders; You have made known Your strength among the peoples. You have by Your power redeemed Your people, the sons of Jacob and Joseph. The waters saw You, O God; The waters saw You; they were in anguish; The deeps also trembled. The clouds poured out water; The skies gave forth a sound; Your arrows flashed here and there. The sound of Your thunder was in the whirlwind; The lightnings lit up the world; The earth trembled and shook. Your way was in the sea and Your paths in the mighty waters, And Your footprints may not be known. You led Your people like a flock by the hand of Moses and Aaron."

READ AND STUDY GOD'S WORD

1. And now let us launch out on the waters of the unfathomable and incomprehensible ways of God and His righteousness as we study The Scope and Plan of God's Righteousness this week. The gospel is "the power of God for salvation to everyone who believes, to the Jew first and also to the Greek" (Romans 1:16). Today you are going to live in Romans 9. Read Romans 9:1-5 and describe in 1 sentence how Paul is burdened for Israel as he begins this section in Romans.

2. Now Paul is going to share the ways of God and His Word with His people historically. We may not understand all of God and His ways, but we can venture out on the vast ocean of His character and sometimes even do some deep sea diving. He begins in Romans 9:6 by saying that God's word hasn't failed. Then, he points out in Romans 9:8 that God's children are not children of the flesh but of the promise. Then in Romans 9:11 we see that God's purpose according to His choice stands. Now, read Romans 9:14-18 and write in short phrases what you learn about God.

3. In this first section of Romans 9, you see some of the mysteries of how God's redemptive plan and purposes are at work in His sovereign choices of mercy and grace. R.C. Sproul writes about God's character: "It is unthinkable that God could ever be unrighteous or unjust: Paul says strongly, 'Not at all!' He bases his argument on an earlier Scripture: For he says to Moses, 'I will have mercy on whom I have mercy, and I will have compassion on whom I have compassion' (verse 15). This is the basic essence of the doctrine of predestination, showing it to be a doctrine of grace…Salvation is by grace and by grace alone. Bless that holy God, who gives his sovereign mercy, bestowing it upon those whom he will… Our only hope is to be found in the God who shows mercy."[2] Sproul continues in talking about God's providential rule even with Pharaoh: "It is not that God creates evil, nor ever does evil, nor even inclines the heart to evil, but rather that God brings good out of evil, overruling the evil machinations of men to bring about his own purposes." Commentator Leon Morris writes: "There is a strong emphasis on mercy, for Paul is not talking about a mighty and arbitrary tyrant, but about a God who loves all that he has made and specifically the people he has chosen. In this section of his argument he first makes the point that God has always worked on the principle of election, of choosing out people through whom he would work his purpose, then he goes on to make it clear that that purpose is mercy… God is out to secure mercy, not condemnation. God is not unjustly condemning some, but in mercy saving some…if we are saved it is because God chooses to show mercy on us."[3] Our sovereign God is always just and merciful, free to choose, and never capricious or arbitrary. God is longsuffering, "not wishing for any to perish, but for all to come to repentance" (2 Peter 3:9) and "desires all men to be saved and to come to the knowledge of the truth" (1 Timothy 2:4). Those who reject and defy God, cannot, with their rebellious attitude and questions, make God answerable to them (Romans 9:20). God is God. God rules and reigns. God has sovereign freedom in all His dealings with man. In fact, Scripture teaches He does not need to answer or be accountable to man (see Job 33:13, Romans 9:20). It has been said that it is incredible that God has mercy on any sinner, for He did not have to be merciful. He possesses the sovereign right of mercy as He chooses (see Romans 9:16-18).

Paul is also showing in this section of Romans that those who are given God's righteousness are not of physical descent or lineage but are those who have spiritual life by faith in Jesus Christ—the Old Testament Jews who exercised faith and the Gentiles and Jews in the New Testament who exercised faith—"the righteous will live by faith" (Romans 1:17).

God's sovereignty—His rule, authority, power, and control over all things—impacts every area of our lives, including our attitudes and actions. His sovereignty helps us understand that salvation is a gift that we receive by grace through faith, and it cannot be earned by works. His sovereignty helps us understand His design of us, for He is the Potter and we are the clay. He is our Maker

(Psalm 95:6, Isaiah 54:5). So we surrender to Him and say, "I am fearfully and wonderfully made" (Psalm 139:14), realizing we are His masterpiece (Ephesians 2:10). He is sovereign in the ordering of our days and the circumstances of our lives (Psalm 139:16), so we surrender every day to His work, His will, and plan for our lives in times of adversity and in times of ease.

In God's sovereignty, man's actions always play into the hands of God. D. Martyn Lloyd Jones writes that Paul is "continuing to establish that God's purpose is absolute and that nothing can frustrate it…he demonstrates the eternal and glorious consistency of God: the consistency of God with Himself, His own nature and His own great and glorious purpose." God's sovereignty encourages our deepest trust in Him even in life-altering events, devastating circumstances and impossible situations. How do you need to trust God and surrender to Him today?

4. And now, in this next section of Romans 9 you will see the great purpose of God carried out in many vessels of mercy. Mercy is an important word in Romans and throughout Scripture. Mercy is the compassionate heart of God and is seen in His active desire to bestow salvation. Read Romans 9:22-26 and write what you learn about the people who are vessels of mercy. If you know Christ, then He is also talking about you, dear friend. You are a vessel of mercy.

5. In Romans 9:29, Paul says that it is because of Yahweh Sabaoth, the Lord of Hosts, that any are saved. In that name we learn that God delivers from giants and works in impossible situations. God has delivered and saved guilty sinners because of His amazing love. Salvation is possible for both Jews and Gentiles because of Jesus Christ. Paul is addressing the question of why so many of the Jews, God's chosen people, have not embraced the gospel of Jesus Christ, and are not yet saved. During His earthly ministry, Jesus said some profound words to the Jews and they are important to think about here: "You search the Scriptures because you think that in them you have eternal life; it is these that testify about Me; and you are unwilling to come to Me so that you may have life" (John 5:39-40). Now, read Romans 9:27-33 and write out what you discover about Israel — God's promise for Israel (v. 27), and how they have missed the truth of the gospel (v. 32).

ADORE GOD IN PRAYER

Blessed are You, O LORD God of Israel our father, forever and ever. Yours, O LORD, is the greatness and the power and the glory and the victory and the majesty, indeed everything that is in the heavens and the earth; Yours is the dominion, O LORD, and You exalt Yourself as head over all. Both riches and honor come from You, and You rule over all, and in Your hand is power and might; and it lies in Your hand to make great and to strengthen everyone. Now therefore, our God, we thank You, and praise Your glorious name.

DAVID IN 1 CHRONICLES 29:10-13

YIELD YOURSELF TO GOD

The mighty liner of God's sovereign design keeps its steady course over the sea of history. God moves undisturbed and unhindered toward the fulfillment of those eternal purposes which He purposed in Christ Jesus before the world began. We do not know all that is included in those purposes, but enough has been disclosed to furnish us with a broad outline of things to come and to give us good hope and firm assurance of future well-being. We know that God will fulfill every promise made to the prophets; we know that sinners will some day be cleansed out of the earth; we know that a ransomed company will enter into the joy of God and that the righteous will shine forth in the kingdom of their Father; we know that God's perfections will yet receive universal acclamation, that all created intelligences will own Jesus Christ Lord to the glory of God the Father, that the present imperfect order will be done away, and a new heaven and a new earth be established forever. Toward all this God is moving with infinite wisdom and perfect precision of action. No one can dissuade Him from His purposes; nothing turn Him aside from His plans. Since He is omniscient, there can be no unforeseen circumstances, no accidents. As He is sovereign, there can be no countermanded orders, no breakdown in authority; and as He is omnipotent, there can be no want of power to achieve His chosen ends. God is sufficient unto Himself for all these things.[4]

A.W. TOZER IN THE KNOWLEDGE OF THE HOLY

ENJOY HIS PRESENCE

What have you learned today that causes you to bow before your God and praise His holy name? Talk with God in awe and worship today as you think about His sovereignty—His rule and control over all things, and His absolute authority and power. Where in your life do you need to surrender to Him as you realize His amazing love for you and His plan and purpose at work in your life by Christ through the power of the Holy Spirit?

REST IN HIS LOVE

"Be still and know that I am God" (Psalm 46:10 NLT).

SIMPLE BEAUTY

Those who know Your name will put their trust in You. Psalm 9:10
Shelter Island, San Diego, California, USA
Nikon D810, ISO 500, f7.1, 1/1250sec, Adobe Photoshop, Nik Silver Efex Pro
MYPHOTOWALK.COM—CATHERINEMARTIN.SMUGMUG.COM

FAITH IN GOD'S RIGHTEOUSNESS

For not knowing about God's righteousness and seeking to establish their own, they did not subject themselves to the righteousness of God."

ROMANS 10:3

PREPARE YOUR HEART

ou might be wondering how in the world any of this in Romans 9-11 has to do with the here and now of today. Well, think about it. How many do you know who seem to be saying "It's my way or the highway. Me first, no rules." Or there are others who say that they have their own beliefs about God based on their own rationale and thoughts, rather than the authority of God and His Word. We learn in Proverbs 14:12 that "there is a way which seems right to a man, but its end is the way of death." The Lord says, "I, even I, am the LORD, and there is no savior besides Me" (Isaiah 43:11). In this section of Scripture, you come away with a new understanding of those who reject Christ or want to come to God their own way. You will also gain a new and greater view of God's supremacy and sovereignty.

Today is the day to think about man's accountability to God, and how a person is saved and made righteous with God's righteousness. There is the need when presented with the gospel of Jesus Christ to respond by grace through faith and believe in Him. Every life tells a story. As you begin your quiet time with the Lord today, take a few moments and think about your own story. How did you come to the place where you put your faith in Christ? Thank the Lord for how you came to know Him and all He has done in your life. Write a prayer to Him, expressing all that is on your heart.

Read and Study God's Word

1. As we think today about how a person is saved, we are given a contrast that is so very helpful in Romans 9:30-33. Read those verses and write what you learn about the Gentiles and Israel. Note how the Gentiles are contrasted with Israel in relation to righteousness, faith, and works.

Gentiles

Israel

2. How is a person saved? Keep in mind that in Romans 9-11 one of the questions Paul is considering is why so many of the Jews, God's chosen people, have not embraced the gospel of Jesus Christ, and are not yet saved. In Romans 10, he takes this opportunity to talk about the details of salvation, especially in verses 9-10. And the point for us is this: We come to God by grace through faith. "Whoever will call on the name of the Lord will be saved" (Romans 10:13). So many throughout history make their our own rules and try to achieve their own salvation. Israel had pursued righteousness by works, not by faith in Christ. Read Romans 10:9-13 and write out what you learn about being saved.

3. Just think about the heart of God for His people and how He longs for us to live with Him forever. Read the following verses and write your favorite insights about the heart of God for His people and for you.

Luke 23:39-43

John 14:1-6

Ephesians 2:4-5

2 Peter 3:9

Revelation 21:6-7

ADORE GOD IN PRAYER

Our Father which art in heaven, we Thy children are often troubled in mind, hearing within us at once the affirmations of faith and the accusations of conscience. We are sure that there is in us nothing that could attract the love of One as holy and as just as Thou art. Yet Thou hast declared Thine unchanging love for us in Christ Jesus. If nothing in us can win Thy love, nothing in the universe can prevent Thee from loving us. Thy love is uncaused and undeserved. Thou art Thyself the reason for the love wherewith we are loved. Help us to believe the intensity, the eternity of the love that has found us. Then love will cast out fear; and our troubled hearts will be at peace, trusting not in what we are but in what Thou hast declared Thyself to be. Amen.[5]

A.W. TOZER IN THE KNOWLEDGE OF THE HOLY

YIELD YOURSELF TO GOD

In two words, "righteousness" and "salvation," we have the very heart of the redemptive work of Christ. Righteousness means, as we have seen, "rightness" with God, and covers past, present, and future. In relation to the past we are "righteous" by justification. In relation to the present we are "righteous" by sanctification. In relation to the future we shall be "righteous" by glorification. Salvation is the same great fact viewed from another standpoint. Salvation means deliverance, and therefore safety, and this also concerns our past, present, and future. In relation to the past, it is salvation from the penalty of sin. In relation to the present, it is salvation from the power of sin. In relation to the future, it is salvation from the presence of sin. Well may the Apostle call this "the glorious Gospel."[6]

W.H. GRIFFITH THOMAS IN ROMANS: A DEVOTIONAL COMMENTARY VI-XI

We take it that, for Paul, the confession that Jesus is Lord meant the acknowledgment that Jesus shares the name and the nature, the holiness, the authority, power, majesty and eternity of the one and only true God. And when, as is often the case, there is joined with the title "Lord" a personal pronoun in the genitive, there is expressed in addition the sense of His ownership of those who acknowledge Him and of their consciousness of being His property, the sense of personal commitment and allegiance, of trust and confidence.[7]

C.E.B. CRANFIELD IN ROMANS: A SHORTER COMMENTARY

ENJOY HIS PRESENCE

What a day it is when a person turns to Christ and puts their faith in Him. If you have ever attended or watched a Billy Graham Crusade, you know the overwhelming emotion as thousands of people pour out of the stands to come to the front and give their lives to Jesus Christ. There is exactly what Cranfield expressed in his commentary—"the sense of personal commitment and allegiance, of trust and confidence." It is clearly the work of the Holy Spirit in hearts. There is no turning back for now you belong to the Lord Jesus Christ. This is at the heart of what we learn here in Romans and it is what Paul wants for those people who are rejecting Christ and trying to get to God by works and their own way. It is as he describes in 2 Corinthians 3:15-16—"a veil lies over their heart; but whenever a person turns to the Lord, the veil is taken away." Perhaps you have family or friends who don't know the Lord. Pray for them, dear friend, that they will turn to the Lord and the veil will be taken away. And now, what is the most important truth you have learned today and how will you apply it to your life? Close by writing a prayer to your Lord. Then, meditate on the words of Just As I Am written by Charlotte Elliott in 1835.

Just as I am - without one plea. But that Thy blood was shed for me,
And that Thou bidst me come to Thee, O Lamb of God, I come!

Just as I am - and waiting not to rid my soul of one dark blot,
To Thee, whose blood can cleanse each spot, O Lamb of God, I come!

Just as I am - though toss'd about with many a conflict, many a doubt,
Fightings and fears within, without, O Lamb of God, I come!

Just as I am - poor, wretched, blind; Sight, riches, healing of the mind,
Yea, all I need, in Thee to find, O Lamb of God, I come!

Just as I am - Thou wilt receive, wilt welcome, pardon, cleanse, relieve;
Because Thy promise I believe, O Lamb of God, I come!

Just as I am - Thy love unknown has broken every barrier down;
Now to be Thine, yea, Thine alone, O Lamb of God, I come!

Just as I am - of that free love the breadth, length, depth, and height to prove
Here for a season, then above, O Lamb of God, I come

REST IN HIS LOVE

"I am the way, and the truth, and the life; no one comes to the Father but through Me" (John 14:6).

THE OPEN GATE

They will come in and go out and find pasture. John 10:9 NIV
Principe Corsini Villa Le Corti, Val Di Pesa, Florence, Tuscany, Italy
Nikon D7000, ISO 250, f7.1, 1/400sec, Adobe Photoshop, Nik Silver Efex Pro
MYPHOTOWALK.COM—CATHERINEMARTIN.SMUGMUG.COM

REVELATION IN GOD'S RIGHTEOUSNESS

So faith comes from hearing, and hearing by the word of Christ."
ROMANS 10:17

PREPARE YOUR HEART

n his book, *A Severe Mercy*, Sheldon Vanauken tells the story of how he came to faith in Christ. He and his wife, Davy, moved to Oxford and became friends with C.S. Lewis. They began their quest and investigation into Christianity by reading Lewis' books. They had many questions and one day, on impulse, Sheldon Vanauken decided to write to C.S. Lewis. He immediately responded. And so, Vanauken wrote again with many deep thoughts and questions. In his second response, C.S. Lewis answered his questions and shared profound theological truths from Scripture. But it is how he ended his letter that is most poignant. He wrote, "But I think you are already in the meshes of the net! The Holy Spirit is after you. I doubt if you'll get away! Yours, C.S. Lewis."[8]

Don't those words make you smile. Often it is so apparent when you are telling someone about Jesus that they are about to embrace the power of the gospel of Christ and enter into a forever relationship with Him. In fact, VanAuken and his wife did become Christians.

Usually there is someone who shares the gospel of Christ with another who does not yet know Him. And it is an amazing moment when that person chooses to put their faith in Jesus Christ for salvation from sins and experience the righteousness of God. It is as though their eyes are opened. There is a moment when the truth is revealed, the scales literally fall from one's eyes, faith is exercised, and a person is saved. As Newton wrote: "I once was lost, but now am found. Was blind, but now I see."

Now in Paul's writing about the message of the gospel to the Jews in Romans 9-11, he is going to talk about whether or not they have heard about Christ. As you begin your quiet time, ask the Lord to give you eyes that see and ears that hear all He is saying in His Word.

READ AND STUDY GOD'S WORD

1. Today as we continue in the words of Paul about Israel and their opportunity for salvation, you will learn what it takes for a person to hear the gospel. And Paul actually deals with the question about whether or not they have heard. Read Romans 10:14-17 and write what you

learn about what is needed for the gospel message to be communicated and a person to come to faith in Christ.

2. In Romans 10:15 Paul asks the question, "How will they preach unless they are sent." And then he shares how beautiful the feet are of those bring good news to others. In Luke 24:47 Jesus shared that forgiveness of sins would be proclaimed in His name to all nations. In Matthew 26:13, He told His disciples that the gospel would be preached to the whole world. You have been learning about the gospel in Romans. How willing are you to share it with others? How does knowing that the Lord wants the gospel proclaimed to the whole world motivate you to tell someone else about Him?

3. Now Paul talks about the response and responsibility of Israel. Read Romans 10:16-21 and note how Israel has responded (see especially verse 21).

4. Two important verses in this passage of Scripture are related to God's revelation. He has revealed Himself in the Word of Christ (Romans 10:17) and in creation (Romans 10:18). Read the following verses and write out what you learn about how God has made Himself known:

Psalm 19:1-6

2 Peter 1:19-21

5. Would you like to grow in your own faith? The secret is found in Romans 10:17. "So faith comes from hearing, and hearing by the Word of Christ." How well do you know your Bible? The

more you know God's Word, the stronger your faith will be. Faith can be defined as "taking God at His Word." Your faith rests on the truth and the authority of God's Word. Read this event in the life of Jesus in Luke 7:1-10, and note why Jesus was so amazed at the faith of the centurion. Are you willing to live in God's Word and have a faith that amazes Jesus?

ADORE GOD IN PRAYER

Pray through the words of this prayer by Lloyd John Ogilvie: "Sovereign God, gracious Father, blessed Redeemer, inspiring Spirit, I worship you for your faithfulness, lovingkindness, judgment, and mercy. The offering I bring to my worship is myself. Nothing in my hands I bring; simply to Your grace I cling. I worship You in wonder and winsomeness, joy and gladness, delight and dependence. The blessedness of belonging to You is the beauty of holiness I have to offer in my worship. All that I have and am belongs to You. The life You have given me is Yours, the blessings You've given me are because of Your goodness, and my triumph in the future is assured only as I trust in You alone. May this whole day be spent in worship of You. I seek to worship You in my work, my talk, and my thoughts. I commit this day to practicing Your presence in the sublime and simple, with people of great and no reputation, and in duties that bring me recognition and those that only You see. To You be the glory!"[9]

YIELD YOURSELF TO GOD

The responsibility for proclaiming it [the gospel of Jesus Christ] rests with us; the responsibility for receiving or rejecting it lies with those who hear it. This is a point of primary importance in the Christian life and experience. Faith comes from the message heard. This message comes by the Word of God. Hence, the more we know of God through His Word, the more faith we shall possess…The longer we spend with our Bible in getting acquainted with God, the stronger, more practical, and more blessed will our faith be.[10]

W.H. GRIFFITH THOMAS IN ROMANS: A DEVOTIONAL COMMENTARY VI-XI

ENJOY HIS PRESENCE

Oh how important the Word of God is for us! Paul points out in this passage that God had been reaching out His hands to His people and yet they were disobedient and obstinate (Romans

10:21). When you read the Word of God, you never read it alone, but with God. You are in His Presence. He is literally reaching out to you and has something to say to you. And it will become a great foundation for your faith. What have you learned today that encourages you to live in God's Word? And what have you learned that encourages you to share your faith with others? Write out your thoughts in your Journal, then talk with God about your desire to know Him.

REST IN HIS LOVE

"So we have the prophetic word made more sure, to which you do well to pay attention as to a lamp shining in a dark place, until the day dawns and the morning star arises in your hearts" (2 Peter 1:19).

A STEP OF FAITH

We walk by faith, not by sight. 2 Corinthians 5:7
Rancho California Vineyards, Temecula, California, USA
Nikon D810, ISO 800, f4.5, AEB, Adobe Photoshop, Nik Silver Efex Pro
MYPHOTOWALK.COM—CATHERINEMARTIN.SMUGMUG.COM

FAITHFULNESS IN GOD'S RIGHTEOUSNESS

For God's gifts and His call can never be withdrawn.
ROMANS 11:29 NLT

PREPARE YOUR HEART

little girl was walking through her house and came to the cellar door and discovered it was open wide, but all she could see was darkness. She heard a noise and asked, "Who is down there?" Her father called out to her, "It's me, Daddy." "I want to be down there with you," she cried. Then he answered, "The ladder is gone, but if you jump, I'll catch you." She was afraid. She couldn't see him because of the darkness, even though the father could see her. She said, "Daddy, I'm afraid, I can't see you." Then, her father asked her four questions: "Do you believe I'm down here? Do you believe I can catch you? Do you believe I love you? Have I ever lied to you?" She told him she believed all those things. He said, "Then jump." "Okay Daddy, here I come!" And then she took the leap, her father caught her, and gave her a big hug.

Think about that story for a moment. The little girl put her faith in the word of her father. And she took the leap. This is a simple illustration of how faith takes God at His Word. God has made so many promises to His people and He always keeps His promises. And He wants us to grab on to His promises and take Him at His Word.

Paul has shared some powerful truths in Romans 9-10. God is sovereign. And Israel has tried to establish her own righteousness her own way, rather than by faith. And in God's sovereign plan, the Jews' rejection opened the way for the Gentiles to be saved. And now, God is going to show that there is a future and a hope for Israel, and a remnant will be saved. He is faithful to keep His promises. Today, ask the Lord to speak to you as you read and study His Word in your quiet time.

READ AND STUDY GOD'S WORD

1. In your study today, the goal is to see the promise God has for Israel. Read Romans 11:1-6 and write what you see about the promise of a remnant (those Jews who will come to Christ by grace through faith in spite of widespread unbelief).

2. Now Paul is speaking to both Jews and Gentiles. Read Romans 11:11-15, 25-26, 32 and write how God's plans and promises impact both Israel and Gentiles.

Israel

Gentiles

3. There is a big promise for Israel found in Romans 11:26-29. Read those verses and write out all that you see is promised. Note that in Romans 11:26, most commentators observe that "all" doesn't mean "every last one." In this passage, there are several possible interpretations, but the one that makes the most sense is that in the final generation, many Jews will be saved "by grace through faith" in Christ.

4. In all of our study today, we see the great faithfulness of God to keep His promises (see especially Romans 11:29). Read the following verses and underline your favorite words and phrases about God's faithfulness.

> Understand, therefore, that the LORD your God is indeed God. He is the faithful God who keeps his covenant for a thousand generations and lavishes his unfailing love on those who love him and obey his commands. Deuteronomy 7:9 NLT

> God is faithful, through whom you were called into fellowship with His Son, Jesus Christ our Lord. 1 Corinthians 1:9

> Now may the God of peace make you holy in every way, and may your whole spirit and soul and body be kept blameless until our Lord Jesus Christ comes again. God will make this happen, for he who calls you is faithful. 1 Thessalonians 5:23-24 NLT

> If we are unfaithful, he remains faithful, for he cannot deny who he is. 2 Timothy 2:13 NLT

ADORE GOD IN PRAYER

Pray the words of the beloved hymn, "Great Is Thy Faithfulness," written by Thomas Chisholm as a prayer to your Lord.

> Great is Thy faithfulness, O God my Father;
> There is no shadow of turning with Thee;
> Thou changest not, Thy compassions, they fail not;
> As Thou hast been, Thou forever will be.

> *Refrain:* Great is Thy faithfulness!
> Great is Thy faithfulness!
> Morning by morning new mercies I see.
> All I have needed thy hand hath provided;
> Great is Thy faithfulness, Lord, unto me!

Summer and winter and springtime and harvest,
Sun, moon and stars in their courses above
Join with all nature in manifold witness
To Thy great faithfulness, mercy and love. *Refrain*

Pardon for sin and a peace that endureth
Thine own dear presence to cheer and to guide;
Strength for today and bright hope for tomorrow,
Blessings all mine, with ten thousand beside! *Refrain*

YIELD YOURSELF TO GOD

God has vast gracious blessing of them (Israel) shortly. "For the gifts and the calling of God are irrevocable" (Romans 10:29). These words are a source of endless joy. We may trust a God who refuses to allow the utter failure of Israel…

WILLIAM NEWELL IN ROMANS VERSE BY VERSE

Contemplate the revelations of the Apostle in this entire chapter:

1. The fall of the Jews was overruled for mercy to the Gentiles.

2. The salvation of the Gentiles was intended to stir the Jews to the acceptance of Christ.

3. The salvation of the Jews is to issue in still greater blessing to the human race.

4. The glorious future that is yet to dawn on the world by the mercy of God.

The more we ponder these profound truths the more deeply we shall enter into the very heart of the Apostle's thought, and, still more, into the very heart of the Divine purposes of love and grace for the entire world.[11]

W.H. GRIFFITH THOMAS IN ROMANS: A DEVOTIONAL COMMENTARY VI-XI

ENJOY HIS PRESENCE

We are nearing the end of this section of Scripture where Paul is sharing the depth of his love for both the Jews and Gentiles in the church at Rome, and showing the greatness and glory of God—His love, mercy, His plans and His purposes. And perhaps you feel a bit silenced and overwhelmed in awe and wonder as you contemplate the unfathomable character of your God. You realize He is infinite and incomprehensible. For all the truths you may not fully understand, the words of Proverbs 3:5 will help you in application of all you have learned thus far: "Trust in the LORD with all your heart and do not lean on your own understanding." What is the most important truth you have learned from your quiet time today? Write your thoughts, and then close by writing a prayer.

REST IN HIS LOVE

"Know therefore that the LORD your God, He is God, the faithful God, who keeps His covenant and His lovingkindness to a thousandth generation with those who love Him and keep His commandments" (Deuteronomy 7:9).

A Firm Foundation

Praise be to the LORD, my Rock. Psalm 144:1 NIV
Monument Valley Navajo Tribal Park, Oljato-Monument Valley, Utah, USA
Nikon D7000, ISO 160, f11, AEB, Adobe Photoshop, Nik Silver Efex Pro
MYPHOTOWALK.COM—CATHERINEMARTIN.SMUGMUG.COM

GLORY IN GOD'S RIGHTEOUSNESS

*For from Him and through Him and to Him are all
things. To Him be the glory forever. Amen.*

ROMANS 11:36

PREPARE YOUR HEART

ne of the most blessed times for any believer is having the opportunity to sing a favorite hymn or worship song with a group of people who love the Lord. Paul encouraged the church at Colossae to "Let the word of Christ richly dwell within you, with all wisdom teaching and admonishing one another with psalms and hymns and spiritual songs, singing with thankfulness in your hearts to God" (Colossians 3:16). A.W. Tozer, author of *The Pursuit Of God*, loved hymns so much that often, on his way to an appointment, he would meditate on the words of a hymn in one of the many old hymnals he collected. Tozer said, "After the Bible . . . the next most valuable book is a good hymnal. Let any new Christian spend a year prayerfully meditating on the hymns of Watts and Wesley alone, and he or she will become a fine theologian...The results will be more wonderful than he could have dreamed."

How does Paul end this section of Romans where he has ventured out into the waters of the mysteries of God, those things that are unfathomable and incomprehensible? He writes a beautiful hymn for the people of God, those he loves with great passion. D. Martyn Lloyd Jones calls this hymn a doxology that is "beyond any question one of the most glorious, wonderful, and exalted statements which is to be found anywhere in the Bible." Alford, another commentator, refers to it as "the sublimest apostrophe existing even in the pages of inspiration itself."

Today as you prepare for quiet time alone with the Lord, meditate on the words of this beloved hymn written by Isaac Watts.

> Alas! And did my Savior bleed
> And did my Sovereign die?
> Would He devote that sacred head
> For such a worm as I?
> *Refrain:* At the cross, at the cross
> Where I first saw the light,

And the burden of my heart rolled away,
It was there by faith I received my sight,
And now I am happy all the day!

Was it for crimes that I had done
He groaned upon the tree?
Amazing pity! Grace unknown!
And love beyond degree! *Refrain*

Well might the sun in darkness hide
And shut his glories in,
When Christ, the mighty Maker died,
For man the creature's sin. *Refrain*

Thus might I hide my blushing face
While His dear cross appears,
Dissolve my heart in thankfulness,
And melt my eyes to tears. *Refrain*

But drops of grief can ne'er repay
The debt of love I owe:
Here, Lord, I give my self away
'Tis all that I can do. *Refrain*

READ AND STUDY GOD'S WORD

1. What a week of study we have had in Romans 9-11. It is time to sit back and just think about all the magnificent truths you have learned in Paul's letter to the Romans. Can you imagine the impact of this letter on the church in Rome, those Paul addressed as "all who are beloved in Rome, called as saints" (Romans 1:7). And now, Paul breaks out in song in Romans 11:33-36. These verses have been regarded as a doxology, but also as a hymn. Take some time now and read Romans 11:33-36. What is your first impression of these verses? How do they impact you?

2. Read Romans 11:33-36 again and write out everything you learn about God.

3. Paul ends his hymn with these words: "To Him be the glory forever. Amen" (Romans 9:36). Charles Ryrie says that the glory of God "is the manifestation of any or all of His attributes. In other words, it is the displaying of God to the world. Thus, things which glorify God are things which show the characteristics of His being to the world." His glory is the splendor and radiance of His Presence. Even "the heavens declare the glory of God" (Psalm 19:1). J. Gresham Machen says, "The ultimate end of all things that come to pass, including the ultimate end of the great drama of redemption, is found in the glory of the eternal God." Read the following verses and write your most significant insights about the glory of God.

1 Corinthians 10:31

Hebrews 1:1-3

1 Peter 1:6-7

1 Peter 5:10

4. What is your favorite truth about God in this beautiful hymn that Paul has written? Why does what you have read mean so much to you today?

ADORE GOD IN PRAYER

Draw near to the Lord and pour out your heart to Him in prayer in response to all you have learned today about the greatness and glory of God. Thank Him for His great and glorious plan that includes you. You are the beloved of God and called a saint, just like those in the church at Rome. May your faith in Christ be strong and your love for Him be the passion of your heart.

YIELD YOURSELF TO GOD

God's universal agency as the first cause, the sovereign ruler, and the last end, ought to be the matter of our adoration. Thus all his works do praise him objectively; but his saints do bless him actively; they hand that praise to him which all the creatures do minister matter for, (Ps. 145:10). Paul had been discoursing at large of the counsels of God concerning man, sifting the point with a great deal of accuracy; but, after all, he concludes with the acknowledgment of the divine sovereignty, as that into which all these things must be ultimately resolved, and in which alone the mind can safely and sweetly rest. This is, if not the scholastic way, yet the

Christian way, of disputation. Whatever are the premises, let God's glory be the conclusion; especially when we come to talk of the divine counsels and actings, it is best for us to turn our arguments into awful and serious adorations. The glorified saints, that see furthest into these mysteries, never dispute, but praise to eternity.

MATTHEW HENRY IN *MATTHEW HENRY'S COMMENTARY ON THE WHOLE BIBLE*

Like a traveller who has reached the summit of an Alpine ascent, the apostle turns and contemplates. Depths are at his feet; but waves of light illumine them, and there spreads all around an immense horizon which his eye commands. The plan of God in the government of mankind spreads out before him, and he expresses the feelings of admiration and gratitude with which the prospect fills his heart… What the apostle was concerned to say in closing, was that all things proceeding from the creative will of God, advancing through His wisdom and terminating in the manifestation of His holiness, must one day celebrate His glory, and His glory only…The glory of God, the reflection of His perfections in all that exists, that glory, now veiled, in so many respects in the universe, must shine forth magnificently and perfectly for ever and ever. For, as Hodge says, "the highest end for which all things can exist and be ordered, is to display the character of God." This goal of history is, as it were, anticipated by the wish and prayer of the apostle: "To Him be glory!"

FREDERIC LOUIS GODET AND ALEXANDER CUSIN IN *ST. PAUL'S EPISTLE TO THE ROMANS*

ENJOY HIS PRESENCE

Oh dear friend, what a study we have had together in Romans thus far. And how fitting to focus on the greatness and glory of God in the hymn Paul has written at the end of Romans 1-11. How well do you know your God, dear friend? A.W. Tozer wrote these words about God in his book, *The Pursuit of God*: "God is a person, and in the deep of His mighty nature He thinks, wills, enjoys, feels, loves, desires and suffers as any other person may. In making Himself known to us He stays by the familiar pattern of personality. He communicates with us through the avenues of our minds, our wills and our emotions. The continuous and unembarrassed interchange of love and thought between God and the soul of the redeemed man is the throbbing heart of New Testament religion."[12] Do you know God this way? Oswald Chambers speaks of his response to the blessed privilege of knowing God: "I delight to know that there is that in me which must fall prostrate before God when He manifests Himself."[13] What is the most important truth you have learned in your study today? How is the Lord speaking to you in His Word? How is He reviving your heart? Worship Him in love and adoration today as you tell Him how much you love Him.

Rest in His Love

"Let the word of Christ richly dwell within you, with all wisdom teaching and admonishing one another with psalms and hymns and spiritual songs, singing with thankfulness in your hearts to God" (Colossians 3:16).

Footprints In The Sea

He alone stretches out the heavens and treads on the waves of the sea. Job 9:8 NIV
Pauoa Bay, Waimea, Island Of Hawaii, Hawaii, USA
Nikon D7000, ISO 100, f5.6, 1/500sec, Adobe Photoshop, Nik Silver Efex Pro
myPhotoWalk.com—catherinemartin.smugmug.com

DEVOTIONAL READING
BY C.E.B. CRANFIELD

Dear Friend,

Think about all you have learned this week as we have continued on this journey in Paul's letter to the Romans. Write a prayer to the Lord thanking Him for all that He is teaching you.

What were your most meaningful discoveries this week as you spent time with the Lord?

Most meaningful insight:

Most meaningful devotional reading:

Most meaningful verse:

aul has certainly not provided neat answers to the baffling questions which arise in connection with the subject matter of these three chapters [Romans 9-11]. He has certainly not swept away all the difficulties. But, if we have followed him through these chapters with serious and open-minded attentiveness, we may feel that he has given us enough to enable us to repeat the "Amen" of his doxology in joyful confidence that the deep mystery which surrounds us is neither a nightmare mystery of meaninglessness nor a dark mystery of arbitrary omnipotence but the mystery which will never turn out to be anything other than the mystery of the altogether good and merciful and faithful God.[14]

C.E.B. Cranfield in *Romans: A Shorter Commentary*

❧ WEEK SIX ☙

Knowing God And His Unfathomable Ways

In Week Six of *The Proof of God's Amazing Love*, you had the opportunity to study Romans 9-11 and learn about the plan of God's righteousness. Today I want to look the unfathomable ways of God and how there is always so much more to know about God. Grab your Bibles, and let's dig in more deeply together as we study knowing God.

"Oh, the depth of the riches both of the wisdom and knowledge of God! How unsearchable are His judgments and unfathomable His ways!" (Romans 11:33).

"The man who has God for his treasure has all things in One." A.W. Tozer

"I am not the center of things, but God is, and I as His creature and child exist for Him rather than He for me." J.I. Packer

What can we learn in Romans 9-11 about God and His unfathomable ways?

1. God is a ___________________________God—Father, Son, and Holy Spirit. Romans 9:1-5

2. God always keeps His ____. Romans 9:6

3. God is ____. Romans 9:11

4. God is ____. Romans 9:14

5. God is ____. Romans 9:18-20

6. God has a _______________________________and carries out that plan. Romans 9:23-24

7. God is Yahweh Sabaoth, the Lord of Hosts, who delivers us from giants and works in ____ situations. Romans 9:29

8. We are made righteous with the righteousness of God by _______________________________.
Romans 9:30-32

9. Salvation is all about _______________________and God's righteousness to everyone who
believes. Romans 10:4, 9-10

10. God is Lord of _______________________. There is no distinction. Romans 10:12-13

11. Faith comes from hearing and hearing from the _______________of Christ. Romans 10:17

12. God gives all an opportunity to be _______________________. Romans 10:18-21
The Lord…is not willing that any should perish but that all should come to repentance.
2 Peter 3:9, 1 Timothy 2:4, John 1:11-13, 3:16

13. God is _______________________________always, not sometimes. Romans 11:5

14. God's plan and purpose make it possible for _______________to be saved. Romans 10:18-21

15. God is ____. Romans 11:22

16. God is ____ to save. Romans 11:23

17. God's ways are a ____. Romans 11:25

18. God is merciful, and His choosing, gifts and calling are _______________________.
Romans 11:29

*Video messages are available on DVDs or as Digital M4V Video. Audio messages are
available as Digital MP3 Audio. Visit the Quiet Time Ministries Online Store at www.quiettime.org.*

Week Seven

THE LIFE OF GOD'S RIGHTEOUSNESS

Romans 12

The greatest practical teacher of Christian truth in the history of the church is the apostle Paul…Whenever he gives us deep and profound doctrinal teaching he always follows it with very specific, concrete, practical application. In chapter 12, we see that remarkable transition in style which is so typical of the apostle. For eleven chapters he has taken us through the weightiest type of doctrinal study, and he ended that doctrinal section at the end of chapter 11, fitly and appropriately, with a doxology. But what does it mean for our lives? What should be our response in terms of our hearts, in terms of our behavior, in terms of lifestyle?[1]

R.C. Sproul

SURRENDER

Therefore, I urge you, brethren, by the mercies of God, to present your bodies a living and holy sacrifice, acceptable to God, which is your spiritual service of worship.

Romans 12:1

PREPARE YOUR HEART

young girl sat at a board room table at Biola University for an interview to teach Bible and Theology in a Christian university, something she had always dreamed of for her life. At the table were professors and other leaders, ready to ask questions related to her experience, beliefs, relationship with God, commitment to God and His Word, and academic history. At the head of the table was a man who stood out because of his demeanor, humility, and a sparkle in his eyes. The young interviewee couldn't take her eyes off of this one man. He was Clyde Cook, the President of Biola University. And he was clearly in charge of the interview. He asked most of the questions. And just when it seemed as though the interview had only just begun, he pushed his chair back, stood up, and with a wide and generous smile, he looked around the table and rested his eyes on the young girl who was the subject of the conversation. He said decisively, and loudly enough for all to hear, "Well, I've heard enough. Welcome to Biola University. You are now our newest professor." He held out his hand and shook hers. As for this young girl, she could hardly believe it. She was so excited as it had always been her dream to teach in a Christian University. Little did she know at the time the great privilege she had just experienced. She had been interviewed by Clyde Cook, who was a hero of the faith for many including Chuck Swindoll, Luis Palau, Chuck Colson, Dallas Willard, and Josh McDowell.

How does a person become someone like a Clyde Cook, whose life is so influential that only heaven will tell the story of the ripple effect that results from it? It all comes down to God and His plan for each of us, His work in us through the power of the Holy Spirit, and then the decisions that result from an intimate, ongoing, vibrant relationship with Him.

Clyde Cook has an incredible testimony of his own salvation and resulting commitment to Christ. He grew up in Hong Kong with Christian parents, lived for a time in a concentration camp during World War II, and ultimately moved with his parents to California. He remembers a time in Hong Kong at the beginning of World War II when he and his mother were huddled under a staircase where they read Daily Light scriptures, and sang He Leadeth Me, with the sound of falling bombs all around them. He knew the fear of impending danger, the insecurity of the future, and had the influence of Christian parents. And yet, he himself had never come to know Christ personally. In high school during a Forest Home summer camp, he realized he was a sinner, and invited Christ into his life. There came a very important day when the Lord gave Clyde Cook a verse that brought him to a decision that changed the course of his life. While pursuing a basketball scholarship, he read 1 Peter 1:24— "For all flesh is as grass and all the glory of man like the flower of grass. The grass withereth and the flower fadeth away but the Word of the Lord endures forever." When he read that verse he realized he could live for what fades away or he could live for what lasts forever. He said, "I wanted to spend my time in something that endured forever." And it was then that he surrendered himself to the Lord, and committed himself to the leadership of the Lord all the rest of his days. Once the Lord was leading him in things that last forever, he attended Biola University, met his wife Anna Belle, attended Talbot School of Theology, did mission work in the Philippines, taught at Biola and Talbot, and finally, became President of Biola University.

That is one man's story. And you can see that the direction and result of his life came down to the influence of the Lord in his life. It was not how much he had of the Lord, but how much the Lord had of him. Ultimately, it was not Clyde Cook's life, but Christ's life in him. With the Lord at the helm, Christ could take him in His direction, and accomplish His plans and purposes.

The same was true with Corrie ten Boom, who suffered in Ravensbruck concentration camp, was released on a clerical error, and spent many years traveling worldwide sharing the gospel of Jesus Christ. Her last five years of life were spent in silence as she suffered a devastating stroke. She is such a picture of surrender for the Lord knew He could do anything He pleased with Corrie because she made no demands of Him with her will. She delighted to say yes to Him and to His will. She was open and unencumbered and entertained no desires outside of the Lord's desires. And so, He could speak through her as a prisoner in Ravensbruck concentration camp, as a tramp for Him all over the entire world, and as an invalid lying in a bed, paralyzed and unable to speak.

And now, what about you? What is the story of your life? Who is at the helm? You or the Lord? Those are the questions at the heart of where Paul is going to take us now in Romans 12. We have been looking at the great power of the gospel as we saw the need for God's righteousness in Romans 1-3, the way of God's righteousness in Romans 4-5, the union, power and provision of God's righteousness in Romans 6-8, and the scope and plan of God's righteousness in Romans 9-11. And now in Romans 12-16, we are going to see the practical applications of God's righteousness as we learn about service. God has a ministry for you now that you know Him. Jesus Christ lives in you and wants to touch lives in and through you. We have been looking at doctrine, but you can know that doctrine always leads to devotion. Principles always lead to practice. Now we are going to look at the life of God's righteousness. As you begin your quiet time, ask the Lord to speak to you in His word.

READ AND STUDY GOD'S WORD

1. It is difficult to believe we are already in Romans 12 and there are only two more weeks of study in this letter written by Paul to the church in Rome. As we arrive at Romans 12, it's important to make note of the transition from doctrinal truth to practical application. The way we know that this transition is occurring is the use of the word "Therefore." Whenever you see the word, "Therefore," you need to find out what it's "there for."

Paul writes in Romans 12:1—"Therefore, I urge you, brethren, by the mercies of God, to present your bodies a living and holy sacrifice, acceptable to God, which is your spiritual service of worship." Now Paul is bringing all of us to a point of decision. What does God want more than anything? You. Your very body becomes the place where the Lord Himself lives in and through you in the power of the Holy Spirit. No wonder Paul says in 1 Corinthians 6:19-20, "Or do you not know that your body is a temple of the Holy Spirit who is in you, whom you have from God, and that you are not your own? For you have been bought with a price: therefore glorify God in your body." You see, it's not your life—it's His life.

This surrender of our bodies is a very real choice to make and Paul is calling us to make it. He uses as the motivation, "the mercies of God." So as you begin thinking about the meaning of this verse in your own life, it's important to begin by thinking about the mercies of God. Paul is now inviting you to think back through all you have learned in Romans to this point—and he is calling all those truths of the gospel "the mercies of God." Take some time to list as many of the mercies of God that you can think of from Romans 1-11, especially related to the work of Christ on your behalf. You may want to leaf back through the weeks of study and write what you see in single words and small phrases to describe the many mercies. You may use your Journal if you need more space. This will be a treasured collection of mercies you can look at again and again.

2. In Romans 12:1, you learn that you are to "present your bodies a living and holy sacrifice." The New Living Translation writes it this way: "Give your bodies to God because of all He has done for you. Let them be a living and holy sacrifice—the kind He will find acceptable. This is truly the way to worship Him." What do you think it means to present your body a living and holy sacrifice and why do you think this is important in your life with Christ?

3. How does Romans 12:1 involve surrender to the Lord on your part? Can you think of a time in your life when you have surrendered your life to Christ and what happened as a result?

4. Read the following verses and write out how your very body relates to each of these verses:

Galatians 2:20

Philippians 1:21

Colossians 1:27

5. When you are in an intimate, ongoing relationship with Christ, you will hear Him calling you with the same invitation He gave His first-century disciples. "Follow Me, and I will make you fishers of men" (Matthew 4:19). He described in even more detail all that is involved in being His disciple when He said, "If anyone wishes to come after Me, he must deny himself, and take up his cross daily and follow Me" (Luke 9:23). The great commission of Jesus involves making disciples. He said, "All authority has been given to Me in heaven and on earth. Go therefore and make disciples of all the nations, baptizing them in the name of the Father and the Son and the Holy Spirit, teaching them to observe all that I commanded you; and lo, I am with you always even to the end of the age" (Matthew 28:18-20). How do these words of Jesus to take up your cross, follow Him, and make disciples call for a Romans 12:1 surrender?

ADORE GOD IN PRAYER

Draw near to the Lord in prayer and talk with Him about presenting yourself to God, giving Him your very body, that He may work in and through you to touch a lost and hurting world. You may use the words of Frances Ridley Havergal as your prayer to the Lord today.

Take my life and let it be
consecrated, Lord, to thee.
Take my moments and my days;
let them flow in endless praise,
let them flow in endless praise.

Take my hands and let them move
at the impulse of thy love.
Take my feet and let them be
swift and beautiful for thee,
swift and beautiful for thee.

Take my voice and let me sing
always, only, for my King.
Take my lips and let them be
filled with messages from thee,
filled with messages from thee.

Take my silver and my gold;
not a mite would I withhold.
Take my intellect and use
every power as thou shalt choose,
every power as thou shalt choose.

Take my will and make it thine;
it shall be no longer mine.
Take my heart it is thine own;
it shall be thy royal throne,
it shall be thy royal throne.

Take my love; my Lord, I pour
at thy feet its treasure store.
Take myself, and I will be
ever, only, all for thee,
ever, only, all for thee.

YIELD YOURSELF TO GOD

Well you cannot live this life, but Christ can. CHRIST IN US can live this life anywhere and everywhere…The Christian on earth is the visible part of Christ. This is a staggering thought. Its plain import is that you and I are to bring Christ down from heaven to earth that men may see who He is and what He can do in a human life. It is to have Christ's life lived out in us in such fullness that seeing Him in us men are drawn to Him in faith and love.

RUTH PAXSON IN RIVERS OF LIVING WATER

It is our privilege to glorify Christ in our body and magnify Christ in our body (Phil. 1:20–21). Just as Jesus Christ had to take on Himself a body in order to accomplish God's will on earth, so we must yield our bodies to Christ that He might continue God's work through us…For many years I have tried to begin each day by surrendering my body to the Lord. Then I spend time with His Word and let Him transform my mind and prepare my thinking for that new day. Then I pray, and I yield the plans of the day to Him and let Him work as He sees best. I especially pray about those tasks that upset or worry me—and He always sees me through. To have a right relationship with God, we must start the day by yielding to Him our bodies, minds, and wills… If you begin each day by surrendering your body to Christ, it will make a great deal of difference in what you do with your body during the day.[2]

WARREN WIERSBE IN BIBLE EXPOSITION COMMENTARY

You are called to be a home for Christ, a place where He can live while you are on this earth.…In Ephesians 4:12-16 Paul speaks of us as the body of Christ and the need to "grow up in all aspects into Him who is the head, even Christ, from whom the whole body, being fitted and held together by what every joint supplies, according to the proper working of each individual part, causes the growth of the body for the building up of itself in love." William O. Carver, Professor of Missions in the early 20th Century, in his Commentary on Ephesians, writes: "You are to be made so strong by His Spirit coming into and working within you that Christ may have in you—the Church—a place to dwell, a sphere to work in, and instrument of action."[3] Carver made a daring declaration in the classes he taught: "The calling of the Christian and the church is to be the continuation of the incarnation of Jesus Christ." In that one statement, he was pointing out that Christ was continuing His life and work on earth in and through those who are spiritually born again and have entered into a relationship with Him.[4]

CATHERINE MARTIN IN THE CALLING

ENJOY HIS PRESENCE

Oh what a day of study today! You are being taken deeper by the Lord through Paul in Romans 12:1 as you understand what it means to live with Christ during your brief stay on earth. Just think about the early church and all that they experienced with Christ. Their ministry seen in the book of Acts was His ministry. It was Jesus Christ in action. S.D. Gordon, in his book *Quiet Talks On John's Gospel*, describes it this way: "These men learned to live always in the presence of a Jesus whom their outer eyes saw not…He would be with them continually manifesting Himself in rarest power of action, in tenderest personal care, in talking and walking with them. They would see the power plainly at work; then they would say in a soft hush, He is here. They would find new bodily strength, new guidance in perplexity, new peace in the midst of confusion, and they would say to each other in awed tones, He is here: it's the Master's touch. And so it would come to be a habit to anticipate His presence. They would figure Him in, and figure Him in big, as big as He is, in all sorts of circumstances and planning and meeting of difficulties."

Think about all you have learned today. Why is presenting your body to Christ as a living and holy sacrifice so important? In light of the mercies of God, will you present your body to Christ as a living and holy sacrifice today? Will you answer the call of Jesus to take up your cross, follow Him and be His disciple? Tozer writes about how Christ's disciples are facing one direction only, have stopped looking back, and have no further plans of their own. Oh, how true this is! Close by writing your thoughts and a prayer to the Lord in your Journal, expressing all that is on your heart.

REST IN HIS LOVE

"And this is the secret: Christ lives in you" (Colossians 1:27 NLT).

HE STRENGTHENS ME

I can do all things through Him who strengthens me. Philippians 4:13
Corona Del Mar State Beach, Corona Del Mar, Newport Beach, California, USA
Nikon D810, ISO 100, f8, 1/160sec, Adobe Photoshop, Nik Silver Efex Pro
MYPHOTOWALK.COM—CATHERINEMARTIN.SMUGMUG.COM

TRANSFORMATION

And do not be conformed to this world, but be transformed
by the renewing of your mind, so that you may prove what
the will of God is, that which is good and acceptable and perfect.

ROMANS 12:2

PREPARE YOUR HEART

Dr. Henry M. Morris has been called the "father of modern scientific creationism" and is the founder of the Institute for Creation Research. He has often been described as a humble man of God, a godly role model, and helped hundreds of thousands throughout the world to rely on God's Word as the authority for their belief. When he went home to be with the Lord in 2006, a devotional written by G.D. Watson entitled "Others May, You Cannot" was pasted in the flyleaf of his Bible. The words reveal his deep commitment to live for the Lord and not the things of the world. Begin your quiet time today thinking about these words from "Others May, You Cannot."

"If God has called you to be really like Jesus, He will draw you into a life of crucifixion and humility, and put upon you such demands of obedience, that you will not be able to measure yourself by other Christians; and in many ways, He will seem to let other good people do things which He will never let you do. Other Christians and ministers, who seem very religious and useful, can push themselves, pull wires and work schemes to carry out their Christian goals, but these things you simply cannot do. Others may boast of their work or their writings or their success, but the Holy Spirit will not allow you to do any such thing, and if you ever try it, He will lead you into some deep mortification that will make you despise yourself and all your good works. Others may be allowed to succeed in making money, but most likely God will keep you poor, because He wants you to have something far better than gold, namely, a helpless dependence on Him and the joy of seeing Him supply your needs day by day out of an unseen Treasury. The Lord may let others be honored and keep you hidden and unappreciated because He wants to produce some choice, fragrant fruit for His coming glory, which can only be produced in the shade. He may let others do a work for Him and get the credit for it, but He will make you work on and on without others knowing how much you are doing; and then, to make your work still more precious, He may let others get the credit for the work which you have done, and thus make your reward ten times greater when Jesus comes. The Holy Spirit will rebuke you for little words or deeds or even feelings, or for wasting your time, which other Christians never seem to be concerned about, but you must make up your mind that God is an infinite Sovereign and He has a right to do whatever He pleases with His own. He may not explain to you a thousand things which puzzle your reason in the way He deals with you, but if you will just submit yourself to Him in all things, He will wrap you up in a jealous love and bestow upon you many blessings which come only to those who are very near to His heart. Settle it then, that He is to have the privilege of tying your tongue, or chaining your hand, or closing your eyes, in ways that He does not seem to use with others. Now, when you are so possessed with the living God that your secret heart becomes pleased and delighted with this peculiar, personal, private, jealous guardianship and management of the Holy Spirit over your life, then you will have entered the very vestibule of heaven itself."

Dear friend, treasure this special moment of reflection and preparation for your quiet time alone with your Lord.

Read and Study God's Word

1. Romans 12:2 gives two imperatives, meaning these are commands for us. "Do not be conformed to this world, but be transformed…" Conformed is an outward action and transformed is an inward action. Then, we learn how to do this i.e. "by the renewing of your mind." And finally, we see the result: "so that you may prove what the will of God is, that which is good and acceptable and perfect." Read the following translations and paraphrases of Romans 12:2 and underline your favorite words and phrases that help you understanding its meaning.

> Don't copy the behavior and customs of this world, but let God transform you into a new person by changing the way you think. Then you will learn to know God's will for you, which is good and pleasing and perfect. Romans 12:2 NLT

> Do not conform any longer to the pattern of this world, but be transformed by the renewing of your mind. Then you will be able to test and approve what God's will is—his good, pleasing and perfect will. Romans 12:2 NIV

> Don't let the world around you squeeze you into its own mould, but let God re-mould your minds from within, so that you may prove in practice that the plan of God for you is good, meets all his demands and moves towards the goal of true maturity. Romans 12:2 Phillips

Do not be conformed to this world (this age), [fashioned after and adapted to its external, superficial customs], but be transformed (changed) by the [entire] renewal of your mind [by its new ideals and its new attitude], so that you may prove [for yourselves] what is the good and acceptable and perfect will of God, even the thing which is good and acceptable and perfect [in His sight for you].
Romans 12:2 AMPLIFIED

2. The first command is "Do not be conformed to this world." Kenneth Wuest in his *Word Studies in the Greek New Testament* explains this command: "Paul exhorts the saints, 'Stop assuming an outward expression which is patterned after this world, an expression which does not come from, nor is it representative of what you are in your inner being as a regenerated child of God.' One could translate, 'Stop masquerading in the habiliments [devices and things] of this world, its mannerisms, speech expressions, styles, habits.'"[5] Read 1 John 2:15-17 and write what stands out to you about the world. Note also how the world is contrasted with the will of God and living for the will of God.

3. What are ways we become conformed to the world and allow the world around us to squeeze us into its own mold?

4. Instead of being conformed to this world, you are to "let God transform you into a new person by changing the way you think." The Greek word for "transform" is *metamorphoo* and means a complete change into another form. It carries the idea of metamorphosis. The picture of a caterpillar becoming a butterfly helps in understanding this command. The Lord wants to make you a new person from the inside out, and He does it by changing the way you think through the power of the indwelling Holy Spirit. This change is not about imitation but transformation. The Bible speaks often of paying attention to all that you think about. Read Philippians 4:8 and

Colossians 3:2 and write your insights about your thoughts. What are you to think about? How do you think the Bible helps you think about these things?

Philippians 4:8

Colossians 3:2

5. D.L. Moody once said, "The Scriptures were not given for our information, but for our transformation." Read 2 Timothy 3:16-17 and Hebrews 4:12 and write out how God uses the Bible to change us. Personalize what you learn.

2 Timothy 3:16-17

Hebrews 4:12

6. In 2 Corinthians 3:18 we learn more about our transformation. It is so beautiful to watch the Spirit at work in us as He transforms us and make us more like Christ. Read this verse and write out your insights about the Spirit at work in us and the result of our transformation. "But we all, with unveiled face, beholding as in a mirror the glory of the Lord, are being transformed into the same image from glory to glory, just as from the Lord, the Spirit" (2 Corinthians 3:18).

7. The Lord is doing a mighty and powerful work in and through you. He is the Master Artist, making you into a beautiful Masterpiece. Spurgeon writes: "You never see the Great Artist's masterpiece. You only see the rough marble and mark the chips that fall to the ground. You have felt the edge of His chisel; you know the weight of His hammer. If you could see the glorious

image as it will be when He has put the finishing blows to it, you would better understand the chisel, the hammer, and the Artist." Read Ephesians 2:10 and underline words and phrases that teach you about what God is doing in and through you.

> For we are God's masterpiece. He has created us anew in Christ Jesus, so we can do
> the good things he planned for us long ago. Ephesians 2:10 NLT

8. Finally, in Romans 12:2 we see that the result is "that you may prove in practice that the plan of God for you is good, meets all his demands and moves towards the goal of true maturity" (PHILLIPS). Have you ever had a time in your life when things did not work out as you planned, but in time, as the Lord changed you and you grew spiritually, then you saw His plan and purpose in your life? Remember, in Romans 12:2 we see that the will of God is good, acceptable, and perfect. Write your thoughts in the space provided.

ADORE GOD IN PRAYER

O LORD OF THE OCEANS,
My little boat sails on a restless sea,
Grant that Jesus may sit at the helm and steer me safely;
allow no adverse currents to divert my heavenward course,
let not my faith be wrecked amid storms and shoals;
bring me to harbor with flying pennants,
hull unbreached, cargo unspoiled.
I ask great things,
expect great things,
shall receive great things.
I venture on You wholly, fully,
my wind, sunshine, anchor, defense.
The voyage is long, the waves high, the storms pitiless,
but my helm is held steady,
Your Word secures safe passage,
Your grace wafts me onward,

my haven is guaranteed.
This day will bring me nearer home,
Grant me holy consistency in every transaction,
my peace flowing as a running tide,
my righteousness as every chasing wave.
Help me to live circumspectly,
with skill to convert every care into prayer,
Halo my path with gentleness and love,
smooth every asperity of temper;
let me not forget how easy it is to occasion grief;
may I strive to bind up every wound,
and pour oil on all troubled waters.
May the world this day be happier and better because I live.
Let my mast before me be the Savior's cross,
and every oncoming wave the fountain in His side.
Help me, protect me in the moving sea
until I reach the shore of unceasing praise.[6]

THE VALLEY OF VISION

YIELD YOURSELF TO GOD

Remember that the Spirit of God inspired the Word and He will be revealed in the Word. I really have no place in my sympathies for those Christians who neglect the Word or ignore the Word or get revelations apart from the Word. This is the Book of God, after all, and if we know the Book well enough, we will have an answer to every problem in the world. Every problem that touches us is answered in the Book—stay by the Word! I want to preach the Word, love the Word and make the Word the most important element in my Christian life. Read it much, read it often, brood over it, think over it, meditate over it—meditate on the Word of God day and night. When you are awake at night, think of a helpful verse. When you get up in the morning, no matter how you feel, think of a verse and make the Word of God the important element in your day. The Holy Ghost wrote the Word, and if you make much of the Word, He will make much of you. It is through the Word that He reveals Himself. Between those covers is a living Book. God wrote it and it is still vital and effective and alive. God is in this Book, the Holy Ghost is in this Book, and if you want to find Him, go into this Book. Let the old saints be our example. They came to the Word of God and meditated. They laid the Bible on the old-fashioned, handmade chair, got down on the old, scrubbed, board floor and meditated on the Word. As they waited, faith mounted. The Spirit and faith illuminated. They had only a Bible with fine print, narrow margins and poor paper, but they knew their Bible better than some of us do with all of our helps. Let's practice the art of Bible meditation. But please don't grab that phrase and go out and form a club—we are organized to death already. Just meditate. Let us just be plain, thoughtful Christians. Let us open our Bibles, spread them out on a chair, and meditate on the Word of God. It will open itself to us, and the Spirit of God will come and brood over it. I do challenge you to meditate, quietly, reverently, prayerfully, for a month. Put away questions and answers and the filling in of blank lines in the portions you haven't been able to understand. Put all of the cheap trash away and take the Bible, get on your knees, and in faith, say, "Father, here I am. Begin to teach me!" He will surely teach you about Himself and about Jesus and about the Spirit and about life and death and heaven and hell, and about His own presence.[7]

A.W. Tozer in Tozer Speaks, Volume 1

Enjoy His Presence

Think now about how the Lord has been working in your life. How has He been moving you from the world to the Word and changing the way you think? And how have you seen Him moving you from a temporal view to His eternal perspective? The eternal perspective is "the ability to see all of life from God's point of view, and have what you see affect how you live in the present." How has this eternal perspective and the transformation God has been working in you led you to live out His will, His plan and His purpose in your life? How does what you have learned today help stop the habit we sometimes adopt of telling ourselves untrue stories in our minds that eventually cause constant worry and fear? With these questions in mind, think about all that the Lord is teaching you. "Times of refreshing do come from the presence of the Lord" (Acts 3:19). May He refresh and revive you today as you draw near to Him. Close your time by writing a prayer expressing all that is on your heart.

Rest in His Love

"But we all, with unveiled face, beholding as in a mirror the glory of the Lord, are being transformed into the same image from glory to glory, just as from the Lord, the Spirit" (2 Corinthians 3:18).

Renewed Day By Day

Our inner man is being renewed day by day. 2 Corinthians 4:16
St. Mary Valley, Glacier National Park, Montana, USA
Nikon D7000, ISO 100, f29, 1/15sec, Adobe Photoshop, Nik Silver Efex Pro
myPhotoWalk.com—catherinemartin.smugmug.com

HUMILITY

For through the grace given to me I say to everyone among you not to think more highly of himself than he ought to think; but to think so as to have sound judgment, as God has allotted to each a measure of faith.

ROMANS 12:3

PREPARE YOUR HEART

What does a Christian look like? The short and truly profound answer is that a Christian looks more and more like Christ. In Romans 8:29 we see that we are "predestined to become conformed to the image of His Son [Christ]." We learn in 2 Corinthians 3:18 that "we all, with unveiled face, beholding as in a mirror the glory of the Lord, are being transformed into the same image from glory to glory, just as from the Lord, the Spirit." And what is Christ like? One of the qualities that is spoken of related to Jesus is humility. We see in Philippians 2:8 that "He humbled Himself by becoming obedient to the point of death, even death on a cross." Jesus described Himself as humble when He said, "Learn from me, for I am gentle and humble in heart" (Matthew 11:29).

Andrew Murray, in his little book, *Humility: The Beauty of Holiness*, expressed the importance of humility in the life of Christians. He wrote, "When I look back upon my own Christian experience, or at the church of Christ as a whole, I am amazed at how little humility is seen as the distinguishing feature of discipleship. In our preaching and in our living, in our daily interaction in our families and in our social life, as well as fellowship with other Christians, how easy it is to see that humility is not esteemed the cardinal virtue, the root from which grace can grow and the one indispensable condition of true fellowship with Jesus. The fact that it is possible for anyone to say of those who claim to seek holiness that the profession has not been accompanied with increasing humility, is a loud call to all earnest Christians, whatever truth there be in the charge, to prove that meekness and lowliness of heart are the chief marks by which they who follow the Lamb of God are to be known."

The great F.B. Meyer wrote about the importance of humility in his own life: "I used to think that God's gifts were on shelves one above the other and that the taller we grew in Christian character, the more easily we should reach them. I find now that God's gifts are on shelves one beneath the other and that is not a question of growing taller, but of stooping lower and that we have to go down, always down to get His best ones." Humility in the Greek actually means "not rising far from the ground" and is a lowliness of mind. Spurgeon said that humility is the proper estimate of oneself. And, so it is.

Jesus Himself said that "The greatest among you shall be your servant. Whoever exalts himself shall be humbled; and whoever humbles himself shall be exalted" (Matthew 23:11-12). Jesus was the great example for this strong exhortation when He said, "For even the Son of Man did not come to be served, but to serve, and to give His life a ransom for many" (Mark 10:45).

We are now launching out into the sacred ground of humility, and Paul obviously puts this beautiful characteristic of a Christian at the top of the list when he writes in Romans 12:3, "For through the grace given to me I say to everyone among you not to think more highly of himself than he ought to think; but to think so as to have sound judgment, as God has allotted to each a measure of faith." Leon Morris, in his Romans Commentary, says that the very Greek construction in this verse is making a powerful exhortation to humility.

So today, dear friend, draw near to the Lord and ask Him to prepare your heart to meet with Him today.

READ AND STUDY GOD'S WORD

1. As you begin your time in Romans 12:3, keep in mind that one of the goals of Paul in the letter to the Romans was to see them established and encouraged in the faith (Romans 1:11-12). So these verses in Romans 12 are given with that goal in mind. Read Romans 12:3 and write out what Paul wants for the Romans and for you.

2. Jesus "humbled Himself by becoming obedient to the point of death, even death on a cross" (Philippians 2:8). Read Isaiah 53:4-5, 7 and write out what humility looked like in Jesus Christ, our Lord and Savior. Personalize what you learn.

3. We are encouraged to humility throughout the New Testament. Read the following verses and write out what you learn about humility and humbling yourself before the Lord.

Ephesians 4:1-2

Philippians 2:3

Colossians 3:12

James 1:21

James 4:10

1 Peter 5:5-6

4. What is the most important truth you have learned about humility and in what way do you need to humble yourself before the Lord today?

Adore God in Prayer

Help me to meditate more intently on your humility and patience, O my Savior, so that almost unconsciously these traits may reappear in my own character.

F.B. Meyer in Daily Prayers

Yield Yourself to God

Here is the path to the higher life. It is the lowest path! This was what Jesus said to the disciples who were thinking of being great in the kingdom and of sitting on His right hand and His left. Ask not for exaltation. That is God's work. See that you humble yourselves, and take no place before God or man but that of a servant. That is your work; let that be your one purpose and prayer. God is faithful. Just as water seeks and fills the lowest place, so the moment God finds the creature empty, His glory and power flow in to exalt and to bless. He that humbles himself—that must be our one aim—shall be exalted; that is God's aim. By His mighty power and in His great love He will do it. People sometimes speak of humility and meekness as something that would rob us of what is noble and bold. Oh, that all would realize that this is the nobility of the kingdom of heaven, that this is the royal spirit that the King of heaven displayed, that this is godlike, to humble oneself and to become the servant of all! This is the path to the gladness and the glory of Christ's presence in us, of His power resting upon us. Jesus, the meek and lowly One, calls us to learn of Him the path to God. Let us study the words we have been reading until our heart is filled with the thought: My one need is humility. And let us believe that what He shows He gives, and what He is He imparts. As the meek and lowly One, He will come into and dwell within the longing heart.

Andrew Murray in Humility: The Beauty Of Holiness

Enjoy His Presence

What is the most important truth the Lord has taught you today? Think especially about how humility helps us serve the Lord and live out His plans and purposes for our lives. Close your time today by writing a prayer to the Lord.

REST IN HIS LOVE

"Learn from me, for I am gentle and humble in heart" (Matthew 11:29).

LOOKING TO THE LORD

Look to the LORD and his strength, seek his face always. Psalm 105:4 NIV
Corona Del Mar State Beach, Corona Del Mar, Newport Beach, California, USA
Nikon D810, ISO 1600, f11, 1/5000sec, Adobe Photoshop, Nik Silver Efex Pro
MYPHOTOWALK.COM—CATHERINEMARTIN.SMUGMUG.COM

DAY 4

SERVING

Be devoted to one another in brotherly love; give preference to one another in honor; not lagging behind in diligence, fervent in spirit, serving the Lord.

ROMANS 12:10-11

PREPARE YOUR HEART

How much do you love the church? And by church, we mean not just one church, or a building, but the body of believers. The Apostle Paul loved the church. He expresses this love again and again throughout all his letters. In 2 Corinthians 11, Paul was candid about the many ways he had suffered as a servant of the Lord. But perhaps his greatest burden and focus in ministry was the church. He wrote: "Apart from such external things, there is the daily pressure on me of concern for all the churches" (2 Corinthians 11:28). We know that he longed to visit the church in Rome, and planned on doing so. In Romans 1, Paul spoke of those in the church at Rome as "saints" (Romans 1:7). And now, in Romans 12, he once again focuses on the church, calling it "one body in Christ" (Romans 12:5) and again, the "saints" (Romans 12:13). So our eyes should open wide and our ears should listen carefully, for the Lord has something powerful to say to us.

What does the life of God's righteousness look like and how will it act in the church? Paul is going to show us. And oh, how important this is for us, especially today, as we live in a lost and hurting world. The church is the place where people come to know Christ, know and love God's Word, grow in their relationship with the Lord, use their Holy Spirit-given gifts for God's glory, and minister to one another with Christ's love, care, and concern in the power of the Holy Spirit.

Begin your quiet time by asking the Lord to give you eyes to see and ears to hear all He has for you in His Word today. You might write a short prayer expressing all that is on your heart.

READ AND STUDY GOD'S WORD

1. In Romans 12:4-13, we are going to see what the life of God's righteousness looks like among believers i.e. the church, as we are transformed through the power of the Holy Spirit. Read these exhortations of Paul and write out who we are, what we have been given, and what we are to do.

Who we are (Romans 12:5)

What we have been given (Romans 12:6)

What we are to do (Romans 12:6-13)

2. In these verses, you learned that "we, who are many, are one body in Christ." Read 1 Corinthians 12:4-7, 11-14, 25-26 and write your insights about the body of Christ and spiritual gifts.

3. How important is the church, His Bride, to the Lord Jesus Christ? Read the following verses and write your most significant insights about Christ and the church.

Ephesians 5:23-30

Colossians 1:18

4. As you think about the body of Christ, how has your study helped you see your own significance as a part of the body of Christ? What is the most important truth you have learned today?

ADORE GOD IN PRAYER

Take some time now to thank the Lord for how He loves the church. Pray through all you have learned about the church as the body of Christ and how He has gifted you according to the grace given to you. Then, each day, always ask the Lord how you can serve Him in the strength of the Holy Spirit.

> The church's one foundation is Jesus Christ, her Lord;
> she is His new creation, by water and the word.
> From heav'n He came and sought her to be His holy bride;
> with His own blood He bought her, and for her life He died.
>
> SAMUEL JOHN STONE

Yield Yourself to God

> The Church is an organism rather than an organization, and this figure of the body with its several members is a definite reminder of the place and limits of each individual Christian…We may vary the old phrase and say that in the Church of Christ there is "a place for everyone and everyone in his place," and the more thoroughly we face this two-fold truth the more effectively will the work of the church be done.[8]

W.H. Griffith Thomas in Romans: A Devotional Commentary XII-XVI

> You may say that you are not important. But you are! That part next to you is more important, perhaps, but he cannot go on without you and he is dependent upon you, and he will suffer if you are not in a fit condition to do your part. So all of us are vital, all of us are essential, all of us have a great privilege, and the way to avoid problems and disasters is always to be thinking of the whole body and especially of the Head. Then you will always be looking at Him, keeping your eye on Him, ready, sensitive, responsive, so that when He initiates an action, it is carried out. That is the great New Testament doctrine of the Christian church and her unity and functioning.[9]

D. Martyn Lloyd-Jones in Romans: Christian Conduct, Exposition of Chapter 12

Enjoy His Presence

As you think through all you learned today, especially in Romans 12, what has God put on your heart? Perhaps the Lord has given you an idea for ministry that is larger than anything you could have imagined. How will you live it out in your life? As you live it out, you are "serving the Lord" (Romans 12:11). Paul is such an example of what it means to serve the Lord. In writing to the church in Ephesus, he said, "You yourselves know, from the first day that I set foot in Asia, how I was with you the whole time, serving the Lord with all humility and with tears and with trials which came upon me…But I do not consider my life of any account as dear to myself, so that I may finish my course and the ministry which I received from the Lord Jesus, to testify solemnly of the gospel of the grace of God" (Acts 20:18-19, 24).

Think today especially of Romans 12:9-13: "Let love be without hypocrisy. Abhor what is evil; cling to what is good. Be devoted to one another in brotherly love; give preference to one another in honor; not lagging behind in diligence, fervent in spirit, serving the Lord; rejoicing in hope, persevering in tribulation, devoted to prayer, contributing to the needs of the saints, practicing hospitality." Underline or highlight those areas that are especially on your heart today. Is there someone in your life who needs the love of the Lord, or you need to give honor to today? Who can you pray for or help out? Who does the Lord want to reach out to in your life today? Do you need to encourage someone today with a note or phone call? Are there any ideas the Lord has given you for ministry? Write your thoughts and insights, then close your time in prayer to the Lord.

REST IN HIS LOVE

"Christ also loved the church and gave Himself up for her, so that He might sanctify her, having cleansed her by the washing of water with the word, that He might present to Himself the church in all her glory, having no spot or wrinkle or any such thing; but that she would be holy and blameless" (Ephesians 5:25-27).

A Good Work In You

He who began a good work in you will perfect it until the day of Christ Jesus. Philippians 1:6
Golden Pebble Habitat, Palm Desert, California, USA
Nikon D810, ISO 800, f2.2, 1/400sec, Adobe Photoshop, Nik Silver Efex Pro
MyPhotoWalk.com—CatherineMartin.smugmug.com

INFLUENCE

*Bless those who persecute you; bless and do not curse...Do not
be overcome by evil, but overcome evil with good.*
ROMANS 12:14, 21

PREPARE YOUR HEART

hat happens when a person lives the life of God's righteousness? Lives are influenced by
the Lord Jesus Christ as He lives in and through them. The life of God's righteousness
shining in a person looks magnificently brighter and different than the darkness and desolation
of the world. Jesus said, "Let your light shine before men in such a way that they may see your
good works, and glorify your Father who is in heaven" (Matthew 5:16). So many who have gone
before us have been such bright lights for the Lord. And their lives have created a ripple effect of
influence down through the years.

One of the best examples of a life of influence and the ripple effect is seen in the life of Henrietta
Mears. The story begins with Reverend Stuart MacLennan, pastor of Hollywood Presbyterian
Church more than a hundred years ago. One day he was invited to preach at a small church in
Minneapolis. How could he have possibly known that this one sermon would eventually impact
hundreds of thousands throughout the world? In the audience that day was Henrietta Mears, in
her thirties, a high school principal and an organizer and teacher in Sunday School classes. Mears
was so moved by MacLennan's sermon that she invited him to lunch after church. MacLennon
was so impressed with Mears that he invited her to visit his church sometime. Well, "sometime"
became years. In 1927, Henrietta Mears took a sabbatical and visited Hollywood Presbyterian
in southern California. MacLennan invited her to join the staff as Christian Education Director.
She prayed about the invitation and knew it was God's work and His will for her. She served there
until she went home to be with the Lord in 1963.

What is most profound is the influence of her life. One of her students was Bill Bright, who
ultimately became the co-founder of Campus Crusade for Christ, along with his wife, Vonette
Bright. Mears encouraged a young Billy Graham with the authority of God's Word and pushed
him to lead the 1949 evangelistic crusade in Los Angeles, which launched the Billy Graham

ministry. Another student of hers was Richard Halverson who became the minister of Fourth Presbyterian Church in Bethesda, Maryland, and also was Chaplain of the United States Senate.

When you think of influence, you can't forget the ripple effect. This ripple effect is apparent in the life of Richard Halverson, who impacted so many people over the course of his life. In 1995 he stepped from earth to heaven, and the memorial tributes in his honor stretched to 99 pages of words from hundreds who were influenced by him. One woman remarked, "If you ran around with Dick on Capitol Hill you saw that he knew the name of every policeman, every page, every person who cooked, because people mattered to him. The Gospel was not about what he preached, his talk and his walk were the same." Dr. Billy Graham shared how Richard Halverson impacted him back in the early Forest Home days. He wrote: "They had a campfire, and if you wanted to re-dedicate your life to the Lord, or go into Christian service, you would pick up a little stick of wood and put it on that fire. And I remember somebody had pointed out Dick Halverson to me, and I had met him at that conference, and he was one of the first people to get up and go and put that stick on that fire. And I thought, my goodness, if he needs to do that, I need to put a whole load of wood on the fire because already, his godliness, his prayer life, his study of scripture had affected me."

Oh how the light of Henrietta Mears was shining during her life. And how bright was the light of Christ in Richard Halverson. And now, dear friend, it is your time to shine with the light of Jesus Christ. Do you realize how important you are to the Lord as you live out each day? In fact, a scroll of remembrance is written in God's presence "concerning those who feared the LORD and honored His name" (Malachi 3:16 NIV). As you begin your quiet time today, ask God to feed you with His Word and give you a heart to shine for Him everywhere He leads you each day.

READ AND STUDY GOD'S WORD

1. In Romans 12:14-21, Paul is going to show the influence of the life of God's righteousness in you with everyone around you, whether friends or enemies. Read Romans 12:14-21 and write out your most significant insights about how you live your life as the Lord transforms you through the power of the Holy Spirit. Personalize your discoveries in God's Word.

2. How do the words of Romans 12:14-21 help you when you suffer unjustly at the hands of another? Write out the strong encouragement that is most significant to you related to times if and when someone comes against you.

3. How does Romans 12:15-16 make a difference in the life of someone who is hurting or who needs comfort and encouragement? How has someone encouraged you in this way when you were hurting?

4. In Hebrews 13:7 you are encouraged to "Remember those who led you, who spoke the word of God to you; and considering the result of their conduct, imitate their faith." God has brought important heroes of the faith into your life who have had a great influence in leading you to Christ and teaching you the essentials of the Christian life. Each hero has come to deep commitments and surrenders all along their way and are teachers for all of us. One great example is author and speaker Elisabeth Elliot, who wrote these powerful words in her book, *Discipline: The Glad Surrender*: "When I know myself called, summoned, addressed, taken possession of, known, acted upon, I have heard the Master. I put myself gladly, fully, and forever at His disposal, and to what He says my answer is yes."[10] Someone who can say such powerful words like those will have a profound influence in many lives. And Elisabeth Elliot influenced thousands in her lifetime.

Who has influenced you for Jesus Christ and what was it about them that had the greatest impact?

5. How is the Lord speaking to you today in His Word?

ADORE GOD IN PRAYER

Pray the words of F.B. Meyer today: "Make me a bright Christian, I entreat you, not morbid and austere and silent, not foolish and frivolous, but radiant, glad, and happy."

YIELD YOURSELF TO GOD

You go no place by accident this week; wherever you go, Christ is sending you. You are no place by accident this week; wherever you are, Christ has placed you, has planted you. A little statement from my favorite devotional writer, Oswald Chambers: "Never allow the thought 'I am of no use where I am.' You certainly are of no use where you are not." You go nowhere by accident; you are nowhere by accident. Wherever you go, wherever you are, Christ is placing you or sending you because Christ has a job He wants to do there and He can only do it in your body. Think. Wherever you are, Jesus Christ is literally present in the flesh. Believe that, and go in that confidence.

BENEDICTION OF DR. RICHARD C. HALVERSON

ENJOY HIS PRESENCE

Dear friend, as you think about all you have studied today, do you see how your life makes a difference, whether you are at home, in the grocery store, in line at the bank, sitting in church next to someone who may be discouraged and crushed in spirit, or at a desk in an office? May you take the words of Romans 12 to heart and live them out as the Lord leads you, moment by moment. And may you rest in the hope that someday the Lord Himself will wipe every tear from your eyes (Revelation 21:4). Close your time today by writing a prayer to the Lord, expressing all that is on your heart:

REST IN HIS LOVE

"Let your light shine before men in such a way that they may see your good works, and glorify your Father who is in heaven" (Matthew 5:16).

NO MORE TEARS

He will wipe every tear from their eyes. Revelation 21:4
The Rose Garden, Newport Beach, California, USA
Nikon D810, ISO 400, f5.6, 1/250sec, Adobe Photoshop, Nik Silver Efex Pro
MYPHOTOWALK.COM—CATHERINEMARTIN.SMUGMUG.COM

DEVOTIONAL READING
BY HENRIETTA C. MEARS

DEAR FRIEND,

This week you had the opportunity to study in depth Romans 12 and the Life of God's Righteousness. Look over your quiet times from Week Seven. What was the most profound truth you learned from the Lord?

What were your most meaningful discoveries this week as you spent time with the Lord?

Most meaningful insight:

Most meaningful devotional reading:

Most meaningful verse:

s you think about all that you have learned this week, meditate on these words by Henrietta Mears: "In this appeal, Paul urges us to have our lives measure up to our beliefs. He shows that the doctrine of justification by faith will not allow laxity in life or conduct. We are saved to serve. The Christian life must be lived in its relation to God, self and others. It may surprise you to find out that up to this point [Romans 12] we have not had to do a thing but believe in Christ and yield ourselves to Him to use as He wills. Now we are to serve…Until we have been saved by His grace and transformed by His love, we can do little for God…When we present ourselves to Christ and become filled with His love, we can find a lot to do. Christ wants a "living sacrifice," not a dead one (Romans 12:1). Many will die for Christ. Few will live for Him…Let others see Jesus in you! Live for Him."[11]

HENRIETTA C. MEARS IN WHAT THE BIBLE IS ALL ABOUT

The Power Of A Surrendered Life

In Week Seven of *The Proof of God's Amazing Love*, we studied Romans 12 and looked at the life of God's righteousness. Today we are going to look at the twofold surrender God is asking of us and the amazing results when we say yes to the Lord. So grab your Bible, these notes, and let's dig in to the amazing Word of God and learn about the power of a surrendered life.

"Therefore I urge you, brethren, by the mercies of God, to present your bodies a living and holy sacrifice, acceptable to God, which is your spiritual service of worship. And do not be conformed to this world, but be transformed by the renewing of your mind, so that you may prove what the will of God is, that which is good and acceptable and perfect" (Romans 12:1-2).

Surrender is not passive resignation, but a ____ to God's ways and God's will. There is a resulting ____ with joy along life's journey with Jesus.

What is the twofold surrender?

1. Surrender your ____ to God. Romans 12:1
1 Corinthians 6:19-20

"You are nothing but gloves." Corrie ten Boom

When you surrender yourself to God, giving yourself to Him, then He can have His way with you. You are the glove, and He is the hand in that glove, through the power of the Holy Spirit.

2. Surrender your ____ to God. Romans 12:2

Give your mind to God and live in the Word of God. Study His Word—Observation study, Translation study, Verse study, Word study, Reference study, Character study, Doctrine/Ethics study.

What are the amazing results of this twofold surrender?

1. You will _______________________________the Lord. Romans 12:1, Colossians 3:23-24, Matthew 6:24

2. You will _______________________________the Lord. Romans 12:1, 1 Corinthians 6:19, 2 Corinthians 4:6-7

3. You will be ____. Romans 12:2, Romans 8:29, 2 Corinthians 3:18

4. You will experience God's ____. Romans 12:2

"When I know myself called, summoned, addressed, taken possession of, known, acted upon, I have heard the Master. I put myself gladly, fully, and forever at His disposal, and to what He says my answer is yes." Elisabeth Elliot in *Discipline: The Glad Surrender*

Video messages are available on DVDs or as Digital M4V Video. Audio messages are available as Digital MP3 Audio. Visit the Quiet Time Ministries Online Store at www.quiettime.org.

THE IMPACT OF GOD'S RIGHTEOUSNESS

Romans 13-16

Paul spoke from the white-hot conviction that is born of experience. On the road to Damascus, he had in a single instant all the artificial props of works, race and character knocked out from under him. He caught a full glimpse of the glorified Christ. From then on, he had but one message: faith in the crucified and risen Lord. He would hear nothing else; he spoke nothing else; he lived nothing less…Paul was proud of the gospel because he had proved its power in his own life and in the lives of all who would believe…Romans is Paul's shout of joy to a lost world. The first three chapters describe the hell of sin. The last five chapters describe the heaven of holiness. The intervening chapters describe Christ, the Way.[1]

HENRIETTA C. MEARS

BEHAVIOR IN THE WORLD

*Let us behave properly as in the day…put on the Lord Jesus Christ,
and make no provision for the flesh in regard to its lusts.*
ROMANS 13:13-14

PREPARE YOUR HEART

magine what it would be like if you could sit down with Paul and just hear him share things with you that are on his heart as a result of all he has learned from the Lord about the gospel, God's righteousness, and living by faith. He has been faithful in ministry for many years. Now he is going to wax eloquently about the impact of God's righteousness, not just in the lives of those around you, but also in your own life. When the Lord Jesus lives in you, you are changed, transformed, and you act differently in all kinds of situations. We learn from Jesus that we, as Christians, are in the world, but not of the world (John 17:14-16). And that's what we are going to see in greater detail in Romans 13-16. You will be different even as you live in the world of governments and nations, different with your neighbors, and different in your own life-style. Paul touches on these things. You will live a life of hope and encouragement, and joy and peace as you are conformed to the image of Christ in the power of the Holy Spirit. You are like Christ everywhere and in every way. And then, near the end of Romans, Paul just gets personal with many people in Rome. We see he was all about people. He knew their names and you will see it when we get to Romans 16. And finally, with a pastoral heart, he gives the saints in Rome a gospel benediction. Imagine them holding out their hands to God and receiving this benediction as if Christ was giving it to them Himself.

So today, dear friend, ask God to speak to your heart as you begin this last week of study in *The Proof Of God's Amazing Love.*

READ AND STUDY GOD'S WORD

1. Today we are going to study Romans 13 and in this chapter you are going to see the impact that the Lord makes in your life as you live in the world. Here is what Jesus prayed for His disciples: "But now I come to You; and these things I speak in the world so that they may

have My joy made full in themselves. I have given them Your word; and the world has hated them, because they are not of the world, even as I am not of the world. I do not ask You to take them out of the world, but to keep them from the evil one. They are not of the world, even as I am not of the world. Sanctify them in the truth; Your word is truth. As You sent Me into the world, I also have sent them into the world" (John 17:13-18). Do you see that we are in the world, but not of it? Read through Romans 13:1-14 in one sitting and write one word descriptions of the kind of behavior we have and the characteristics that will be true of our lives because Christ now lives in us.

2. The first section of Romans 13:1-7 speaks of our behavior as citizens in subjection to governing authorities. And Paul makes a big deal about the authority of God. This is important for us. As you read this section of Scripture, it's important to note what is said and what is not said. W.H. Griffith Thomas in his commentary on Romans points out that Paul is not talking here about persecution or failure of duty by the government or state. Read Romans 13:1-7 and write out what you learn about authority and what behavior on our part honors God.

3. Read 1 Peter 2:13-17 and write out what you learn about submission and how it can impact the world around you. Keep in mind such things as how your obedience can glorify Christ at a place of employment, with your parents, and with government.

4. Read Romans 13:8-10 and write out what you learn about the importance of love and how it is to express itself in our lives as we live in the world but not of the world.

5. In Romans 13:11-14 we learn that "The night is almost gone, and the day is near." What does the Lord want us to do according to those verses?

6. As you think about all these exhortations (strong encouragements) related to living in the world i.e. submission, love, proper behavior, look again at Romans 13:14 — "Rather, clothe yourselves with the Lord Jesus Christ, and do not think about how to gratify the desires of the sinful nature" (NIV). The Greek word for "clothe" means to put on as a garment. The *New American Standard Bible* uses the phrase "put on." It is figurative language meaning identification with Jesus Christ. Remember, you are the Bride of Jesus Christ, and in Revelation 19:7-8 we see that there will be a time when "the marriage of the Lamb has come and His bride has made herself ready. It was given to her to clothe herself in fine linen, bright and clean; for the fine linen is the righteous acts of the saints."

Read the following verses and write what clothing yourself with the Lord Jesus Christ looks like, keeping in mind that someday you will see your Bridegroom face-to-face, and you will be His Bride who has made herself ready.

Isaiah 61:10

Ephesians 4:24

Colossians 3:10-17

ADORE GOD IN PRAYER

Pray the words of this hymn today as you talk with the Lord:

Have thine own way, Lord! Have thine own way!
Thou art the potter, I am the clay.
Mold me and make me after thy will,
while I am waiting, yielded and still.

Have thine own way, Lord! Have thine own way!
Search me and try me, Savior today!
Wash me just now, Lord, wash me just now,
as in thy presence humbly I bow.

Have thine own way, Lord! Have thine own way!
Wounded and weary, help me I pray!
Power, all power, surely is thine!
Touch me and heal me, Savior divine!

Have thine own way, Lord! Have thine own way!
Hold o'er my being absolute sway.
Fill with thy Spirit till all shall see
Christ only, always, living in me!

ADELAIDE A. POLLARD, 1906

YIELD YOURSELF TO GOD

Paul's summary statement encourages Christians to live respectfully and honorably in the eyes of the government, fulfilling all requirements and meeting all obligations. Note that our debt to government includes more than mere taxes and tolls (money); we also owe respect, which Paul describes as "fear" and "honor." The apostle is simply applying an earlier principle to our relationship with government: "So far as it depends on you, be at peace with all men" (12:18). As we fulfill all the requirements of good citizenship, we cast Jesus Christ in a positive light and, perhaps, create opportunities to share the good news with greater freedom.[2]

Charles R. Swindoll in Insights On Romans

Remember that Paul is writing to people who were living under a government that ultimately beheaded him. Paul was executed by a tyrannical Roman government. The Christians to whom Paul is writing paid with their lives in the Circus Maximus in Rome, when they were used as fodder for the gladiators and the lions. Though Rome had a marvelous legal system, its rulers imposed ruthless policies upon their own people…Paul is saying something very profound. First of all, behind this statement is the absolute conviction of Scripture that God is the Lord of history. In the providence of God there is no government that can ever come to power except through God's ordination. Now we have to make a very crucial distinction here. When Paul says that the powers that be are ordained of God, he does not necessarily mean that the powers that be are approved of by God. [3]

R.C. Sproul in The Gospel of God: An Exposition of Romans

When I get up in the morning I put on my clothes, intending them to be part of me all day, to go where I go and do what I do. They cover me and make me presentable to others. That is the purpose of clothes. In the same way, the apostle is saying to us, "Put on Jesus Christ when you get up in the morning. Make Him a part of your life that day. Intend that He go with you everywhere you go, and that He act through you in everything you do. Call upon His resources. Live your life in Christ."

Ray Stedman

Enjoy His Presence

As you think about all you've studied today, what is the most important truth you have learned today? What is God teaching you from Romans 13? Write your insights, then close by writing a prayer to the Lord expressing all that is on your heart today.

REST IN HIS LOVE

"Live as free men, but do not use your freedom as a cover-up for evil; live as servants of God. Show proper respect to everyone: Love the brotherhood of believers, fear God, honor the king" (1 Peter 2:16-17 NIV).

GOING UP TO GOD

He enables me to tread on the heights. Habakkuk 3:19 NIV
Dixie National Forest, Bryce Canyon National Park, Bryce Canyon, Utah, USA
Nikon D7000, ISO 125, f11, 1/8sec, Adobe Photoshop, Nik Silver Efex Pro
MYPHOTOWALK.COM—CATHERINEMARTIN.SMUGMUG.COM

LOVE IN RELATIONSHIPS

*If we live, we live for the Lord…if because of food, your brother
is hurt, you are no longer walking according to love.*

ROMANS 14:8,15

PREPARE YOUR HEART

What does being clothed in Christ look like in real life, especially in relationships with others around us? That is the great truth and challenge we just read in Romans 13:14. Paul is now going to help us understand what it means to walk in love, day by day. God's love changes everything including you and those around you. No wonder Paul encouraged the church at Ephesus (and us) to "walk in love, just as Christ also loved you and gave Himself up for us, an offering and a sacrifice to God as a fragrant aroma" (Ephesians 5:2). Once you come to know Christ, your life is going to make a great impact on those around you. This is the message he wanted the church in Rome to understand and He wants us to see this truth as well.

Today, draw near to the Lord and ask Him to open your eyes to the truth of His Word and then use it to transform you into His servant as you live life here on earth until that day when you step into heaven.

READ AND STUDY GOD'S WORD

1. Romans 14 is all about love in relationships, both your relationship with Christ and your relationship with others. Read Romans 14:1-9 and notice how Paul describes differences between one person and another. Then, how are we all to live?

2. Now read Romans 14:10-23. What are the ways we can show love to another and make peace? What is Paul encouraging us to do? What are the most important exhortations (strong encouragements) that you see in this passage?

3. In Romans 14:12 Paul says, "So then each one of us will give an account of himself to God." Since Paul includes himself and is writing to the believers in Rome, the believer's eternal destiny is not at issue here as faith has already been placed in Christ and "there is therefore now no condemnation to those who are in Christ Jesus" (Romans 8:1). Our lives of service lived in Christ will be seen (1 Corinthians 3:12-15) and rewards will be given for what remains and endures (1 Corinthians 4:4-5). How does knowing this encourage you to live your life "for the Lord" (Romans 14:8) especially in loving others?

4. In Romans 14 we see a life of sacrifice, selflessness, humility, and love. Jesus shows us how to live this way. Read Philippians 2:1-5 and write what is most significant to you about how to live in relationship with others.

5. How does Romans 14 impact you today? What is the Lord teaching you to apply in your own life and in your relationships with others?

ADORE GOD IN PRAYER

Pray through the words of F.B. Meyer: "My one desire and prayer is that I may be filled with your love. I am bankrupt of love; I have not love enough of my own to love my neighbor as myself. Shed abroad your love in my heart through your Holy Spirit."

YIELD YOURSELF TO GOD

The Christian is always governed by his relationship to the Lord… Every other person, all non-Christians, are living to please themselves, and they live according to their own ideas and theories. But the first thing that is true of Christians is that they cease to do that; they now live to the Lord.[4]

D. MARTYN LLOYD-JONES IN ROMANS: EXPOSITION OF
CHAPTER 14:1-17, LIBERTY AND CONSCIENCE

ENJOY HIS PRESENCE

How has God spoken to you in His Word today, especially in what it means to be governed in everything by your relationship to the Lord. Close your time alone with the Lord by writing a prayer, expressing all that is on your heart.

REST IN HIS LOVE

"Make my joy complete by being of the same mind, maintaining the same love, united in spirit, intent on one purpose. Do nothing from selfishness or empty conceit, but with humility of mind regard one another as more important than yourselves; do not merely look out for your own personal interests, but also for the interests of others" (Philippians 1:2-4).

A GREATER PLAN

Trust in the Lord and do good. Psalm 37:3
Colorado River, Lake Havasu City, Arizona, USA
Nikon D7000, ISO 100, f11, AEB, Adobe Photoshop, Nik Silver Efex Pro
MYPHOTOWALK.COM—CATHERINEMARTIN.SMUGMUG.COM

ABOUNDING HOPE FOR LIFE

Now may the God of hope fill you with all joy and peace in believing, so that you will abound in hope by the power of the Holy Spirit.

ROMANS 15:13

PREPARE YOUR HEART

Have you ever experienced a meaningful time with a friend, and suddenly you sensed that the friend was wrapping things up and preparing to leave? We have been living in this journey in Paul's magnum opus, his very important treatise on the gospel of Christ, and truths that change one's life forever. And now, Paul is going to talk about a most encouraging theme as he nears the close of Romans—hope. We now sense that he is focusing in on something important as he is wrapping up the practical points he is making about faith, righteousness, and the gospel. He says in Romans 15:4 that "whatever was written in earlier times was written for our instruction, so that through perseverance and the encouragement of the Scriptures we might have hope." And then, he closes this section with a prayer of benediction in Romans 15:13. "Now may the God of hope fill you with all joy and peace in believing, so that you will abound in hope by the power of the Holy Spirit." Once again, we see the gospel's power in us and another essential of the Christian life.

How fitting that Paul takes those in the church at Rome (and us) to that prominent distinguishing characteristic for the just people who live by faith. They have hope. In fact, sometimes those around us may wonder how we can possibly keep going or have a smile with such adversity in our lives. What Paul shares in Romans 15:13 is that we "abound in hope by the power of the Holy Spirit." The indwelling Holy Spirit does in us what we can never do for ourselves. He gives us hope.

Hope is the crowning glory for every child of God. It is why a suffering Christian shines as a light in the world. The Greek word for "hope" is *elpis* and means a confident expectation. You might even remember what it means with the acronym HOPE—*Holding On with Patient Expectation*.

Today as we study hope, draw near to the Lord and ask Him to speak to you in His Word. May you have eyes to see and ears to hear all that He has to say to you today. Pray the prayer of the psalmist today: "Open my eyes to see the wonderful truths in your instructions" (Psalm 119:18 NLT). Write a one sentence prayer to the Lord expressing what is on your heart today.

READ AND STUDY GOD'S WORD

1. Today as you think about hope, how do you need hope and how do you think it makes a difference in your own life?

2. Read Romans 15:1-13 and write out those things that seem to be on Paul's mind and his heart in this section.

3. Paul makes a point to talk about bearing with others and not just pleasing ourselves, perseverance, encouragement from the Scriptures, our hope and its impact on relationships, the Gentiles having hope and glorifying God, and our abounding in hope by the power of the Holy Spirit. That's just a quick summary. Let's think about the power of hope in our lives. After reading Romans 15:1-13, what do you learn about hope's impact in our lives and in the lives of those around us?

4. Read Romans 15:4 and 15:13. How can we have hope?

4. Read the following verses and write out all that you learn about hope.

1 Timothy 1:1

Hebrews 6:17-19

Hebrews 10:23

1 Peter 1:3

1 Peter 3:15

5. The Lord gives us hope in the present and also hope for the future. In this hope, we see truths about "now" and also, the "not yet." Paul, in his letter to Titus instructs us how to live during our time on earth, and then speaks of a great hope in the future for all of us. He writes: "For the grace of God has appeared, bringing salvation to all men, instructing us to deny ungodliness and worldly desires and to live sensibly, righteously and godly in the present age, looking for the blessed hope and the appearing of the glory of our great God and Savior, Christ Jesus, who gave Himself for us to redeem us from every lawless deed, and to purify for Himself a people for His own possession, zealous for good deeds" (Titus 2:11-14). This blessed hope is a description of the rapture of the Church according to many commentators, and is cause for great hope. Regardless of the timing of this event, we can look forward to the day when the Lord appears, and we shall see our Lord Jesus face to face, and be with Him forever.

Now you are a pilgrim on earth, a servant of the Lord, and as the Bride making herself ready for her Bridegroom, you are on your way home where you will live with the Lord forever. Here we see hope in the now and the not yet in life. Someday we shall step into heaven and our faith will become sight. "For now we see in a mirror dimly, but then face to face; now I know in part, but then I will know fully just as I also have been fully known" (1 Corinthians 13:12). John tells us "Beloved, now we are children of God, and it has not appeared as yet what we will be. We know that when He appears, we will be like Him, because we will see Him just as He is" (1 John 3:2). Describe in one word how knowing you have such a future gives you hope today.

6. Notice in Romans 15:4 that it is the encouragement of the Scriptures that gives you hope. Think about all the Bible verses you know. What verse in the Bible encourages you the most and gives you hope today? (Here are some favorite verses for encouragement today: Psalm 34:18, Psalm 84:11, Isaiah 41:10, Jeremiah 29:11, John 3:16, Philippians 4:13, 4:19, 1 Peter 5:10, 1 John 5:4).

ADORE GOD IN PRAYER

Take some time now to talk with God about your own need for hope. Take seriously the words of Peter in 1 Peter 5:7. "Give all your worries and cares to God, for he cares about you" (NLT). Pray through the promises of God that are on your heart today and ask the Lord, through the power of the Holy Spirit, to help you "Hold On with Patient Expectation" (HOPE).

YIELD YOURSELF TO GOD

Hope is the ability to listen to the music of the future. Faith is the courage to dance to it in the present.

DR. PETER KUZMIC

Have we not known men whose lives have not given out any entrancing music in the day of a calm prosperity, but who, when the tempest drove against them, have astonished their fellows by the power and strength of their music?[5]

JOHN HENRY JOWETT IN THE SILVER LINING

"Hope thou in God." Oh, remember this: There is never a time when we may not hope in God. Whatever our necessities, however great our difficulties, and though to all appearance help is impossible, yet our business is to hope in God, and it will be found that it is not in vain. In the Lord's own time help will come. Oh, the hundreds, yea, the thousands of times that I have found it thus within the past seventy years and four months! When it seemed impossible that help could come, help did come; for God has His own resources. He is not confined. In ten thousand different ways, and at ten thousand different times God may help us. Our business is to spread our cases before the Lord, in childlike simplicity to pour out all our heart before God, saying, "I do not deserve that Thou shouldst hear me and answer my requests, but for the sake of my precious Lord Jesus; for His sake answer my prayer, and give me grace quietly to wait till it please Thee to answer my prayer. For I believe Thou wilt do it in Thine own time and way." "For I shall yet praise him." More prayer, more exercise of faith, more patient waiting, and the result will be blessing, abundant blessing. Thus I have found it many hundreds of times, and therefore I continually say to myself, "Hope thou in God."

George Mueller in Streams in the Desert

Enjoy His Presence

Oh dear friend, today is the day to think about your hope. Are you abounding in that confident expectation that Paul talks about in the verses we have studied today? Have you held on to the promises of God with a patient expectation? Will you run to the God of hope and ask Him to fill you with joy and peace so that you may abound in hope by the power of the Holy Spirit? Take comfort in this wonderful promise from the Lord. "For I know the plans that I have for you,' declares the LORD, 'plans for welfare and not for calamity to give you a future and a hope'" (Jeremiah 29:11). You can know that no matter what you are facing today "after you have suffered a little while, the God of all grace, who called you to His eternal glory in Christ, will Himself perfect, confirm, strengthen, and establish you" (1 Peter 5:10). Close by writing a prayer to the Lord expressing all that is on your heart today.

REST IN HIS LOVE

"Let us hold fast the confession of our hope without wavering, for He who promised is faithful" (Hebrews 10:23).

THE GIFT OF GRACE

The God of all grace…will Himself perfect, confirm, strengthen, and establish you. 1 Peter 5:10
Hawaii Tropical Botanical Gardens, Papaikou, Island Of Hawaii, Hawaii, USA
Nikon D7000, ISO 160, f16, 1/600sec, Adobe Photoshop, Nik Silver Efex Pro
MYPHOTOWALK.COM—CATHERINEMARTIN.SMUGMUG.COM

GETTING PERSONAL WITH THE CHURCH

I am fully convinced, my dear brothers and sisters, that you are full of goodness. You know these things so well you can teach each other all about them. Even so, I have been bold enough to write about some of these points, knowing all you need is this reminder…after all these long years of waiting, I am eager to visit you."

ROMANS 15:14-15,23 NLT

PREPARE YOUR HEART

o you remember as a child learning this little rhyme about the church? "Here is the church. Here is the steeple. Open the doors and see all the people." It wasn't only words. There were also hand gestures to illustrate what we were saying. You locked your fingers together and closed your hands. When you opened up your hands, all your fingers represented the people in the church.

We learn from the Bible that the church is not about buildings, but people. We are the church. In fact, Paul states it so very well in Ephesians 5:25-27—"Christ also loved the church and gave Himself up for her, so that He might sanctify her, having cleansed her by the washing of water with the word, that He might present to Himself the church in all her glory, having no spot or wrinkle or any such thing; but that she would be holy and blameless." Paul loved the church. In fact, he expresses how significant the church was to him when he wrote, "There is the daily pressure on me of concern for all the churches" (2 Corinthians 11:28).

As Paul closes out this wonderful letter to the Romans, he is now going to get personal with things that come from his heart. And then, he gets personal by naming certain people in the church and why they are important to him. And finally, he shares some warnings before giving a beautiful benediction that we will look at tomorrow, in the last full day of this study.

Just think, we have the opportunity to learn from Paul what was on his heart to say personally to those in the church after writing such an incredible letter concerning the gospel of Christ.

So now, dear friend, once again, as you draw near to the Lord, ask Him to speak to you in His Word, and help you grow more intimate in your relationship with Him, your Lord and Savior Jesus Christ.

READ AND STUDY GOD'S WORD

1. What was on the heart of Paul for the churches, and especially for the church in Rome near the end of his letter? This is so valuable for us to learn, because it is our chance to be discipled by the one and only Paul, the Apostle. We can learn from him how to encourage others in the church. Just imagine that you are walking side by side with him in ministry. Read Romans 15:14-33 and write in words and short phrases your most significant insights about what was most on the heart of Paul for those in the church as he gets deep and personal with them.

2. Near the end of Romans, Paul gives some warnings to the church. Read Romans 16:17-20 and write out your most significant insight about his warnings to the church.

3. Finally, in getting personal with the church, Paul actually mentions names. This helps us see that Paul wasn't obscure and far-removed from people. No. He knew them intimately and served with them as co-laborers for the gospel of Christ. Imagine what it would have meant to you to have Paul mention your name and what you mean to him! Read Romans 16:1-16 and note all the people he greeted and the reasons he mentions related to why they were important and what they meant to him. (Note: if you have time, you might find a good Bible dictionary, Study Bible, or an online Bible study reference to look up these different people who received greetings from Paul.)

Phoebe, verses 1-2

Prisca and Aquila, verses 3-4

Epaenetus, verse 5

Mary, verse 6

Andronicus and Junias, verse 7

Ampliatus, verse 8; Urbanus, verse 9; Stachys, verse 9

Apelles and the household of Aristobulus, verse 10

Herodian and the household of Narcissus, verse 11

Tryphaena and Tryphosa, Persis, verse 12

Rufus, verse 13

Romans 16:14-16

Romans 16:21-23 those with Paul who greet the church, including Timothy, Lucius, Jason, Sosipater, and Tertius, Paul's secretary

4. After reading all of these closing greetings and personal words, what stands our to you and impresses you the most about Paul? And what is significant to you about those in the church?

ADORE GOD IN PRAYER

Talk with God about everything you have learned from Him today in His Word.

YIELD YOURSELF TO GOD

The more we ponder the Apostle's words the more deeply we are impressed with the reality of his service extending over so many years. There was a deep hunger for the souls of men that prompted him to preach fully the Gospel of Christ in such a remarkable way and to such a wide extent. He eagerly longed for everyone to know that which was everything to him…we do well to pray that God will constantly put and keep this earnest desire and definite aim in the hearts of His people. It must be an exquisite joy to tell someone of Christ who has never before heard of him: to be the first to narrate "the Sweet Story of Old" to some heart which without knowing it may have been longing for the satisfaction that Christ alone can give.[6]

W.H. GRIFFITH THOMAS IN ROMANS: A DEVOTIONAL COMMENTARY XII-XVI

ENJOY HIS PRESENCE

In the Introduction to this study of Romans in *The Proof of God's Amazing Love,* we were encouraged with these words of W.H. Griffith Thomas: "It is the heart that must penetrate most deeply into the secrets of this doctrinal, theological, and yet always personal Epistle. The Apostle's own spiritual experience is the main key to his meaning, and those who enter into similar experiences of the profound truths here recorded will possess the best clue to the interpretation."[7] We have indeed penetrated deeply into the secrets of the letter to the Romans. And we have truly seen the heart of Paul throughout Romans; in the words he uses, the themes he emphasizes, and here at the end in his exhortations and greetings. Paul was faithful to carry out all that the Lord entrusted to him, and according to tradition, Paul was martyred for his faith by the emperor Nero in approximately AD 62-64.

As you think about all you have seen in the heart of Paul, if you could write a thank you letter to him, what would you say? Take some time now to write out what you would say. This will help you in thinking about what you have learned from Paul about the Lord, the Gospel, and about ministry.

REST IN HIS LOVE

"I know that when I come to you, I will come in the fullness of the blessing of Christ" (Romans 15:29).

ALWAYS HOPE

I have hope in Him. Lamentations 3:24
Oak Creek Canyon, Sedona, Arizona, USA
Nikon D800E, ISO 1000, f11, 1/25sec, Adobe Photoshop, Nik Silver Efex Pro
MYPHOTOWALK.COM—CATHERINEMARTIN.SMUGMUG.COM

BENEDICTION OF THE GOSPEL

Now to Him...to the only wise God, through Jesus Christ, be the glory forever. Amen.
ROMANS 16:25,27

PREPARE YOUR HEART

hroughout the history of the church, the benediction comes at the end of a church service. It is a gospel blessing. Derek Thomas, a minister and professor, writes that a benediction says to the people of God: "You have worshiped. You're going out for the rest of the week to work and labor. Go in peace. Go with the blessing and the assurance of God's covenant promises upon you that He will never leave you nor forsake you, that you are Christ's, and that you will be Christ's forever. You may experience trials and difficulties this week, but you are covenant children underneath the umbrella of the covenant blessings. You are not under the covenant curses. Remind yourself that you're under the sunlight of the gospel this coming week."[8] He concludes by saying that the benediction is "a glorious moment."

We have indeed felt "the sunlight of the gospel" in Romans, haven't we! It is fitting that Paul would conclude his epistle to the Romans all about the gospel of Christ with a beautiful benediction that would encourage, bless and lead this Roman church (and us) to a glorious moment of worship and praise.

So today, dear friend, on your last full day of quiet times in Romans, there is a bittersweet feeling as we leave the place where we have truly seen the proof of God's amazing love. Just think about all you have learned about the good news of the Gospel, that it was "while we were yet sinners Christ died for us" (Romans 5:8). We are going to spend this day of quiet time living in the benediction of Paul. So hold out your hands, dear friend, and receive this benediction of Romans 16:25-27 from the Lord today.

Draw near now to your Lord and ask Him to reveal Himself to you anew and revive and refresh your heart as you spend quiet time with Him today.

READ AND STUDY GOD'S WORD

1. Read the benediction of Paul in Romans 16:25-27. What is your favorite phrase in these words from Paul?

2. Read Romans 16:25-27 in the following paraphrases and translations and underline your favorite words and phrases.

> Now to Him who is able to establish you according to my gospel and the preaching of Jesus Christ, according to the revelation of the mystery which has been kept secret for long ages past, but now is manifested, and by the Scriptures of the prophets, according to the commandment of the eternal God, has been made known to all the nations, leading to obedience of faith; to the only wise God, through Jesus Christ, be the glory forever. Amen. NASB

> Now all glory to God, who is able to make you strong, just as my Good News says. This message about Jesus Christ has revealed his plan for you Gentiles, a plan kept secret from the beginning of time. But now as the prophets foretold and as the eternal God has commanded, this message is made known to all Gentiles everywhere, so that they too might believe and obey him. All glory to the only wise God, through Jesus Christ, forever. Amen. NLT

> Now to him who is able to establish you by my gospel and the proclamation of Jesus Christ, according to the revelation of the mystery hidden for long ages past, but now revealed and made known through the prophetic writings by the command of the eternal God, so that all nations might believe and obey him—to the only wise God be glory forever through Jesus Christ! Amen. NIV

> Now to Him Who is able to strengthen you in the faith which is in accordance with my Gospel and the preaching of (concerning) Jesus Christ (the Messiah), according to the revelation (the unveiling) of the mystery of the plan of redemption which was kept in silence and secret for long ages, but is now disclosed and through the prophetic Scriptures is made known to all nations, according to the command of the eternal God, [to win them] to obedience to the faith, To [the] only wise God be glory forevermore through Jesus Christ (the Anointed One)! Amen (so be it). AMP

> All of our praise rises to the One who is strong enough to make you strong, exactly as preached in Jesus Christ, precisely as revealed in the mystery kept secret for so long but now an open book through the prophetic Scriptures. All the nations of

the world can now know the truth and be brought into obedient belief, carrying out the orders of God, who got all this started, down to the very last letter. All our praise is focused through Jesus on this incomparably wise God! Yes! MSG

3. Why do you think these words are such an encouragement after all you have learned and read about the gospel in Romans?

4. Some stand-out words in this beautiful benediction are "eternal" and "forever" and they are related to your God who establishes you in your faith, gives you forgiveness of sins and eternal life through the Lord Jesus Christ who is your Savior and Lord. Think about these words from Revelation 22:3-5 revealing your future life with your Lord: "There will no longer be any curse; and the throne of God and of the Lamb will be in it, and His bond-servants will serve Him; they will see His face, and His name will be on their foreheads. And there will no longer be any night; and they will not have need of the light of a lamp nor the light of the sun, because the Lord God will illumine them; and they will reign forever and ever." Why does the promise of forever bring hope to you today?

5. Leaf through the weeks of quiet times in *The Proof of God's Amazing Love*. What is one of the most important insights you have learned? What is one truth the Lord taught you in your study of Romans that you will carry with you as you continue on in the great adventure of knowing God?

6. One more question. How have you seen the proof of God's amazing love in all you have learned in Romans?

7. Go back to the Introduction and read your Letter to the Lord. How has the Lord answered your prayer?

ADORE GOD IN PRAYER

Pray the words of F.B. Meyer today: "Gracious Father, I thank you for the Son of your love, for all that he has done for us, and will do; for all that he has been to us, and will be. I thank you that he holds me in his strong, pierced hand, loving me with the love that cannot let me go."[9]

YIELD YOURSELF TO GOD

At length, the end of the Epistle is near. St. Paul has now done his utmost by letter, but as he closes he remembers that God alone can establish the Roman Christians in the faith. And so, as Godet remarks, we have in these verses "the look upwards"…" "To God be glory through Jesus Christ for ever." This is the culminating point of the Christian life. The close of the Epistle suggests the course of Christian experience. God is to be glorified by our daily living, and if only we manifest that steadfastness which the Apostle desires, there can be no doubt that it will glorify God as perhaps nothing else can do. Men are impressed by strength, and when they realize that "our help cometh from the Lord" They too will be led to enter into personal relations with Him through the everlasting Gospel. Day by Day, hour by hour, and even moment by moment, may we never forget the supreme purpose of everything in life: "that God may be all in all."[10]

W.H. GRIFFITH THOMAS IN ROMANS: A DEVOTIONAL COMMENTARY XII-XVI

ENJOY HIS PRESENCE

And now, dear friend, what is your story? How has the Lord spoken to you as you have spent quiet times alone with Him in the letter to the Romans in *The Proof of God's Amazing Love*? Think about all those great Christians whose lives were changed forever by the book of Romans—people like Martin Luther, Charles Spurgeon, Augustine, and others. You have had the opportunity to live in the words of Romans and also to know Paul the Apostle better. Paul was overwhelmed with the love of Christ and wanted to know Him more and more each day. He wrote: "Yes, furthermore, I count everything as loss compared to the possession of the priceless privilege (the overwhelming preciousness, the surpassing worth, and supreme advantage) of knowing Christ Jesus my Lord and of progressively becoming more deeply and intimately acquainted with Him [of perceiving and recognizing and understanding Him more fully and clearly]" (Philippians 3:8 AMP).

As you close your quiet time today at the end of this study, read and meditate once again on those words written by Charles Wesley in the hymn, "And Can It Be" on page 10. Write a prayer to the Lord expressing all that is on your heart today including your great love for Him. Finally, hold your hands out and receive this benediction from Paul and celebrate your Lord who loves you with His amazing love.

> Now to Him who is able to establish you according to my gospel and the preaching of Jesus Christ, according to the revelation of the mystery which has been kept secret for long ages past, but now is manifested, and by the Scriptures of the prophets, according to the commandment of the eternal God, has been made known to all the nations, leading to obedience of faith; to the only wise God, through Jesus Christ, be the glory forever. Amen. Romans 16:25-27

REST IN HIS LOVE

"Now to him who is able to establish you by my gospel and the proclamation of Jesus Christ" (Romans 16:25).

SET FREE

The Spirit of life in Christ Jesus has set you free. Romans 8:2
Corona Del Mar State Beach, Corona Del Mar, Newport Beach, California, USA
Nikon D810, ISO 100, f5.6, 1/400sec, Adobe Photoshop, Nik Silver Efex Pro
MYPHOTOWALK.COM—CATHERINEMARTIN.SMUGMUG.COM

DEVOTIONAL READING
BY JOHN OXENHAM

DEAR FRIEND,

In your quiet times this week you impact of God's righteousness. What were your most meaningful discoveries this week as you spent time with the Lord?

Most meaningful insight:

Most meaningful devotional reading:

Most meaningful verse:

Look back through the weeks of study and write your thoughts on the following questions. How did *The Proof of God's Amazing Love* help you the most in your relationship with Christ?

What helped you experience God's amazing love the most as you studied *Romans*?

What was your favorite week of study in *The Proof Of God's Amazing Love* and why?

What was the most important truth you learned in *The Proof of God's Amazing Love*?

What will you take with you and always remember from this study?

As you come to the end of this study in the letter to the Romans, it is important to say that we have only "touched the merest fringe of it; the study is for a lifetime," as W.H. Griffith Thomas points out in his commentary. You can go back to Romans again and again to be refreshed, encouraged, revived, and established in the faith.

Always remember that you are never alone. The Lord Jesus Christ is with you and promises to "never leave you nor forsake you" (Hebrews 13:5 ESV). S.D. Gordon puts it this way: "Jesus never sends a man ahead alone. He blazes a clear way through every thicket and woods, and then softly calls, 'Follow me. Let's go on together, you and I.' He has been everywhere that we are called to go. His feet have trodden down smooth a path through every experience that comes to us. He knows each road, and knows it well: the valley road of disappointment with its dark shadows; the steep path of temptation down through the rocky ravines and slippery gullies; the narrow path of pain, with the brambly thornbushes so close on each side, with their slash and sting; the dizzy road along the heights of victory; the old beaten road of commonplace daily routine. Everyday paths He has trodden and glorified, and will walk anew with each of us. The only safe way to travel is with Him alongside and in control."

Mrs. Charles Cowman shares the story about an explorer in great peril. She wrote: "After a long trying march over perilous Antarctic mountains and glaciers a South Pole explorer said to his leader, 'I had a curious feeling on the march that there was another Person with us!'" She continues with these words of encouragement: "Another Person! He is ever there to march side by side with those who trust Him! Take His Hand and Walk with Him!" Close your time with the Lord by meditating on these words about you and Jesus by John Oxenham entitled "Roadmates."

> Come, share the road with Me, My own,
> Through good and evil weather;
> Two better speed than one alone,
> So let us go together.
>
> Come, share the road with Me, My own,
> You know I'll never fail you,
> And doubts and fears of the unknown
> Shall never more assail you.

Come, share the road with Me, My own,
I'll share your joys and sorrows.
And hand in hand we'll seek the throne
And God's great glad tomorrows.

Come, share the road with Me, My own,
And where the black clouds gather,
I'll share thy load with thee, My son,
And we'll press on together.

And as we go we'll share also
With all who travel on it.
For all who share the road with Me
Must share with all upon it.

So make we—all one company,
Love's golden cord our tether,
And, come what may, we'll climb the way
Together—aye, together!

❧ **WEEK EIGHT** ❧

Getting Dressed For Eternity

It's hard to believe that we have completed our last week of study in *The Proof of God's Amazing Love*. What an adventure we have had together in Romans! Today I want to look at Romans 13-16 and the eternal perspective of our lives here on earth. Paul takes the Roman church and us all the way to forever. Grab your Bibles and these notes as we look at the impact of God's righteousness in our lives.

"Clothe yourselves with the Lord Jesus Christ, do not think about how to gratify the desires of the sinful nature" (Romans 13:14 NIV).

Who You Are

1. You are the _______________________ of Jesus Christ. Romans 5:8, Ephesians 5:22-33, Revelation 19:7, 21:2

2. You are a citizen of _______________________. Romans 14:17, Philippians 3:20-21, Colossians 1:13

Where You Are Going

1. You are on your way _______________________. Romans 13:11-12, 2 Corinthians 5:8, Revelation 21-22

2. There will be a _______________ heaven and _______________ earth. Revelation 21:1

3. Heaven will be a place of _______________________. Romans 14:17, Luke 23:43

How To Live in the Now and Not Yet

1. Think about _______________________. Colossians 3:2

2. ____the heavenly country. Hebrews 11:16

How Shall We Dress For Eternity?

1. When you are clothed with Jesus Christ, you are clothed with _______________________
and righteousness. Isaiah 61:10

2. When you are clothed with Jesus Christ, His character _______________________________ in
us and becomes our clothing. Colossians 3:10-17

3. The Bride is clothed in fine linen—the righteous _________________________________ of the
saints. Revelation 19:7-8, Ephesians 2:10

4. Your veil is the amazing _________________________________of Jesus Christ. Romans 5:8,
Song of Solomon 2:3-4

What do you have to look forward to as you are getting dressed for eternity?

1. Seeing your Lord's ____. Revelation 22:3-4

2. There will be no more crying, mourning, death or _________________. Revelation 21:4

3. You will see and experience the _______________________________of God. Romans 5:2,
Revelation 21:9-11, 23

4. All things are _______________________and the old has passed away. Revelation 21:5

5. You will experience eternal bliss and _______________ forever living with your Lord.
Revelation 21:3

6. You will _________________forever and ever with your Bridegroom. Revelation 22:5

NOW THAT YOU HAVE COMPLETED THESE QUIET TIMES

You have spent eight weeks consistently drawing near to God in quiet time with Him. That time alone with Him does not need to come to an end. What is the next step? To continue your pursuit of God, you might consider other books from the A Quiet Time Experience series, including *A Heart that Hopes in God, Run Before the Wind, Trusting in the Names of God, Passionate Prayer,* and *Walk on Water Faith.* The Quiet Times For The Heart series are also books of quiet times with titles such as *Pilgrimage of the Heart, Revive My Heart, A Heart that Dances, A Heart on Fire,* and *A Heart to See Forever.* To learn more about quiet time, read signature books from the A 30-Day Journey series such as *Six Secrets to a Powerful Quiet Time* and *Knowing and Loving the Bible.* DVD and HD Digital Leader's Kits with inspirational messages and Leader's Guides are available for many books. Quiet Time Ministries online has exciting resources like *The Quiet Time Notebooks* to encourage you in your quiet time with God. Find daily encouragement from Cath's Blog at www.quiettime.org and view A Walk In Grace, the devotional photo journal featuring Catherine's myPhotoWalk.com photography. Join hundreds of other women online to study God's Word and grow in God's grace at Cath's Online Bible Studies. Resources may be ordered online from Quiet Time Ministries at www.quiettime.org or by calling Quiet Time Ministries directly. For more information, you may contact:

Quiet Time Ministries
P.O. Box 14007
Palm Desert, California 92255
(800) 925-6458, (760) 772-2357
E-mail: catherine@quiettime.org
Website: www.quiettime.org

ABOUT THE AUTHOR

Catherine Martin is a summa cum laude graduate of Bethel Theological Seminary with a Master of Arts degree in Theological Studies. She is founder and president of Quiet Time Ministries, a director of women's ministries for many years, and an adjunct faculty member of Biola University. She is the author of *Six Secrets to a Powerful Quiet Time, Knowing and Loving the Bible, Walking with the God Who Cares, Set my Heart on Fire, Trusting in the Names of God, Passionate Prayer, Quiet Time Moments for Women, Drawing Strength from the Names of God, A Woman's Heart that Dances,* and *A Woman's Walk in Grace* published by Harvest House Publishers, and *Pilgrimage of the Heart, Revive My Heart* and *A Heart that Dances,* published by NavPress. She has also written *The Quiet Time Notebooks, A Heart on Fire, A Heart to See Forever, Run Before the Wind, A Heart That Hopes in God, Walk on Water Faith, One Holy Passion,* and *The Calling* published by Quiet Time Ministries Press. She is founder of myPhotoWalk.com dedicated to the art of devotional photography, publishing *myPhotoWalk: Quiet Time Moments, Savoring God's Promises of Hope, The Story of Your Life,* and *A Day in the Life of God.* As a popular keynote speaker at retreats and conferences, Catherine challenges others to seek God and love Him with all of their heart, soul, mind, and strength. .

ABOUT QUIET TIME MINISTRIES

Quiet Time Ministries is a nonprofit religious organization under Section 501(c)(3) of the Internal Revenue Code. Cash donations are tax deductible as charitable contributions. We count on prayerful donors like you, partners with Quiet Time Ministries pursuing our goals of the furtherance of the Gospel of Jesus Christ and teaching devotion to God and His Word. Visit us online at www.quiettime.org to view special funding opportunities and current ministry projects. Your prayerful donations bring countless project to life!

Quiet Time Ministries | P.O. Box 14007 | Palm Desert, California 92255
1.800.925.6458 | catherine@quiettime.org | www.quiettime.org | www.myphotowalk.com

APPENDIX

Introduction

   egin your class with prayer and then welcome everyone to this new book of quiet times. Have
the people in your group share their names and what brought them to the study. Make sure
each person in your group has a book. Also, gather contact information for all participants in
your group including name, address, phone number, and e-mail. That way you can keep in touch
and encourage those in your group.

   Familiarize your group with the layout of the book. Each week consists of five days of quiet
times, as well as a devotional reading and response for days 6 and 7. Each day follows the PRAYER
quiet time plan:

   Prepare Your Heart

   Read and Study God's Word

   Adore God in Prayer

   Yield Yourself to God

   Enjoy His Presence

   Rest in His Love

Journal and prayer pages are included in the back of the book. Note that the quiet times offer
devotional reading, Bible study, prayer, and practical application. Some days are longer than others
and therefore, they should study at their own pace. Days 6-7 are for catching up, review, etc. This is
a concentrated, intentional, journey in the book of Romans with a special focus on God's amazing
love as seen in the gospel of Jesus Christ. As you and your group see God's amazing love more
and more throughout the study, the result is a growing passionate love for God. Encourage your
group to interact with the study, underlining significant insights and writing comments in the
margins. Ask your group to read the Introduction sometime in their first day of study. Also point
out that the Introduction includes a place where they will write a letter to the Lord. Encourage
them to draw near to God each day and ask Him to speak to their hearts.

   You can determine how to organize your group sessions, but here's one idea: Discuss the week
of quiet times together in the first hour, break for ten minutes, and then watch the video message
on the companion DVD or HD Digital M4V. There are nine messages for *The Proof of God's
Amazing Love*—one for the introduction and one for each week. You might also share with your

group a summary of how to prepare for their quiet time by setting aside a time each day and a place. Consider sharing how time alone with the Lord has made a difference in your own life. Let your class know about Quiet Time Ministries Online, quiet time resources, and Catherine Martin's A Walk In Grace Photo Journal at www.quiettime.org.

Another option is to divide each week (completing the study in 16 weeks) by discussing days 1–3 one week and days 4–7 another week. This allows your group to journey through each quiet time at a slower pace.

Pray for one another by offering a way to record and exchange prayer requests. Some groups like to pass around a basket with cards that people can use to record prayer requests. Then, people take a request out of the basket and pray for someone during the week. Others like to use three by five cards and then exchange cards on a weekly basis.

Close this introductory class with prayer, take a short break, and then show the companion DVD or HD Digital M4V video message.

Week One: For Such A Time As This

This week, the goal of your discussion is to study the background of Romans and understand some of its main themes. You might even give the example of the value of preparation for a trip. Describe how studying a guidebook helps in understanding the best places to visit and important stops along the way. You will understand the background of Romans by studying Romans 1:1-17 as you look at the author of Romans, the recipients, the occasion and purpose of the letter, and the main theme of Romans.

DAY 1: The Need Of The Hour

1. Open your discussion with prayer. Ask any new members of your group to introduce themselves. Share the goal of these quiet times: to study the proof of God's amazing love and embrace the power of the gospel of Christ.

2. What did you learn from the Introduction about this study? What is our study going to be about? What excited you the most about embarking on this study after reading the Introduction?

3. Day 1 began with the story of John and Charles Wesley. What is your favorite phrase in the song written by Charles Wesley, "And Can It Be That I Should Gain" found on page 10?

4. What did you learn about the author, recipients, occasion and purpose, and the theme of Romans on page 25?

5. What did you learn about the gospel from the verses you studied in Day 1 and especially from Romans 1:1-2, and 16-17?

6. What did you learn about truth and how did that motivate you to study God's Word, especially Romans?

7. What encouraged you the most in Day 1?

DAY 2: The Man For The Hour

1. In Day 2 we studied the life of Paul. Why was Paul the least likely candidate to be chosen by the Lord to share the gospel with Jews and Gentiles?

2. What did you learn about Paul's conversion to Christ and what stood out to you the most in your study of Paul?

3. Share what you saw about Paul's heart for his ministry from the Lord?

4. Why is he such a great example for Christians today?

5. What was he the perfect choice to preach and write about the gospel?

DAY 3: The People Of The Hour

1. On Day 3 we focused on the recipients of Romans. What did you learn about them?

2. In your study of some of the important phrases describing the church at Rome, what did you learn about being the called of Jesus Christ, beloved of God, and called as saints?

3. What was most significant to you in this day of study?

DAY 4: What Is On The Heart Of God?

1. In Day 4 you had the opportunity to spend more time thinking about the heart of God and His amazing love for you. What did you see in His plan described in Prepare Your Heart that meant the most to you about God?

2. What did you learn about God's love in Romans 5:1-9 and Romans 8:38--39?

3. How did you see His great love in all you read about His plan for you seen even in the Old Testament and in Hebrews 9:11-12?

4. You had the opportunity to spend time in the parable of the Prodigal Son. How did this parable show you the Lord's heart and love for you even more? What did Jesus want us to know about His love?

5. What was most significant to you in the verses in Ephesians and in the Romans Road to Salvation?

6. What was your favorite quote or insight from today's study

DAY 5: How Then Shall You Live?

1. In Day 5 we began with the story of Francis Scheaffer. Have you ever experienced a time of crisis when you realized in your own life in a new and deeper way the need for faith in God's Word?

2. What did you learn about the righteousness of God in today's study? How can we experience the righteousness of God?

3. What did you learn about faith?

4. What was your favorite quote in the devotional reading?

DAYS 6 AND 7: Devotional Reading by A.W. Tozer

1. What was your favorite verse, insight, or quote from your quiet times this week?

2. What did you learn from the excerpt written by William Newell in Day 6 and 7?

3. What was your favorite photo this week in your quiet times?

4. Close your time together in prayer.

Week Two: The Need For God's Righteousness

This week you read and studied Romans 1:18-3:31 focusing on our need for the righteousness of God. In our five days of study, we looked at the revelation of God in the book of Romans: God Revealed, Sin Revealed, Law Revealed, Savior Revealed, and Salvation Revealed. What a powerful week of study!

DAY 1: God Revealed

1. Open your discussion with prayer. Then share that this week you had the opportunity to look at why we need the righteousness of God. Have someone read Romans 1:18-20 and ask why we are accountable to God whether we believe in God or not.

2. What was your most significant insight about God from Romans 1:18-23?

3. What did you learn about God and His creation from the verses on page 63?

4. We had a sneak peak into future discoveries in Romans by looking at Romans 5:8-10. How is it that one can be saved? What did you learn?

5. What was your favorite quote or insight from today's study?

DAY 2: Sin Revealed

1. In Day 2 you studied the sin of man and his need for God's righteousness. What did you learn about sin? What is it about God that humbles us and make us feel a need for mercy?

2. How did you summarize what you read in Romans 1:18-32 about unrighteousness and its results? How do you see the wreck and ruin of sin and evil in the world today?

3. We studied the phrase "God gave them over" in Romans 1. What does that phrase mean and what did you learn about why He gave them over in verses 21-23, 25, 28, and 32?

4. On page 71 in Day 2 you studied some verses about the work of God in your life. What was your favorite insight from these verses?

5. What was your favorite quote from the devotional reading?

DAY 3: Law Revealed

1. In Day 3 you learned more about the law. Have someone read Romans 3:20 and ask what is the purpose of the Law as seen in this verse.

2. What blessed you the most from the life of Zola Levitt?

3. What was your most significant insight from Romans 2:1-16 about God?

4. What stood out to you in Romans 2:21-23?

5. After reading Romans 3:1-20, what did you discover about who is righteous, who is accountable to God, and the purpose of the Law?

6. We learned from Paul's example. What was your favorite insight from Philippians 3:3-9 on page 75?

7. What was your favorite quote in the devotional reading? Why is knowing you are a sinner important in our understanding of the gospel, the good news of Jesus Christ?

DAY 4: Savior Revealed

1. In Day 4 you studied the word of your Lord and Savior Jesus Christ. Have someone read Romans 3:21-22 and ask what is your favorite part of these verses?

2. What did you learn from your study of Isaiah 53:1-12?

3. Describe the event in Luke 4:14-21. What was most significant to you?

4. What was your favorite phrase in Isaiah 62:1-4? How do you see the heart of the Lord and His love for you in this passage of Scripture?

5. What did you learn about all that the Lord has done for you on page 82?

6. What was your favorite quote in the devotional reading today? What did you learn that would make you sing those words, "Hallelujah, what a Savior!"

DAY 5: Salvation Revealed

1. In Day 5 you studied more in-depth salvation in Jesus Christ. We began with the story of Martin Luther. What did you love about his example?

2. What did you learn in Romans 3:21-31 about why we need the righteousness of God and how we can have it?

3. You had the opportunity to do an in-depth study of important theological terms in this passage of Scripture in Romans. What did you learn about justified and justification, grace, redemption, propitiation?

4. How did the Passover in Exodus 12 help you see in a deeper way all that Christ has accomplished for you? Why is the shed blood important?

5. Paul only wanted to boast in "the cross of Jesus Christ" (Galatians 6:14). You had the opportunity to spend time reading about Jesus on the cross in John 19:16-30. What was most significant to you as you lived in that passage of Scripture?

6. What was your favorite quote in the devotional reading?

7. What meant the most to you from Spurgeon's testimony about his own salvation?

8. What stood out the most to you today about your Savior Jesus Christ?

DAYS 6 AND 7: Devotional Reading by D. Martyn Lloyd-Jones

1. What was your favorite verse, insight, or quote from your quiet times this week?

2. What did you learn from the excerpt by D. Martyn Lloyd-Jones in Days 6-7?

3. What is your favorite phrase from the great hymn, "When I Survey The Wondrous Cross?" Why do the words mean so much more to you now that you have studied Romans 1-3?

4. What was your favorite photo this week in your quiet times?

5. Close your time together in prayer.

Week Three: The Way Of God's Righteousness

We spent the first two weeks of study with an overview of Romans, a look at some of the main themes, and deep study in Romans 1-3. In Week Three we study Romans 4-5 and begin to see why the gospel is such great news. In this week of study we are given a deeper glimpse into the power of the gospel and the eternal security that is ours because of Jesus Christ.

DAY 1: God's Righteousness In Abraham

1. Open your discussion with prayer. Give a brief review of what they've learned in the last two weeks of study. You might share quickly the author, recipients, occasion and purpose of Romans, and the theme. Then you can share that in their study of Romans 1-3 they saw the need for righteousness and the fact that all have sinned and fall short of the glory of God. Then you might begin by sharing that this week

in Romans 4 we studied the example of Abraham and in Romans 5 our unshakeable position and eternal security and assurance in the gospel of Jesus Christ.

2. What did you learn about Abraham's faith and God's righteousness in Romans 4:1-15?

3. Have someone read Romans 4:9 and ask what "credited" means. Then what did you learn in Romans 4:4-8 about works vs. faith?

4. On page 103 we read Romans 4:16 - what did you learn from that verse?

5. What did you learn from Abraham's example of faith in Romans 4:20-25?

6. How did the devotional reading help you in understanding works vs. faith?

DAY 2: The Unshakeable Position

1. What did you learn from the example of the people who had bought tickets for a cruise?

2. What did you learn from Romans 5:1-2 about all that is true of you because you are justified by faith?

3. How did the verses in Romans and 2 Corinthians help you understand what Jesus accomplished on your behalf?

4. Share your favorite part of the words of Kenneth Wuest about standing in grace.

5. What was your favorite quote in the prayer or devotional reading?

6. What is your favorite insight from today's study?

DAY 3: Power In Trials

1. What was your favorite insight from today's study that will help you in the trials you face today?

2. According to Romans 5:3-5 why can you exult or rejoice in tribulations?

3. You learned the definitions and meanings of some of the words in this passage. What was your favorite?

4. Share your favorite verse about trials and rejoicing from your study today.

5. How does the Holy Spirit help in difficult times?

6. Why is Corrie ten Boom such a great example for us, especially in trials?

DAY 4: God's Love In Salvation

1. In Day 4 we focused on the love of God for us. What is your favorite part of the hymn by Matheson, "O Love That Will Not Let Me Go."

2. What did the Lord accomplish on your behalf according to Romans 5:6-11?

3. What was your favorite truth about God's love from the verses you studied today?

4. How does the fact that God loves you encourage you today?

DAY 5: Eternal Assurance And Security

1. How did the story in Prepare Your Heart of the wealthy man and the auction encourage and impact you? Why is it such a good picture of all we have because of Christ?

2. In Romans 5:1-21 what are some of the words and phrases that give you eternal assurance and security?

3. What did you learn about the view of Jesus in heaven from Revelation 5:11-14?

4. What truth encouraged you the most from all the Scripture you studied today?

5. What was your favorite quote in the prayer and devotional reading?

DAYS 6 AND 7: Devotional Reading by Hannah Whitall Smith

1. In Days Six and Seven you had the opportunity to read from Hannah Whitall Smith. What was your favorite truth from his writing?

2. What was your favorite verse, insight, or quote from your study in Week Three?

3. What is the most important truth you will take with you from this week of study? How are you seeing the proof of God's amazing love and the power of the gospel of Christ?

4. What was your favorite photo this week in your quiet times?

Week Four: The Union In God's Righteousness

The goal for your discussion is to lead your group through these powerful chapters in Romans. It may be the first time many in your group have ever studied these chapters and truths in-depth. It will be a most meaningful time as everyone shares what they have learned and how they have personalized these truths in their own lives.

DAY 1: The Great Union

1. Open your discussion with prayer. Share briefly about your discussion last week about Romans 4 and 5, Abraham's faith and their eternal security in Christ. Begin by asking what their study in Romans 6 and 7 meant to them this week.

2. What did you learn about your union with Christ from Romans 6:1-14? What is now true about you because you know Christ?

3. How do you now live because you are crucified with Christ according to Galatians 2:20?

4. We now live in the land of grace. We are not under law of grace. What did you learn about grace? What is it like in the land of grace?

5. How does knowing you are under grace encourage you today? Why did you need to hear about grace today?

6. What was your favorite quote in the devotional reading?

DAY 2: The Great Freedom

1. Have someone read Romans 6:22

2. In Romans 6 we saw that our relationship to sin has changed. What was our previous relationship to sin according to the verses we read in Romans 6 on page 143?

3. What is our relationship to sin now that we know Christ according to the verses in Romans 6?

4. And now here's a big question. How then should we live and why is it possible according to Romans 6?

5. What kind of life is Paul encouraging us to live?

6. What does it mean to live a sanctified life? How did Colossians 3:1-4 and 1 Thessalonians 4:3-7 help you in thinking about how to live?

7. How did this day of study help you in thinking about how to live in light of all that Christ has done for us?

DAY 3: The Great Cry

1. In Day 3 we studied Romans 7 and the example of marriage to understand our relationship with Christ. In Romans 7:1-6 why do you think Paul used the example of marriage?

2. In Romans 7:4-6 what did you see about the impact of being joined to Christ.

3. In Romans 7:7-13 what did you learn about the Law and sin?

4. What meant the most to you in thinking about being the Bride of Jesus Christ?

5. How did the devotional reading help you in understanding what it means for us to be united with Christ?

6. What does knowing that you are joined with Christ forever mean to you today?

DAY 4: The Great Question

1. In Day 4 Paul uses himself as an example What conflict is Paul experiencing? What did you learn about this conflict and why he is experiencing it?

2. What is his great question and what is the answer?

3. How did Chuck Swindoll's words help you in understanding this conflict?

4. What is the most important truth you learned in the study of Romans 6 and 7 that you can apply to your own life?

DAY 5: The Great Promise

1. And now, in Day 5 we had the opportunity to begin our venture into the holy ground of Romans 8. Have someone read Romans 8:1-4.

2. According to these verses, why is there now no condemnation?

3. You learn in these verses that you are now "in Christ." What did you learn from the other verses you studied today about all that is true of you because you are "in Christ?"

4. What did you learn from the devotional reading by Hodge and Wiersbe?

DAYS 6 AND 7: Devotional Reading by W.H. Griffith Thomas

1. In days 6 and 7 you had the opportunity to read from W.H. Griffith Thomas. What was your favorite insight from his writing?

2. Did you have a favorite quote, insight, or verse from Week Four?

3. What was your favorite photo this week in your quiet times?

4. Close your time together in prayer.

Week Five: The Power Of God's Righteousness

Your goal in your discussion this week is to help those in your group learn about the power of the gospel and the work of the Holy Spirit in our lives in probably one of the favorite chapters in the Bible for many people—Romans 8.

DAY 1: Power In The Spirit

1. Open your discussion with prayer. As you begin your time of discussion today, read the quote by A.W. Tozer on the Week Five page.

2. What did you discover about the repeated use of the Holy Spirit in Romans 8? How important do you think the Holy Spirit is if it is repeated that many times?

3. What did you learn about the Spirit and being born again from Jesus in John 3:5-8?

4. In Romans 8:5-13 what did you learn about what is true about you because the Spirit is in your life and how does He help you?

5. From your study in Galatians, what did you learn about the Spirit-filled life?

6. What was the most important truth the Lord taught you in Day 1?

DAY 2: Power As Children Of God

1. In Romans 8:14-17 what did you learn is now true of you because of the Holy Spirit?

2. One of the truths we discovered is that we are led by the Spirit of God. How does that encourage you today?

3. What did you learn from the verses you studied about being an heir of God and fellow-heir with Christ? What was your favorite verse in this study?

4. What was your favorite quote in the prayer or devotional reading?

DAY 3: Power In Suffering

1. What did you learn from the story of Annie Johnson Flint that encouraged you? Why is she such an example of experiencing power in suffering and how did her poem help you today?

2. What did you learn about suffering in Romans 8:18-25?

3. How does the Holy Spirit help us when we suffer?

4. What truth was your favorite in all the verses you read in this day's quiet time?

5. What was your favorite insight from the devotional reading in Day 3?

DAY 4: Power In Prayer

1. In Prepare Your Heart, you read about Catherine Marshall and the prayer of relinquishment. What did you learn from her story?

2. How does the Holy Spirit help us in prayer according to Romans 8:26-27?

3. Romans 8:28-34 was filled with promises. What was your favorite?

4. You had the opportunity to live in some of the promises found in Romans 8:28, Romans 8:29-30, and Romans 8:33. What did you learn that meant the most to you and how did it help you see even more just how amazing God's love is for you?

5. What encouraged you in the prayer and devotional reading?

DAY 5: Power In Christ's Love

1. In Day 5 you spent time reading and thinking about those words at the end of Romans 8 about the love of Christ. What was Paul saying about the love of Christ?

2. What did you learn from the verses you studied about the truth of your victory and the love of Christ?

3. What is a fear you have and how does knowing nothing can separate you from the love of God in Christ Jesus your Lord encourage you?

4. What was your favorite quote in the prayer and/or the devotional reading?

DAYS 6 AND 7: Devotional Reading by Octavius Winslow

1. What was your favorite verse, insight, or quote from your quiet times this week?

2. What did you learn from the excerpt by Octavius Winslow?

3. What was your favorite photo this week in your quiet times?

4. How did your study this week encourage you in a new and deeper way to embrace the power of the gospel of Christ and to walk in newness of life in the power of the Holy Spirit? How did it help you appreciate even more the love of God in Christ Jesus your Lord?

5. Close your time together in prayer.

Week Six: The Plan Of God's Righteousness

In Week Six you are entering a new section of Romans, chapters 9-11 where Paul deals with some questions he has probably been thinking about for a long time. Why have the Jewish people rejected the gospel? And what is their destiny as a people? What powerful quiet times we had this week and you are going to talk about them together with your group.

DAY 1: Sovereignty In God's Righteousness

1. Open your discussion with prayer. Begin by reading the first 4 paragraphs in Prepare Your Heart in Day 1. Ask your group what meant the most to them in this week of quiet times? What was the easiest to understand and what was the most difficult?

2. What did you learn about God in Romans 9:6-18 (page 212).

3. On page 213 you had the opportunity to read some of R.C. Sproul's thoughts about God's mercy and providence and sovereignty. What was most significant to you about God's sovereignty and how did it help you think more deeply about the greatness of your God? How do you need to trust God and surrender to Him today?

4. What encouraged you in Romans 9:22-26 (page 214)?

5. In Romans 9:27-33 you learned about how Israel missed the truth of the gospel. How were they pursuing righteousness?

6. How did Tozer's words about God's sovereign design help you see the greatness and glory of God?

DAY 2: Faith In God's Righteousness

1. In Day 2 we thought more deeply about how a person is saved. What did you learn in Romans 10:1-13?

2. What did you see about the heart of God for His people in the verses you studied?

3. How did the devotional reading help you understand salvation?

4. How did you come to faith in Christ and what was it like when "the veil was taken away" (2 Corinthians 3:15-16)?

5. Have you ever prayed for someone and finally saw them come to the Lord. If you can, share your story with the group.

DAY 3: Revelation In God's Righteousness

1. In Day 3 we continue to think about salvation and the response of Israel. What meant the most to you in the story of Sheldon Van Auken in Prepare Your Heart?

2. What did you learn in Romans 10:14-17 about what is needed to share the gospel message?

3. What did you learn about Israel's response in Romans 10:16-21?

4. How has God revealed Himself? What did you learn in the verses you studied?

5. Oh the power of the Word of God for your faith! It's seen throughout Scripture. You had the opportunity to see an event in the life of Jesus in Luke 7:1-10. Why was Jesus amazed with this man's faith and what made his faith so amazing?

6. What did you learn today that encourages you to spend more time in the Word of God and live by faith?

DAY 4: Faithfulness In God's Righteousness

1. In Day 4 we spent time in Romans 11. We began our quiet time with a story about a little girl and her father. How did it demonstrate what it means to live by faith?

2. What promise stood out to you the most in Romans 11:1-10?

3. What did you see that God promises for Israel in Romans 11:26-29?

4. What did you learn about God's faithfulness in the verses you studied? How does His faithfulness encourage you today?

5. Great Is Thy Faithfulness is a favorite hymn of many. What line in that hymn do you love the most?

DAY 5: Glory In God's Righteousness

1. In Day 5 you spent quiet time in Romans 11:33-36, a doxology that is also a hymn. Begin by having someone in your group read these words.

2. What is your favorite truth about God in these verses?

3. Have someone read question 3 on page 235. Then ask what did you learn from the verses about the glory of God?

4. What was your favorite quote in the devotional reading?

DAYS 6 AND 7: Devotional Reading by C.E.B. Cranfield

1. What was your favorite verse, insight, or quote from your quiet times this week?

2. What did you learn from the excerpt by C.E.B. Cranfield?

3. What was your favorite photo this week in your quiet times? Close your time together in prayer.

Week Seven: The Life Of God's Righteousness'

The goal for your discussion this week is to talk about all that you are learning about the practical life of God's righteousness studied in Romans 12, following the principles of Romans 1-11.

DAY 1: Surrender

1. Open your discussion with prayer. Share briefly about all that we have been learning on this journey in Romans. Once you have reviewed quickly what we have studied thus far, ask your group how they are being encouraged in their relationship with the Lord in this study. Ask them what has impressed them the most about Jesus, the gospel, and God's amazing love seen in all that the Lord has done for us.

2. In Day 1 of Week Seven we begin with the stories of Clyde Cook and Corrie ten Boom. What stood out to you about their lives, their decisions, and how they lived?

3. Have someone in your group read Romans 12:1. You were asked to think through the many mercies of God. Have different ones in your group share the mercies they listed.

4. What do you think it means to present your body a living and holy sacrifice and why do you think this is important in your life with Christ?

5. Can you think of a time when you surrendered your life to Christ and what happened as a result?

6. What was your favorite truth from the verses you studied?

7. What was your favorite part of the devotional reading?

DAY 2: Transformation

1. In Day 2 you began your quiet time in Prepare Your Heart with a powerful reading entitled "Others May, You Cannot" that was written by G.D. Watson and found in the flyleaf of Dr. Henry M. Morris' Bible. What meant the most to you in this reading?

2. Have someone in your group read Romans 12:2. What did you learn about the world and what are ways that we become conformed to it and allow it to squeeze us into its mold?

3. What did you learn about how we are transformed and what it means to be transformed?

4. How does the Bible help in our transformation?

5. What is the result of our transformation?

6. What did you learn about what God is doing in your life from Ephesians 2:10?

7. What was your favorite phrase in the prayer from *The Valley Of Vision*?

8. What did the words of Tozer mean to you and how did they encourage and challenge you?

DAY 3: Humility

1. In Day 3 you studied the character quality of humility. What is humility and why is it important in our lives?

2. What did you see about the humility of Jesus in Isaiah 53? How was it expressed in His life on earth and His work on the cross?

3. What did you learn about humility from the verses you studied?

4. What did you learn from Andrew Murray about humility?

DAY 4: Serving

1. In Day 4, you spent time studying the church. What did you learn from Romans 12:4-13 about what God's righteousness looks like among believers?

2. What did you learn from the verses in 1 Corinthians 12 about being part of the body of Christ and spiritual gifts?

3. What did you learn about Christ and the church from the verses you studied?

4. How did your study today help you understand your service in the church among believers?

DAY 5: Influence

1. In Day 5 you had the opportunity to learn how our lives influence those around us. What did you learn from Romans 12:14-21?

2. You learned about how we can encourage one another. How have you been encouraged by someone else when you were hurting?

3. How did the Lord speak to you in this passage of Scripture?

DAYS 6 AND 7: Devotional Reading by Henrietta Mears

1. What was your favorite verse, insight, or quote from your quiet times this week?

2. What was your favorite insight from the words of Henrietta Mears?

3. How did Romans 12 encourage you to a deeper commitment to Christ as you studied in Week Seven?

4. What was your favorite photo this week in your quiet times?

5. Close your time together in prayer.

Week Eight: The Impact Of God's Righteousness

And now we come to this last week of study in *The Proof Of God's Amazing Love*. The goal of your discussion today is to help your group share what they've learned from Paul, especially from his passion for the church. You want to help them realize their lives make a difference because of the work of Christ in and through them. And then, you will want to allow time for sharing all that those in your group have learned in *The Proof Of God's Amazing Love*.

DAY 1: Behavior In The World

1. Open your discussion with prayer. Begin by expressing how much you've enjoyed leading the group and sharing together during this journey in Romans. And share how wonderful the discussions have been. As you discuss together for one last time in *The Proof Of God's Amazing Love*, ask your group what has been their favorite part of this study.

2. This week we studied the last four chapters in Romans and had the opportunity to hear more of what Paul considers important for us to know about the gospel of

Jesus Christ in our lives. Begin by having someone in your group read the words from Prepare Your Heart as an introduction to today's discussion.

3. What is Paul encouraging in our lives from the words of Romans 13:1-14?

4. What did you learn about authority in these words? And what did you learn about submission from 1 Peter 2:13-17. How can obedience to Christ make a difference where we work, with our family and friends, and even government?

5. How does loving others, as Paul encourages, make a difference?

6. In Romans 13:11-14, what are we encouraged to do?

7. Describe in your own words what it means to clothe ourselves with Jesus Christ?

8. What encouraged you in the devotional reading today?

DAY 2: Love In Relationships

1. In Day 2 we spent time in Romans 14 looking at how our love and being clothed in Christ looks like in life. What did you learn about how we are to live?

2. What are practical ways we can show love to one another?

3. How does knowing God has His eyes on us and that we will give an account for ourselves encourage you in your own service to the Lord?

4. What was the most significant truth you learned in Day 2?

DAY 3: Abounding Hope For Life

1. Day 3 is all about hope as you lived in some of the verses in Romans 15. How did you need this study on hope? How did it encourage you?

2. As you read Romans 15:1-13, what topics were on Paul's mind? Where was his focus?

3. What did you learn about hope from Romans 15:4 and Romans 15:13?

4. What did you learn about hope from the other verses you studied on pages 296-297?

5. What was your favorite quote in the devotional reading?

DAY 4: Getting Personal With The Church

1. In Day 4 we saw some closing remarks from Paul to people in the church. Over all, as you read these verses, what stood out to you about Paul's relationship with those in the church?

2. What was most on the heart of Paul as you read Romans 15:14-33?

3. What did he warn the church about in Romans 16:17-20?

4. And now, we had the opportunity to go through most of the names of people that Paul addressed. What stood out to you in some of the things he said to these people? What blessed you the most?

5. At the end of this day's study, you had the opportunity to write a thank you note to Paul. Who would like to share what you wrote to Paul?

DAY 5: Benediction Of The Gospel

1. And now, we come to the end of Romans. After you open in prayer, have someone read Paul's benediction in Romans 16:25-27.

2. What were your favorite words and phrases in this benediction? And what was your favorite translation?

3. Why does the promise of forever bring hope to you today?

4. What was your favorite quote from your Day 5 quiet time?

5. How have you seen the proof of God's amazing love in all you have studied in Romans?

6. How did God answer the prayer that you wrote in your letter to Him at the beginning of the study?

DAYS 6 AND 7: Devotional Reading by John Oxenham

1. What encouraged you from the words of John Oxenham, "Roadmates?"

2. You had an opportunity to take some time and leaf through these eights weeks of quiet times to look at all you have learned. What are some of the most important principles and truths we've learned from Romans?

3. What is the most important truth you have learned about God in this book of quiet times? What will you take with you? (If you have a visual aid such as a whiteboard, you might even write these truths out for your class to see).

4. What was your favorite week in *The Proof Of God's Amazing Love* and why? Did you have a favorite verse or chapter from Romans?

5. What was your favorite photo in *The Proof Of God's Amazing Love*? In what way was the devotional photography meaningful to you in your quiet times?

6. If you didn't answer before, would you like to share how God answered the prayer that you wrote in your letter to Him at the beginning of the study?

7. What will you take with you from *The Proof Of God's Amazing Love*? What will you always remember?

8. Close your time together in prayer.

I love Romans and have collected many books and commentaries on Romans and books that have helped understand truths taught in Romans over the years. Here are some of the many of books used in the writing of *The Proof of God's Amazing Love*. Some of my favorites are listed including a few study Bibles and Bible study tools that have been helpful for me over the years. I encourage you to study God's Word daily. No time is ever wasted alone with God in His Word.

An Exposition of Romans, 14 Volumes by D. Martyn Lloyd-Jones (Carlisle, PA: The Banner of Truth Trust 1985)

Be Right, NT Commentary Romans by Warren W. Wiersbe (Colorado Springs, CO: David C. Cook 1977)

Expositor's Bible Commentary by Frank Gaebelein, ed. (Grand Rapids, MI: Zondervan Publishing House 1976)

Galatians: The Charter of Christian Liberty by Merrill C. Tenney (Grand Rapids, MI: William B. Eerdmans Publishing Company 1971)

He That Is Spiritual by Lewis Sperry Chafer (Grand Rapids, MI: Zondervan Publishing House 1918)

Insights on Romans by Charles R. Swindoll (Grand Rapids, MI: Zondervan Publishing House 2010)

Keswick's Authentic Voice by Herbert F. Stevenson, ed. (Grand Rapids, MI: Zondervan Publishing House 1959)

Linguistic Key to the Greek New Testament by Fritz Rienecker and Cleon Rogers (Grand Rapids, MI: Zondervan Publishing House 1976, 1980)

Logos Bible Study Software at www.logos.com with training by Morris Proctor at mpseminars.com. I will forever be indebted to both Logos and Morris Proctor for the greatest Bible Study Software on the planet. I spent many hours using the books, commentaries, and Bible study tools in my Logos library.

Men Made New by John R.W. Stott (Grand Rapids, MI: Baker Book House 1966)

Paul: Apostle of the Heart Set Free by F.F. Bruce (Grand Rapids, MI: William B. Eerdmans Publishing Company 1977)

Romans by F.F. Bruce (Downers Grove, IL: Intervarsity Press 1985)

Romans: A Shorter Commentary by C.E.B. Cranfield (Grand Rapids, MI: William B. Eerdmans Publishing Company 1985)

Romans Verse by Verse by William R. Newell (Chicago, IL: Moody Press 1977)

St. Paul's Epistle to the Romans: A Devotional Commentary by W.H. Griffith Thomas (Grand Rapids, MI: William B. Eerdmans Publishing Company 1946, 1974)

Study Bibles: ESV Study Bible (Wheaton, IL: Crossway Bibles 2008), *The Hebrew Greek Key Word Study Bible, NASB Edition* by Spiros Zodhiates (Chattanooga, TN: AMG Publishers 2014), *The New International Inductive Study Bible, Updated New American Standard Bible* (Eugene, OR: Harvest House Publishers 2000), *The NIV Study Bible* (Grand Rapids, MI: Zondervan Publishing House 1985)

The Christian's Secret of a Happy Life by Hannah Whitall Smith (Old Tappan, NJ: Fleming H. Revell Company 1952)

The Epistle to the Romanss by Leon Morris, The Pillar New Testament Commentary (Grand Rapids, MI: Leicester, England: W.B. Eerdmans; Inter-Varsity Press, 1988)

The Gospel of God: An Exposition of Romans by R.C. Sproul (Great Britan: Christian Focus Publications, 1994),

The Green Letters: Principles of Spiritual Growth by Miles J. Stanford (Grand Rapids, MI: Zondervan Publishing House 1975)

The Normal Christian Life by Watchman Nee (Wheaton, IL: Tyndale House Publishers 1957)

Victorious Christian Living by Alan Redpath (Old Tappan, NJ: Fleming H. Revell 1955)

NOTES

INTRODUCTION

1. COVER PHOTOGRAPHY: *God's Smile*, Hebrews 6:10 NLT, Principe Corsini Villa Le Corti, Val Di Pesa, Florence, Tuscany, Italy, Nikon D7000, Nikkor 18-105mm, FL 66.0mm, ISO 250, f/5.3, 1/800sec, Adobe Camera Raw, Adobe Photoshop, Topaz Software, ON1 Software. myPhotoWalk.com—CatherineMartin.SmugMug.com.

2. W.H. Griffith Thomas, D.D., *Romans: A Devotional Commentary I-V* (London: The Religious Tract Society 1911), p. vii.

WEEK 1

1. Dr. Roger J. Green, *Christian History Magazine* (Issue 28, 1990).

2. C.E.B. Cranfield, *Romans: A Shorter Commentary* (Grand Rapids: William B. Eerdmans Publishing Company 1985, 1990), p. ix.

3. W.H. Griffith Thomas, *Romans: A Devotional Commentary I-V* (London: The Religious Tract Society 1911), p. 19.

4. Frederic Louis Godet and Alexander Cusin, *Commentary on St. Paul's Epistle to the Romans, Volume I* (Edinburgh: T & T Clark, 1890) p. 1.

5. D. Martyn Lloyd-Jones, *Romans: Exposition of Chapter 1: The Gospel of God* (Carlisle, PA: The Banner of Truth Trust, 1985, 2020) pp. 23-24.

6. Catherine Marshall, *The Prayers of Peter Marshall*, (Grand Rapids: Chosen Books, 1982) p. 29.

7. F.F. Bruce, *Paul: Apostle of the Heart Set Free* (Grand Rapids: William B. Eerdmans Publishing Company 1989) p. 15.

8. F.B. Meyer, *Great Men Of The Bible, Volume II* (Grand Rapids: Zondervan 1982) pp. 331-332.

9. Merrill C. Tenney, *Galatians: The Charter of Christian Liberty* (Grand Rapids: Eerdmans, 1950), p. 75.

10. W. H. Griffith Thomas, *Romans: A Devotional Commentary I-V*, p. 19.

11. W. H. Griffith Thomas, *Romans: A Devotional Commentary I-V*, p. 47-48.

12. Kenneth E. Bailey, *The Cross and the Prodigal: Luke 15 through the Eyes of Middle Eastern Peasants*, Second Edition (Downers Grove, IL: IVP Books, 2005), p. 68.

13. D. Martyn Lloyd-Jones, *Romans: Exposition of Chapter 5: Assurance* (Carlisle, PA: The Banner of Truth Trust, 1985, 2020) pp. 106-107.

14. Francis A. Schaeffer, *True Spirituality*, (Wheaton, IL: Tyndale House Publishers, 1971), pp. xxix-xxx.

15. Barclay Moon Newman and Eugene Albert Nida, *A Handbook On Paul's Letter to the Romans* (New York: United Bible Societies, 1973) p. 20.

16. Francis A. Schaeffer, *True Spirituality*, pp. 63-64.

17. Warren W. Wiersbe, Be Right (Colorado Springs, CO: David C. Cook 2008), pp. 25-26.

18. Miles J. Stanford, *Principles of Spiritual Growth* (Grand Rapids: Zondervan 1981), p. 11.

19. William R. Newell, *Romans Verse By Verse*, (Chicago: Moody Press 1938, 1977) p. 24.

WEEK 2

1. Stephen Charnock, *The Complete Works of Stephen Charnock, Volume 1* (Edinburgh; London; Dublin: James Nichol; James Nisbet and Co.; W. Robertson; G. Herbert, 1864–1866) p. 128.

2. Viggo Olsen, M.D., *Daktar: Diplomat in Bangladesh* (Chicago: Moody Press 1973) pp. 40-41.

3. Corrie ten Boom, *Each New Day* (Grand Rapids: Revell, 1977).

4. Richard A. Swenson, M.D., *More Than Meets The Eye* (Colorado Springs: NavPress, 2000) pp. 11, 149.

5. Kenneth Barker, General Editor, *The NIV Study Bible* (Grand Rapids: Zondervan, 1985) p. 1707.

6. Leon Morris, *The Epistle to the Romans*, The Pillar New Testament Commentary (Grand Rapids, MI 1988), p.93.

7. William Barclay, ed. The Letter to the Romans, The Daily Study Bible Series (Philadelphia, The Westminster John Knox Press, 1975), p. 32.

8. Everett F. Harrison, *Roman*s in The Expositor's Bible Commentary ed. Frank E. Gabelein (Grand Rapids, MI 1976) pp. 24-25.

9. *Donald Grey Barnhouse, The Invisible War (Grand Rapids, MI: Zondervan Publishing House 1965) p. 51.*

10. Kenneth Barker, General Editor, *The NIV Study Bible..*

11. D. Martyn Lloyd-Jones, *Romans: Exposition of Chapter 1: The Gospel of God* (Carlisle, PA: The Banner of Truth Trust, 1985, 2020) pp. 318-319, 322-323.

12. William R. Newell, *Romans Verse By Verse*, pp. 85-86.

13. Catherine Marshall, *The Prayers of Peter Marshall,*, p. 67.

14. Charles Spurgeon, *All Of Grace* (New Kensington: Whitaker House, 1981) pp. 16-17.

15. Peter Bayne, *The Testimony of Christ to Christianity* (London: James Nisbet & Co., 1862) pp. 150-151.

16. Paul P. Enns, *The Moody Handbook of Theology* (Chicago: Moody Press, 1989) p. 639.

17. Sprios Zodhiates, *The Complete Word Study Dictionary; New Testament*, (Chattanooga, TN: AMG Publishers, 2000).

18. Charles Spurgeon, *Beside Still Waters* (Nashville, TN: Thomas Nelson, 1999) p. 33.

19. D. Martyn Lloyd-Jones, *Romans, Exposition of Chapter 3:20–4:25, Atonement and Justification*, pp. 57, 61

WEEK 3

1. Charles Haddon Spurgeon, *Morning and Evening*, December 17 Evening.

2. William Newell, *Romans Verse By Verse*, pp. 131-132.

3. D. Martyn Lloyd-Jones, *Romans: Exposition of Chapter 1: The Gospel of God* , p. 25.

4. Barclay Moon Newman and Eugene Albert Nida, *A Handbook On Paul's Letter to the Romans*, p. 92.

5. Kenneth S. Wuest, *Wuest's Word Studies From The Greek New Testament, Volume 2*, Grand Rapids: Eerdmans, 1997), pp. 77-78.

6. W. H. Griffith Thomas, *Romans: A Devotional Commentary I-V*, p. 194.

7. Miles J. Stanford, *Principles of Spiritual Growth* (Lincoln: Back to the Bible, 1984) p. 16.

8. William Newell, *Romans Verse By Verse*, pp. 245-247.

9. Fritz Rienecker, Cleon Rogers, Linguistic Key to the Greek New Testament (Grand Rapids: Zondervan Publishing House, 1976), p. 605.

10. Helen Kooiman Hosier, *100 Christian Women Who Changed the 20th Century* (Grand Rapids: Fleming H. Revell, 2000) p. 77.

11. Corrie ten Boom, *Tramp For The Lord*, pp. 57-58.

12. Kenneth W. Osbeck, *101 Hymn Stories*, (Grand Rapids: Kregel Publications, 1982), p. 190.

13. H.A. Ironside, *Addresses on the Song of Solomon*, (Neptune, NJ: Loizeaux Brothers, Inc., 1933, 1978) pp. 30-36.

14. W. H. Griffith Thomas, *Romans: A Devotional Commentary I-V*, pp. 196-197.

15. This story is by an unknown author and is shared multiple times at many different websites on the internet.

16. Ian Thomas *The Saving Life Of Christ* (Grand Rapids: Zondervan Publishing House, 1961), p. 13.

17. Ruth Harms Calkin *Precious Thoughts From The Heart* (New York: Inspirational Press, 1994), p. 18.

WEEK 4

1. William R. Newell, *Romans Verse by Verse* p. 209.

2. Joseph Cooke, *Celebration of Grace* (Milton-Freewater, OR: Outwest Printing, 1991), p. 13.

3. Catherine Martin, A Woman's Walk In Grace (Eugene, OR: Harvest House Publishers 2010).

4. Charles R. Swindoll, *Swindoll's New Testatment Insights* (Grand Rapids, MI: Zondervan, 2010) p. 132.

5. F.B. Meyer, *The Christ Life for Your Life* (Chicago: Moody Press,) p. 61.

6. D. Martyn Lloyd-Jones, *Romans: Exposition of Chapter 1: The Gospel of God* , p. 27.

7. Alan Redpath, *Victorious Christian Living* (Old Tappan, New Jersey 1955) pp. 71-72.

8. Watchman Nee, *The Normal Christian Life*, (Fort Washington: Christian Literature Crusade, 1957) pp. 64-65.

9. W. H. Griffith Thomas, *Romans: A Devotional Commentary VI-XI* (London: The Religious Tract Society 1912), p. 33.

10. Robert Parsons, *Quotes From The Quiet Hour* (Chicago: Moody Press 1949), p. 66

11. Charles R. Swindoll, *Swindoll's New Testament Insights* (Grand Rapids, MI: Zondervan, 2010) pp. 154-155.

12. Leon Morris, *The Epistle To The Romans*, The Pillar New Testament Commentary, (Grand Rapids, MI: Leicester, England: W.B. Eerdmans, Inter-Varsity Press, 1988) pp. 251, 253.

13. Charles Hodge, *Romans, Crossway Classic Commentaries* (Wheaton, IL: Crossway Books, 1993) Romans 8:1.

14. Warren W. Wiersbe, *Wiersbe's Expository Outlines on the New Testament* (Wheaton, IL: Victor Books, 1992) pp. 387-388.

15. John R.W. Stott, *Men Made New: An Exposition of Romans 5-8* (Grand Rapids, MI: Baker Book House 1978) pp. 82-84.

16. W. H. Griffith Thomas, *Romans: A Devotional Commentary VI-XI*, pp. 110-111.

WEEK 5

1. A.W. Tozer, compiled by Warren Wiersbe, *The Best of A.W. Tozer* (Camp Hill: Christian Publications) pp. 60-61.

2. Catherine Martin, *Revive My Heart - Satisfy Your Thirst for Personal Spiritual Revival* (Palm Desert: Quiet Time Ministries 2003) p. 15.

3. Lewis Sperry Chafer, *He That Is Spiritual* (Grand Rapids: Zondervan Publishing House 1918) pp. 43-44.

4. Brian H. Edwards, *Revival: A People Saturated with God* (Darlington: Evangelical Press 1990) pp. 46-48.

5. Oswald Chambers, *My Utmost For His Highest* (Grand Rapids, MI: Oswald Chambers Publications, Marshall Pickering 1986) March 19 selection.

6. Ruth Harms Calkin, *Precious Thoughts From The Heart* (New York: Inspirational Press, 1994), p. 14.

7. W. H. Griffith Thomas, *Romans: A Devotional Commentary VI-XI*, pp. 81-82.

8. D. Martyn Lloyd-Jones *Romans, Exposition of Chapter 8:5-17, The Sons of God* (Carlisle, PA: The Banner of Truth Trust 1974) p. 411..

9. Annie Johnson Flint, *Best-Loved Poems* (London: Marshall, Morgan & Scott) p. 6.

10. Leon Morris, *The Epistle To The Romans*, p. 318.

11. Amy Carmichael, *Gold By Moonlight*, (Fort Washington: Christian Literature Crusade) p. 75.

12. James Montgomery Boice, *Romans: The Reign Of Grace, Volume 2* (Grand Rapids, MI: Baker Book House, 1991), p. 912.

13. Catherine Marshall, *The Prayers of Peter Marshall*, p. 15.

14. Amy Carmichael, *Gold By Moonlight*, pp. 70-71.

WEEK 6

1. Charles R. Swindoll, *Insights On Romans*, p. 189.

2. R.C. Sproul, *The Gospel of God: An Exposition of Romans* (Great Britain: Christian Focus Publications, 1994), p. 168.

3. Leon Morris, *The Epistle To The Romans,* pp. 351, 359-360.

4. A.W. Tozer, *The Knowledge Of The Holy* (New York: Harper & Row 1961) pp. 118-119.

5. A.W. Tozer, *The Knowledge Of The Holy*, p. 104.

6. W. H. Griffith Thomas, *Romans: A Devotional Commentary VI-XI,* pp. 175-176.

7. C.E.B. Cranfield, *Romans: A Shorter Commentary* (Grand Rapids: William B. Eerdmans Publishing Company 1985) p. 259.

8. Sheldon Vanauken, *A Severe Mercy* (San Francisco: Harper & Row 1977) p. 93.

9. Lloyd John Ogilvie, *Quiet Moments With God*, (Eugene, Oregon, 1997) p. April 29.

10. W. H. Griffith Thomas, *Romans: A Devotional Commentary VI-XI*, p. 185.

11. W. H. Griffith Thomas, *Romans: A Devotional Commentary VI-XI*, pp. 214-215.

12. A.W. Tozer, The Pursuit of God (Camp Hill, PA: WingSpread, 2006), pp. 13-14.

13. Oswald Chambers, My Utmost For His Highest, (Grand Rapids, MI: Oswald Chambers Publications; Marshall Pickering, 1986).

14. C.E.B. Cranfield, *Romans: A Shorter Commentary* pp.289-290.

WEEK 7

1. R.C. Sproul, *The Gospel of God: An Exposition of Romans*, (Great Britain: Christian Focus Publications, 1994) p. 194.

2. Warren Wiersbe, *The Bible Exposition Commentary, Volume 1* (Wheaton, IL: Victor Books 1996) pp. 554-555, 589.

3. W.O. Carver, *Ephesians: The Glory of God in the Christian Calling*, (Nashville: Broadman Press 1949) p. 51.

4. Catherine Martin, *The Calling* (Palm Desert, CA: Quiet Time Ministries 2019) p. 56.

5. Kenneth Wuest, *Wuest's Word Studies from the Greek New Testament, Vol. 2*, (Grand Rapids: Eerdmans 1997) pp. 206-207.

6. Arthur Bennett ed., *The Valley Of Vision* (Carlisle, PA: The Banner Of Truth Trust 1975), pp. 202-203.

7. A.W. Tozer, Tozer Speaks, Volume 1 (Chicago, IL: WingSpread Publishers 2010), p. 117.

8. W. H. Griffith Thomas, *Romans: A Devotional Commentary XII-XVI* (London: The Religious Tract Society 1912), pp. 23-24.

9. D. Martyn Lloyd-Jones, *Romans: Exposition of Chapter 12: Christian Conduct*, p. 210.

10. Elisabeth Elliot, *Discipline: The Glad Surrender* (Old Tappen, NJ: Fleming H. Revell Company, 1960) p. 18.

11. Henrietta C. Mears, *What The Bible Is All About* (Ventura, CA: Regal, 2011) pp. 530-531.

WEEK 8

1. Henrietta C. Mears, *What The Bible Is All About*, pp. 533-534.

2. Charles R. Swindoll, *Insights On Romans*, page 274.

3. R.C. Sproul, *The Gospel of God: An Exposition of Romans,* pp. 212-213.

4. D. Martyn Lloyd-Jones, *Romans: Exposition of Chapter 14:1-7 Liberty and Conscience*, pp. 100-101

5. John Henry Jowett, *The Silver Lining* (New York: Flaming H. Revell, 1907) pp. 133-134.

6. W. H. Griffith Thomas, *Romans: A Devotional Commentary XII-XVI ,* pp. 125-126.

7. W. H. Griffith Thomas, *Romans: A Devotional Commentary I-V ,* p.vii.

8. Quoted from https://www.ligonier.org/learn/qas/what-is-a-benediction-why-does-it-appear-in-so-many-worship-services

9. F.B. Meyer, *Daily Prayers*, (Wheaton, IL: Harold Shaw Publishers 1995) p. 137.

10. W. H. Griffith Thomas, *Romans: A Devotional Commentary XII-XVI ,* pp. 176, 183-184.

ACKNOWLEDGMENTS

ow does a book like *The Proof Of God's Amazing Love* come to life? It takes years of God etching these principles from the Word of God on the heart in such a way that it is lived out in life. In this case, the Lord has been teaching me from the book of Romans ever since I first became a Christian more than forty years ago. I have a family friend, Thea Dryfhout (now with the Lord), to thank for inviting me to her home shortly after I became a Christian, giving me lots of good food, and teaching me from the book of Romans. I began my journey with the Lord in Romans and I am still in that wonderful book of the Bible today. This is the seventh in the A Quiet Time Experience series—quiet times for the busy person to use in their quiet time to go deep with God and grow in their intimate relationship with Him.

Thank you to my precious family; David, Mother and Dad (both now with the Lord), Robert, Kayla, Linda, Christopher, Andy, Keegan, and James. Thank you especially for your unconditional love and encouragement as I write books and share the messages that God has laid on my heart in my quiet times alone with Him.

I want to especially thank my husband, David, for your love, wisdom, and brilliance as together we run this race set before us and serve in Quiet Time Ministries. And thank you for the beautiful cover design of *The Proof Of God's Amazing Love*.

I am so very thankful over these many years for the Quiet Time Ministries team for serving the Lord together with me—Kayla Branscum, Shirley Peters, Conni Hudson, Cindy Clark, Sandy Fallon, Paula Zillmer, Karen Darras Hawley, and Kelly Wysard.

And then, thank you for my dear friends who have offered such words of truth, encouragement, and hope that I have needed all along the way: Beverly Trupp, Conni Hudson, Cindy, Clark, Andy Kotner, Julie Airis, Stefanie Kelly, Joe and Judy Patti, Betty Mann, Kelly Wysard, Jan Lupia, Barbara Waddell, and Vonette Bright. Thank you to all the women throughout North America who are in our Quiet Time Ministries Online Bible Study for praying together with me as I wrote *The Proof of God's Amazing Love*. I love studying God's Word together with you.

Thank you to the Board of Directors of Quiet Time Ministries: David Martin, Conni Hudson, Andy Kotner, and Jane Lyons, for your faithfulness in this ministry. And thank you to all who partner with me both financially and prayerfully in Quiet Time Ministries. You have helped make possible this idea the Lord gave me so many years ago called Quiet Time Ministries and have allowed us to continue to spread God's Word to men and women throughout the world. I also want to thank those who have partnered financially with Quiet Time Ministries to sponsor myPhotoWalk photo shoots and purchase photographic equipment including my Nikon cameras, lenses, tripods, and filters.

Thank you to my Bethel Seminary professors who gave me such a love for God's Word and helped me learn to study with excellence, especially Dr. Ronald Youngblood, Dr. Walt Wessel, Dr. James Smith, and Dr. Al Glenn. A special thanks to Dr. Walt Wessel for all his teaching in the Romans class in seminary. I had all those wonderful notes to consult as I wrote this study.

Thank you to those who have been such a huge help to me in the writing and publishing of books: Jim Smoke whose advice and help have, by God's grace, completely altered the course of my life and Greg Johnson, my agent, who has come alongside me and Quiet Time Ministries to help in the goals that the Lord has laid on my heart.

Thank you to those who have encouraged me in devotional photography through workshops, conferences, books, videos, examples, portfolios, and personal training — I am so very thankful for you — Bill Fortney, Dr. Charles Stanley, Laurie Rubin, Kevin Toohey, Kathleen Reeder, Kathleen Clemons, Trey Ratcliff, Scott Kelby, Matt Kloskowski, Sebastian Michaels, R.C. Concepcion, Karen Hutton, His Light Friends, Ben Long, Harold Davis, Art Wolfe, Tom Mangelsen, Chris Orwig, David DuChemin, Bryan Peterson, and April Milani.

A special thanks to all those leaders who answer God's call to lead others and challenge them to draw near to God, study His Word, and live for His glory. Thank you to all the women I've been privileged to serve with in leadership over the years. Thank you to the Women's Ministries Directors and leaders in churches who encourage their amazing women to live in God's Word and love Him with all their hearts. And a special thanks to all the groups worldwide who are drawing near to God in quiet time using the many quiet time studies from Quiet Time Ministries.

I am so very grateful to those women of God who love His Word and teach it every day of their lives, especially Anne Graham Lotz and Kay Arthur.

Finally, thank you to all those saints who have lived our their lives with a passion for God and have encouraged me to love the Lord with all my heart and spend daily quiet time with Him: especially Corrie ten Boom, Charles Haddon Spurgeon, Oswald Chambers, F.B. Meyer, Octavius Winslow, Amy Carmichael, Lilias Trotter, Annie Johnson Flint, A.W. Tozer, Andrew Murray, and Mrs. Charles Cowman.

Thank You, Lord, for Your amazing, extravagant, immeasurable, unconditional love—for saying yes, loving us so much that you gave Yourself up for us, and now live in us and walk with us, moment by moment, through the power of the Holy Spirit. Thank You for the gospel. It is truly good news that I will hold on to with all my heart until that day when I see You face to face. As Paul so fittingly closed the letter to the Romans: "All glory to the only wise God, through Jesus Christ, forever. Amen."

JOURNAL
"Pour out your heart like water in the
presence of the Lord" — Lamentations 2:19 NIV
SIX SECRETS TO A POWERFUL QUIET TIME ©2005

JOURNAL

"Pour out your heart like water in the presence of the Lord" — Lamentations 2:19 NIV

JOURNAL

"Pour out your heart like water in the presence of the Lord" — Lamentations 2:19 NIV

Journal

"Pour out your heart like water in the presence of the Lord" — Lamentations 2:19 NIV

JOURNAL

"Pour out your heart like water in the presence of the Lord" — Lamentations 2:19 NIV

SIX SECRETS TO A POWERFUL QUIET TIME ©2005

JOURNAL

"Pour out your heart like water in the presence of the Lord" — Lamentations 2:19 NIV

SIX SECRETS TO A POWERFUL QUIET TIME ©2005

ADORE GOD IN PRAYER

*Prayer for*____

Date: Topic:

Scripture:

Request:

Answer:

____

Date: Topic:

Scripture:

Request:

Answer:

____

Date: Topic:

Scripture:

Request:

Answer:

____

Date: Topic:

Scripture:

Request:

Answer:

____

Date: Topic:

Scripture:

Request:

Answer:

____

ADORE GOD IN PRAYER

*Prayer for*____

Date: Topic:

Scripture:

Request:

Answer:

Date: Topic:

Scripture:

Request:

Answer:

Date: Topic:

Scripture:

Request:

Answer:

Date: Topic:

Scripture:

Request:

Answer:

Date: Topic:

Scripture:

Request:

Answer:

ADORE GOD IN PRAYER

"Don't worry about anything; instead, pray about everything" — Philippians 4:6 NIV

*Prayer for*____

Date: Topic:

Scripture:

Request:

Answer:

____

Date: Topic:

Scripture:

Request:

Answer:

____

Date: Topic:

Scripture:

Request:

Answer:

____

Date: Topic:

Scripture:

Request:

Answer:

____

Date: Topic:

Scripture:

Request:

Answer:

____

ADORE GOD IN PRAYER

Prayer for ____

Date: Topic:

Scripture:

Request:

Answer:

Date: Topic:

Scripture:

Request:

Answer:

Date: Topic:

Scripture:

Request:

Answer:

Date: Topic:

Scripture:

Request:

Answer:

Date: Topic:

Scripture:

Request:

Answer:

ADORE GOD IN PRAYER

"Don't worry about anything;
instead, pray about everything" — Philippians 4:6 NIV

*Prayer for*____

Date: Topic:

Scripture:

Request:

Answer:

Date: Topic:

Scripture:

Request:

Answer:

Date: Topic:

Scripture:

Request:

Answer:

Date: Topic:

Scripture:

Request:

Answer:

Date: Topic:

Scripture:

Request:

Answer:

---

*Prayer for*____

Date: Topic:
Scripture:
Request:

Answer:

____

Date: Topic:
Scripture:
Request:

Answer:

____

Date: Topic:
Scripture:
Request:

Answer:

____

Date: Topic:
Scripture:
Request:

Answer:

____

Date: Topic:
Scripture:
Request:

Answer:

____

A Quiet Time
EXPERIENCE
WALK ON WATER FAITH
Discovering Power
in the Promises of God
Catherine Martin
Author of Run Before the Wind
MARTIN
WALK ON WATER FAITH
A QUIET TIME EXPERIENCE

CATHERINE MARTIN
Author of myPhotoWalk — The Story of Your Life
THE CALLING
The Story of Who You Are
and Why You Are Here
THE CALLING
MARTIN

THE STORY OF YOUR LIFE

Discovering a Heart to Follow the Master

CATHERINE MARTIN

A Quiet Time
EXPERIENCE

One
Holy
Passion

A Sacred Journey in Exodus to God's Amazing Love

Catherine Martin
Author of Walk on Water Faith